**COMPUTER BOOK SERIES FROM IDG**

# Upgrading and Fixing PCs For Dummies

## Ten Steps for Working on Your PC

1. Back up any important information on your hard drive to a floppy disk for safekeeping. (To be really safe, back up the whole hard drive, including any last minute instructions on any floppy disks.)

2. Read any instructions that came with your new part.

3. Exit any running programs, turn off your PC, and unplug it from the wall.

4. Clean off the desk space next to your computer.

5. Put your tools next to the computer.

6. Remove your PC's cover.

7. Remove the old item and insert the new one.

8. Plug in the PC, turn it on, and carefully test the new part to see whether it works.

9. Turn off the PC, unplug it, and put the case back together.

10. Plug in the PC and put away your tools.

## Always Remember These Things

**Turn off and unplug your computer before taking off its cover.**

Please. This one's the most important step of all. You can damage both yourself *and* your computer if you forget to turn off and unplug the computer.

**The red (or colored) wire is positive.**

Look for a little + sign on the socket that the wires plug into. The red or colored wire plugs into the pin marked by the + sign.

**The positive/red wire connects to Pin 1.**

Look for little numbers printed along the edge of a socket.

The positive wire — always the red or colored wire — always fits onto the pin marked as number 1.

Can't see the number 1? Then push the plug into the socket with the red wire facing toward the *low* numbers on the socket.

**The two black wires almost always go next to each other on a motherboard's power connector.**

When pushing power-supply cables into the motherboard's sockets, arrange the two cables so the two black wires are next to each other.

## Cheat Sheet

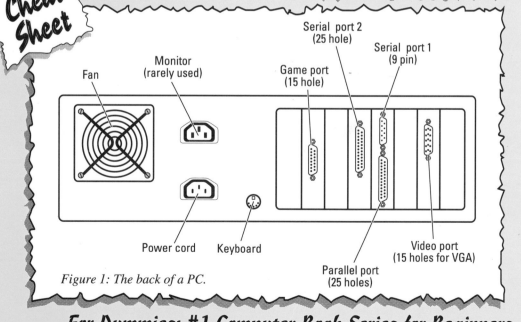

*Figure 1: The back of a PC.*

## ... For Dummies: #1 Computer Book Series for Beginners

JUL. 1 9 1994

# Upgrading and Fixing PCs For Dummies

## How to Remove a PC's Case

1. Turn off the computer, monitor, and peripherals (modem, CD-ROM, and so on). Make sure that everything attached to your computer is turned off and unplugged.

2. Unplug your computer. Unplug your computer's power cord from the wall.

3. Remove four or five screws from the outside edges. The older your PC, the more screws you'll find on the back of it. See the four screws closest to each corner, like in Figure 2? Those outside-edge screws hold the cover onto the case; ignore the others. Turn each screw counterclockwise to loosen it. If there's a screw along the top edge, midway between the corners, remove that one, too.

   Place the screws in a safe place, where you'll be able to find them later (and where they won't fall and lodge themselves in your PC's guts).

4. Slide off the cover. On some computers, the cover slides toward the front. You may need to pull pretty hard. Try lifting up a little on the cover from the back.

   On other computers, the cover lifts up and off.

5. Clean inside the computer. Use a can of compressed air to blow out all the dust while you're in there. Clean any dust remnants from where they cling to the power supply's fan in the back.

   To replace the cover, reverse these steps. (Don't put the dust back in, though.)

## I Can Access My PC's CMOS or Setup Program by Doing This

*(circle one)*

Pressing the Delete key when the computer boots up

Pressing Ctrl-Alt-Enter simultaneously

Pressing Ctrl-Alt-Esc simultaneously

*(write your own method here)*

_____

_____

_____

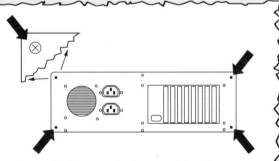

Figure 2: Remove the four outside-edge screws that hold the cover onto the case.

**. . . For Dummies: #1 Computer Book Series for Beginners**

# Say What You Think

Listen up, all you readers of IDG's ...*For Dummies* books! It's time to take advantage of the direct reader pipeline to the authors and editors of IDG Books.

We would like your input for future printings and editions of this title. Tell us what you liked about this book, how you think the book can be improved, and anything else you'd like to share. Did you like a particular chapter more than any other? And how about the chapters you didn't like? We want to know it all.

Please send your comments, questions, and suggestions to:

Reprint Coordinator
IDG Books Worldwide
3250 N. Post Road, Ste. 140
Indianapolis, IN 46226

Please be sure to include your name, address, and phone number.

Thanks for your input.

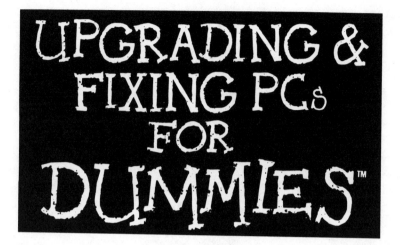

# UPGRADING & FIXING PCs FOR DUMMIES™

**by Andy Rathbone,**
author of best-selling
*Windows For Dummies*
and *OS/2 For Dummies*
and coauthor of *PCs For Dummies*

**IDG**
**BOOKS**

IDG Books Worldwide, Inc.
An International Data Group Company

San Mateo, California ♦ Indianapolis, Indiana ♦ Boston, Massachusetts

# Upgrading and Fixing PCs For Dummies

Published by
**IDG Books Worldwide, Inc.**
An International Data Group Company
155 Bovet Road, Suite 310
San Mateo, CA 94402

Library of Congress Catalog Card No.: 93-79179

ISBN: 1-56884-002-0

Printed in the United States of America

10 9 8 7 6 5 4 3 2 1

Distributed in the United States by IDG Books Worldwide, Inc.

Distributed in Canada by Macmillan of Canada, a Division of Canada Publishing Corporation; by Woodslane Pty. Ltd. in Australia and New Zealand; and by Computer Bookshops in the U.K. and Ireland.

For information on translations and availability in other countries, contact Marc Jeffrey Mikulich, Foreign Rights Manager, at IDG Books Worldwide. Fax: 415-358-1260.

For sales inquiries and special prices for bulk quantities, write to the address above or call IDG Books Worldwide at 415-312-0650.

 is a trademark of IDG Books Worldwide, Inc.

# About the Author

Andy Rathbone started geeking around with computers in 1985 when he bought a boxy CP/M Kaypro 2X with lime-green letters. Like other nerds, he soon began playing with null-modem adapters, dialing up computer bulletin boards, and working at Radio Shack.

In between playing computer games, he served as editor of the *Daily Aztec* newspaper at San Diego State University. After graduating with a comparative literature degree, he went to work for a bizarre underground coffee-table magazine that sort of disappeared.

Andy began combining his two interests, words and computers, by selling articles to a local computer magazine. During the next few years, Andy started ghostwriting computer books for more famous computer authors, as well as writing several hundred articles about computers for technoid publications like *Supercomputing Review, CompuServe, ID Systems, DataPro,* and *Shareware.*

In 1992, Andy and *DOS For Dummies* author Dan Gookin teamed up to write *PCs For Dummies,* which was a runner-up in the Introductory How-To Book - Systems category of the Eighth Annual Computer Press Awards (1993). Andy subsequently wrote *Windows For Dummies* and *OS/2 For Dummies.*

Andy is currently writing *More Windows For Dummies,* as well as contributing regularly to *CompuServe* magazine, mailed monthly to CompuServe members. (Feel free to drop him a line at 75300,1565.)

Andy lives with his most-excellent wife, Tina, and their cat in San Diego, California. When not writing, Andy fiddles with his MIDI synthesizer and tries to keep the cat off both keyboards.

# About IDG Books Worldwide

Welcome to the world of IDG Books Worldwide.

IDG Books Worldwide, Inc., is a division of International Data Group, the world's largest publisher of computer-related information and the leading global provider of information services on information technology. IDG publishes over 194 computer publications in 62 countries. Forty million people read one or more IDG publications each month.

If you use personal computers, IDG Books is committed to publishing quality books that meet your needs. We rely on our extensive network of publications, including such leading periodicals as *Macworld*, *InfoWorld*, *PC World*, *Computerworld*, *Publish*, *Network World*, and *SunWorld*, to help us make informed and timely decisions in creating useful computer books that meet your needs.

Every IDG book strives to bring extra value and skill-building instruction to the reader. Our books are written by experts, with the backing of IDG periodicals, and with careful thought devoted to issues such as audience, interior design, use of icons, and illustrations. Our editorial staff is a careful mix of high-tech journalists and experienced book people. Our close contact with the makers of computer products helps ensure accuracy and thorough coverage. Our heavy use of personal computers at every step in production means we can deliver books in the most timely manner.

We are delivering books of high quality at competitive prices on topics customers want. At IDG, we believe in quality, and we have been delivering quality for over 25 years. You'll find no better book on a subject than an IDG book.

John Kilcullen
President and C.E.O.
IDG Books Worldwide, Inc.

IDG Books Worldwide, Inc. is a division of International Data Group. The officers are Patrick J. McGovern, Founder and Board Chairman; Walter Boyd, President. International Data Group's publications include: **ARGENTINA's** Computerworld Argentina, InfoWorld Argentina; **ASIA's** Computerworld Hong Kong, PC World Hong Kong, Computerworld Southeast Asia, PC World Singapore, Computerworld Malaysia, PC World Malaysia; **AUSTRALIA's** Computerworld Australia, Australian PC World, Australian Macworld, Network World, Reseller, IDG Sources; **AUSTRIA's** Computerwelt Oesterreich, PC Test; **BRAZIL's** Computerworld, Mundo IBM, Mundo Unix, PC World, Publish; **BULGARIA's** Computerworld Bulgaria, Ediworld, PC & Mac World Bulgaria; **CANADA's** Direct Access, Graduate Computerworld, InfoCanada, Network World Canada; **CHILE's** Computerworld, Informatica; **COLUMBIA's** Computerworld Columbia; **CZECH REPUBLIC's** Computerworld, Elektronika, PC World; **DENMARK's** CAD/CAM WORLD, Communications World, Computerworld Danmark, LOTUS World, Macintosh Produktkatalog, Macworld Danmark, PC World Danmark, PC World Produktguide, Windows World; **EQUADOR's** PC World; **EGYPT's** Computerworld (CW) Middle East, PC World Middle East; **FINLAND's** MikroPC, Tietoviikko, Tietoverkko; **FRANCE's** Distributique, GOLDEN MAC, InfoPC, Languages & Systems, Le Guide du Monde Informatique, Le Monde Informatique, Telecoms & Reseaux; **GERMANY's** Computerwoche, Computerwoche Focus, Computerwoche Extra, Computerwoche Karriere, Information Management, Macwelt, Netzwelt, PC Welt, PC Woche, Publish, Unit; **HUNGARY's** Alaplap, Computerworld SZT, PC World, ; **INDIA's** Computers & Communications; **ISRAEL's** Computerworld Israel, PC World Israel; **ITALY's** Computerworld Italia, Lotus Magazine, Macworld Italia, Networking Italia, PC World Italia; **JAPAN's** Computerworld Japan, Macworld Japan, SunWorld Japan, Windows World; **KENYA's** East African Computer News; **KOREA's** Computerworld Korea, Macworld Korea, PC World Korea; **MEXICO's** Compu Edicion, Compu Manufactura, Computacion/Punto de Venta, Computerworld Mexico, MacWorld, Mundo Unix, PC World, Windows; **THE NETHERLAND'S** Computer! Totaal, LAN Magazine, MacWorld; **NEW ZEALAND's** Computer Listings, Computerworld New Zealand, New Zealand PC World; **NIGERIA's** PC World Africa; **NORWAY's** Computerworld Norge, C/World, Lotusworld Norge, Macworld Norge, Networld, PC World Ekspress, PC World Norge, PC World's Product Guide, Publish World, Student Data, Unix World, Windowsworld, IDG Direct Response; **PANAMA's** PC World; **PERU's** Computerworld Peru, PC World; **PEOPLES REPUBLIC OF CHINA's** China Computerworld, PC World China, Electronics International, China Network World; **IDG HIGH TECH BEIJING's** New Product World; **IDG SHENZHEN's** Computer News Digest; **PHILLIPPINES'** Computerworld, PC World; **POLAND's** Computerworld Poland, PC World/Komputer; **PORTUGAL's** Cerebro/PC World, Correio Informatico/Computerworld, MacIn; **ROMANIA's** PC World; **RUSSIA's** Computerworld-Moscow, Mir-PC, Sety; **SLOVENIA's** Monitor Magazine; **SOUTH AFRICA's** Computing S.A.; **SPAIN's** Amiga World, Computerworld Espana, Communicaciones World, Macworld Espana, NeXTWORLD, PC World Espana, Publish, Sunworld; **SWEDEN's** Attack, ComputerSweden, Corporate Computing, Lokala Natverk/LAN, Lotus World, MAC&PC, Macworld, Mikrodatorn, PC World, Publishing & Design (CAP), Datalngenjoren, Maxi Data, Windows World; **SWITZERLAND's** Computerworld Schweiz, Macworld Schweiz, PC & Workstation; **TAIWAN's** Computerworld Taiwan, Global Computer Express, PC World Taiwan; **THAILAND's** Thai Computerworld; **TURKEY's** Computerworld Monitor, Macworld Turkiye, PC World Turkiye; **UNITED KINGDOM's** Lotus Magazine, Macworld, Sunworld; **UNITED STATES'** AmigaWorld, Cable in the Classroom, CD Review, CIO, Computerworld, Desktop Video World, DOS Resource Guide, Electronic News, Federal Computer Week, Federal Integrator, GamePro, IDG Books, InfoWorld, InfoWorld Direct, Laser Event, Macworld, Multimedia World, Network World, NeXTWORLD, PC Games, PC Letter, PC World Publish, Sumeria, SunWorld, SWATPro, Video Event; **VENEZUELA's** Computerworld Venezuela, MicroComputerworld Venezuela; **VIETNAM's** PC World Vietnam.

# Dedication

To that sense of satisfaction felt when fixing it yourself

# Acknowledgments

Special thanks to Sandy Blackthorn, Julie King, Darrin Strain, Tracy Barr, Sandy Grieshop, Michael Partington, Dan Gookin, John Honeycutt, Ken Kaiser, Tina Rathbone, Scott Stern, and Matt Wagner. Thanks also to the production staff of Beth Baker, Cindy Phipps, Tony Augsburger, Drew Moore, Mary Breidenbach, Valery Bourke, and Accent Technical Communications.

The publisher would like to give special thanks to Patrick J. McGovern, without whom this book would not have been possible.

# Credits

**Publisher**
David Solomon

**Acquisitions Editor**
Janna Custer

**Managing Editor**
Mary Bednarek

**Project Editor**
Sandra Blackthorn

**Editors**
Tracy L. Barr
Julie King
Darrin Strain

**Technical Reviewer**
Michael Partington

**Editorial Assistant**
Patricia R. Reynolds

**Proofreader**
Sandy Grieshop

**Production Manager**
Beth J. Baker

**Production Coordinator**
Cindy L. Phipps

**Production Staff**
Tony Augsburger
Mary Breidenbach
Drew R. Moore
Valery Bourke

**Indexer**
Sharon Hilgenberg

# Contents at a Glance

• • • • • • • • • • • • • • • • • • • • • • • • • • • • • • • • • • • • • •

*Introduction* ........................................................................................... 1

*Part I: Biting Your Fingernails* ........................................................ 7

    Chapter 1: Are You Nerdy Enough to Do It Yourself? ...................... 9
    Chapter 2: The *Right* Way to Fix Your PC ...................................... 17
    Chapter 3: Where Does This Piece Go? (Basic Computer Anatomy) .......... 29
    Chapter 4: Figuring Out What's Broken .......................................... 67

*Part II: The PC Parts You Can See (Peripherals)* ...................... 79

    Chapter 5: The Sticky Keyboard ...................................................... 81
    Chapter 6: Of Mice and Modems ..................................................... 89
    Chapter 7: Tweaking the Monitor .................................................. 103
    Chapter 8: Printers (Those Paper Wasters) .................................... 117

*Part III: The Stuff Hiding Inside Your PC* .................................. 131

    Chapter 9: The Motherboard (and its CPU, Math Coprocessor, BIOS,
       and Even a Battery) .................................................................. 133
    Chapter 10: Memory Stuff You'll Wish You Could Forget ............. 155
    Chapter 11: Floppy Drives ............................................................. 175
    Chapter 12: Hard Drives, CD-ROM Drives, and Tape Backup Drives .......... 187
    Chapter 13: Power Supplies ........................................................... 205
    Chapter 14: Stuff on Cards ............................................................ 215

*Part IV: Telling Your Computer What You've Done* ................... 225

    Chapter 15: That AUTOEXEC.BAT and CONFIG.SYS File Stuff .......... 227
    Chapter 16: Telling Windows about a New Part .......................... 239
    Chapter 17: Fiddling with Settings ............................................... 253

*Part V: The Part of Tens* ................................................................. 271

    Chapter 18: Ten Cheap Fixes to Try First .................................... 273
    Chapter 19: The Ten Hardest Upgrades ....................................... 279
    Chapter 20: The Ten Easiest Things to Upgrade .......................... 283
    Chapter 21: Ten Ways to Make Your PC Run Better ..................... 287
    Chapter 22: Ten Confusing Things Your Computer May Say When
       You Turn It On .......................................................................... 293
    Chapter 23: Ten Common Warning Beeps and What They Mean ......... 297
    Chapter 24: Ten Common Error Messages (and How to Avoid Them) ........ 303

*Index* ................................................................................................. 309

# Cartoons at a Glance

page 79

page 292

page 205

page xxiv

page 174

page 7

page 225

page 131

page 252

page 262

# Table of Contents

*Introduction* ............................................................................................. 1
   About This Book ...................................................................................... 1
   How to Use This Book ............................................................................ 2
   Type This Stuff Here .............................................................................. 3
   Read These Parts .................................................................................... 3
   Don't Read These Parts ......................................................................... 3
   How This Book Is Organized ................................................................. 4
       Part I: Biting Your Fingernails ..................................................... 4
       Part II: The PC Parts You Can See (Peripherals) ....................... 4
       Part III: The Stuff Hiding Inside Your PC ................................... 4
       Part IV: Telling Your Computer What You've Done ................... 4
       Part V: The Part of Tens ............................................................... 5
   Icons Used in This Book ......................................................................... 5
   Where to Go from Here ......................................................................... 6

*Part I: Biting Your Fingernails* ..................................................... 7

## Chapter 1: Are You Nerdy Enough to Do It Yourself? ................................ 9
   You Probably Won't Kill Your PC by Accident ..................................... 9
   Upgrading a PC Is Much Easier Than Working on a Car ................... 11
   Can You Really Save Bundles of Money? ............................................ 11
   PCs Aren't as Scary After You've Fixed One ...................................... 12
   When Should You Upgrade? .................................................................. 13
       When Windows or other programs demand it ........................... 13
       When you keep waiting for your PC to catch up ...................... 13
       When you can't afford a new computer ..................................... 13
       When your old equipment becomes tired ................................. 13
       When you want a new part in a hurry ....................................... 14
   When Shouldn't You Upgrade? .............................................................. 14
       When a computer part breaks while your
           computer is under warranty ................................................ 14
       When the dealer says, "I'll install the part
           for free, within 15 minutes!" .............................................. 14
       On a Friday ................................................................................... 14
       When you need your computer up
           and running within 90 minutes .......................................... 15
   Beware of the Chain Reaction ............................................................... 15

**Chapter 2: The Right Way to Fix Your PC** ..................................................... **17**

The Ten Steps for Upgrading Your PC ........................................................ 17
Making a Garage for Your PC ...................................................................... 20
What Tools Do You Need? ............................................................................ 20
    Small Phillips screwdriver ....................................................................... 20
    Itty-bitty flathead screwdriver ................................................................ 21
    Medium Phillips screwdriver .................................................................. 21
    Paper clip .................................................................................................. 21
    Other handy tools .................................................................................... 21
Making a System Disk ................................................................................... 23
Upgrade Do's and Doughnuts ..................................................................... 24
    Do upgrade one thing at a time ............................................................. 25
    Do watch out for static ........................................................................... 25
    Do hang on to your old boxes and manuals ......................................... 25
    Don't force parts together ...................................................................... 25
    Don't bend stuff that comes on cards ................................................... 26
    Don't use head-cleaning disks ............................................................... 26
    Don't rush yourself ................................................................................. 26
    Don't open up monitors or power supplies ......................................... 27
How to Fish Out Dropped Screws .............................................................. 27

**Chapter 3: Where Does This Piece Go?**
**(Basic Computer Anatomy)** ........................................................................ **29**

The Types of PCs ........................................................................................... 29
    Original IBM PC (1981) ............................................................................ 30
    IBM XT (early 1980s) ................................................................................ 31
    IBM AT (mid-1980s) ................................................................................. 31
    386 class (late 1980s) ............................................................................... 31
    PS/2 (1987) ................................................................................................ 32
    A look at laptops ..................................................................................... 33
    PCjr ............................................................................................................ 33
The Case ......................................................................................................... 34
    Big .............................................................................................................. 34
    Little (also called small footprint) ......................................................... 34
    Tower ........................................................................................................ 34
Case Lights and Buttons .............................................................................. 35
    Power light ............................................................................................... 35
    Power switch ............................................................................................ 35
    Reset button ............................................................................................. 36
    Floppy drive lights .................................................................................. 36
    Hard drive light ....................................................................................... 36
    Digital readout ......................................................................................... 37
    Key and lock ............................................................................................ 37

Those Port Things ................................................................37
   Power cord ...............................................................37
   Keyboard cord .........................................................39
   Serial port ...............................................................39
   Parallel port ............................................................40
   Game port ...............................................................41
   Video port ...............................................................42
   Other ports .............................................................42
Keyboards .........................................................................42
Mice, Scanners, and Modems ........................................44
   Mice .........................................................................44
   Scanners ..................................................................45
   Modems ...................................................................46
Monitors ............................................................................46
Printers ..............................................................................47
The Motherboard ............................................................48
   Central processing unit (CPU) .............................49
   Math coprocessor ..................................................50
   BIOS .........................................................................50
   Expansion slots and cards ....................................51
   What cards does your computer have?.................53
   Battery .....................................................................54
   Memory (random-access memory, or RAM).......54
   All those other little parts on the motherboard ...............56
Disk Drives .......................................................................57
   Floppy drives .........................................................57
   Combo drives ..........................................................59
   Hard drives (hard disks) ......................................59
   Other data storage tanks .....................................60
The Power Supply ...........................................................62
How Do I Know Which Parts I Have? ...........................64

**Chapter 4: Figuring Out What's Broken** .................................**67**

It Doesn't Work Anymore! .............................................67
   Make sure that the computer is plugged in and turned on ...............68
   Make sure that the cables are fastened securely ...................................68
   Turn the computer off, wait 30 seconds,
      and turn it back on again .................................................................68
Narrowing Down the Problem ......................................69
   Have you added new software lately? ................................................69
   Have you discovered a weird file that didn't do
      anything and deleted it? ....................................................................70
   Have you moved any files or directories around?
      Changed any of their names? .............................................................70
   Have you changed the computer's location on your desktop? .........70

Trying a Different Part ..................................................................71
Watching the Screen When You Turn On Your PC .......................71
Listen to the Beeps, Luke! ............................................................73
Calling In Doctor Software ............................................................73
Buying Replacement Parts ............................................................74
Calling Technical Support ............................................................75
The part's serial number ........................................................75
Information about your computer ..........................................75
The version of the operating system ......................................75
A copy of your CONFIG.SYS and AUTOEXEC.BAT files .......76

## *Part II: The PC Parts You Can See (Peripherals)* .................. 79

### Chapter 5: The Sticky Keyboard ..................................................81

When I Turn On My Computer, the Screen Says Keyboard Not
Found, Press <F1> to Continue or Something Equally Depressing! .........81
Some of the Keys Stick After I Spilled a
Hansen's Natural Raspberry Soda over Them! ..............................82
My Arrow Keys Don't Move the Cursor — They Make Numbers! ................83
All the Letters and Numbers Wore off My Keys! ..........................83
My Keyboard Doesn't Have F11 and F12 Keys,
and Microsoft Word for Windows Uses Those! ..........................84
How Can I Change to a Dvorak Keyboard? ..................................84
Every Time I Press a Key, the Computer Beeps at Me! .................85
How Do I Install a New Keyboard? ...............................................86

### Chapter 6: Of Mice and Modems ..................................................89

My Mouse's Arrow or Cursor Is Starting to Jerk Around ..............89
My Computer Says That It Can't Find My Mouse ........................90
I Installed a Modem (or Scanner or Sound Card or Weird Network
Thing), and Now My Mouse Cursor Jerks Around or Disappears ..........91
My Cordless Mouse Sometimes Acts Weird ................................92
My Friend's Mouse Won't Work on My Computer ........................92
After Installing a Modem and a Mouse,
I Don't Have a Serial Port Left for My Other Gizmos! ...............93
Which Is Better — a Bus Mouse or a Serial Mouse? ...................93
Why Is All This COM and Serial Port Stuff So Difficult? ...............94
How Do I Install or Replace a Serial Mouse? ..............................94
Who Can Understand What All That Modem Stuff Means? .........96
My Modem Hangs Up Whenever Anybody Calls Me ...................98
How Do I Install or Replace an External Modem? .......................98

## Chapter 7: Tweaking the Monitor ........................................ 103

The Screen Has Dust All over It .............................................. 103
It Doesn't Turn On! ................................................................ 104
What Do All Those Funny Video Words Mean? ........................ 104
I Bought an Expensive New Monitor, but My Screen Still Looks Ugly ....... 108
    The monitor's screen looks washed out ............................. 108
    The colors look awful in one of my programs .................... 109
How Do I Know That My Old Monitor
    Will Work with My New Video Card? ................................ 110
    My computer doesn't have a video card! ........................... 110
    Should I buy an accelerator card? .................................... 110
I Bought a Fancy New Card and Monitor,
    but All My Programs Look the Same! ................................ 111
My Cursor Disappeared! .......................................................... 111
My Monitor Makes Weird Noises! ............................................ 112
I Don't Want My Screen to Burn In ......................................... 112
My Laptop's Screen Looks Weird ............................................. 113
How Do I Install a New Monitor? ............................................. 113

## Chapter 8: Printers (Those Paper Wasters) ........................ 117

My Printer Doesn't Print Anything .......................................... 117
The Page Looks Blotchy .......................................................... 118
Everything's Double-Spaced or
    Everything's Printing on the Same Line ........................... 119
How Do I Install a New Toner Cartridge? ................................ 120
I Dunno What All This Printer Stuff Means ............................. 121
    When I try to print something, I get Greek! ..................... 123
    The paper keeps jamming in my laser printer! ................. 124
    My printer says that it has 35 built-in fonts — where? ..... 124
    How can I add PostScript to my LaserJet? ....................... 125
Can I Upgrade My Laser Printer? ............................................ 125
Why Is My Printer Cable So Short? .......................................... 126
How Can Two Computers Share One Printer? ........................... 126
My Laser Printer Smells Funny ............................................... 126
Can I Save Money by Refilling My Cartridges and Ribbons? ..... 127
How Do I Install a New Printer? .............................................. 127

## *Part III: The Stuff Hiding Inside Your PC* ................... *131*

## Chapter 9: The Motherboard (and Its CPU,
## Math Coprocessor, BIOS, and Even a Battery) ................. 133

My Computer Forgot That It Has a Hard Drive,
    and It Doesn't Know What Day It Is! ................................ 134
    I can't find my computer's battery! .................................. 135
    How do I install a new battery? ....................................... 136
    Don't forget what your computer is supposed to remember ... 136

To Ignore This, Press Enter ................................................................138
Can a Math Coprocessor Really Speed Up My Computer? ........................138
    Can I get a math coprocessor for my older computer? ....................140
    How do I install a math coprocessor? ..........................................140
Can I Put a 486 Chip in My 386 Computer to Make It Go Faster? ...............142
Can I Put a 486 Motherboard into My Old IBM PC or XT? ........................143
    Uh, should I really install the motherboard myself? ......................144
    I just installed a new 486 motherboard,
        and it's slower than my old 386! ......................................144
    What's that Overdrive stuff? ....................................................145
    How do I install a new motherboard? ..........................................145
What's This BIOS Business? ..............................................................150
How Do I Replace My BIOS? ..............................................................151

### Chapter 10: Memory Stuff You'll Wish You Could Forget ...................155

My Computer Keeps Saying Parity Error or Something
    Just as Mind-Numbing ..............................................................156
Windows Keeps Saying Not Enough Memory or Insufficient Memory ......156
How Much Memory Do I Have? ..........................................................158
I Installed a Bunch of Memory,
    but My Computer Doesn't Know That It's There! ............................159
Why Can't I Move Memory off My Old Motherboard and Stick
    It onto My New Motherboard? ....................................................161
Geez, What Memory Should I Buy? ....................................................164
    Memory type ........................................................................165
    Memory speed ......................................................................166
    Memory capacity ..................................................................167
How Do I Install More Memory? ........................................................168

### Chapter 11: Floppy Drives ......................................................175

My Computer Barfs on My Friend's Disks! ............................................175
When I Put in a New Disk, it Says Invalid Something or Other ..................176
What's an Extended-Capacity Disk? ....................................................178
My Computer Says That My Sector Isn't Found or My FAT Is Bad! ..........178
How Do I Install a New Floppy Drive? ................................................179

### Chapter 12: Hard Drives, CD-ROM Drives,
### and Tape Backup Drives ........................................................187

What's This CHKDSK Stuff? ..............................................................187
My Hard Disk Sure Isn't as Fast as It Used to Be ..................................188
What's a Controller Card? ................................................................189
Should I Buy an ST506, a SCSI, an ESDI, or an IDE Drive? ....................190
How Do I Get the Drive Lights to Turn On and Off? ..............................192
How Do I Install or Replace an IDE Hard Drive? ..................................192
Breaking in a New Hard Drive ..........................................................198

How Do I Install a CD-ROM Drive? .................................................200
    Installing an external CD-ROM drive .................................200
    Installing an internal CD-ROM drive .................................201
How Do I Install a Tape Backup Unit? ...........................................202

## Chapter 13: Power Supplies ...........................................205

My Computer Makes a Constant Whining Noise ...........................205
Nothing Happens When I Turn On My Computer .........................206
My Computer Forgets the Date, Even After I Changed the Batteries! .......207
What's a UPS or Backup Power Supply? .......................................208
What Kind of Power Supply Should I Buy? ...................................209
Installing a New Power Supply ....................................................209

## Chapter 14: Stuff on Cards ...........................................215

My Card Doesn't Fit! ..................................................................215
My Card Doesn't Work! ...............................................................218
What Kinds of Cards Can I Buy? ...................................................218
How Do I Install a New Card? ......................................................220

# Part IV: Telling Your Computer What You've Done ..............225

## Chapter 15: That AUTOEXEC.BAT and CONFIG.SYS File Stuff ...........227

What's a CONFIG.SYS File? ...........................................................227
What's an AUTOEXEC.BAT File? ....................................................229
What's a Path? ..............................................................................230
How to Edit a CONFIG.SYS or AUTOEXEC.BAT File ........................232
What Are Those Weird Sounds and Words When I Turn On
    My Computer? ..........................................................................236

## Chapter 16: Telling Windows about a New Part ...................239

Introducing Windows to a New Mouse, Keyboard,
    Video Card, or Monitor .............................................................240
I Want More Colors and Higher Resolution! ..................................244
I Changed Video Modes, and Now Windows Is Broken! ..................245
Introducing Windows to a Sound Card (or CD-ROM Drive
    or Other Gadget) .......................................................................246
My Driver's Too Old and Cruddy to Work Right! .............................249
Adding a New Printer ....................................................................250

## Chapter 17: Fiddling with Settings .................................253

My COM Ports Are Arguing! ..........................................................253
How to Resolve Irritating IRQ Conflicts ..........................................256
Address and DMA Stuff ..................................................................259

Jumper Bumping and DIP Switch Flipping .........................................260
    Moving jumpers around .............................................260
    Flipping a DIP switch ...............................................262
Sailing the CMOS Sea .........................................................263
How Do I Change My CMOS? .................................................265

## *Part V: The Part of Tens* ................................. *271*

### Chapter 18: Ten Cheap Fixes to Try First ...............................273

Plug It In ................................................................273
Turn the Computer Off, Wait 30 Seconds, and Turn It Back On .............274
Remove Your WordPerfect Floppy and Then Turn On Your Computer ...274
Check for Overheating .....................................................275
Boot from a System Floppy Disk .........................................275
Reseat Cards, Chips, and Connectors ...................................276
Clean Card Connectors with a Pencil Eraser ...........................276
Install a New Power Supply ..............................................277
Run the Weird-Sounding CHKDSK Program .............................277

### Chapter 19: The Ten Hardest Upgrades ...............................279

Upgrading Ancient Computers Like the Original IBM PC, XT, or PCjr ......279
Installing Those Confounded Internal Modems ........................280
Replacing the Motherboard ..............................................281
Adding a Second Hard Drive to an Older First Hard Drive .............282
Adding Memory to an Old Motherboard ................................282

### Chapter 20: The Ten Easiest Things to Upgrade ....................283

Adding a Keyboard .......................................................283
Adding a Mouse ...........................................................284
Adding Cards ..............................................................284
Replacing a Monitor .......................................................285
Installing a Floppy Drive .................................................285
Adding a Power Supply ..................................................286
Upgrading to the Latest Version of DOS ...............................286

### Chapter 21: Ten Ways to Make Your PC Run Better ...............287

Buy Some Utility Programs ..............................................287
Write Down Your CMOS Information ...................................288
Buy More RAM ...........................................................288
Buy a Graphics Accelerator Card .......................................289
Don't Smoke around Your PC ...........................................289
Keep the Turbo Switch On ..............................................289
Avoid Really Cheap Parts ...............................................290
Don't Flip the Computer On and Off a Lot .............................290
Hang on to Your Old Parts for Emergencies ...........................291

**Chapter 22: Ten Confusing Things Your
Computer May Say When You Turn It On** ...............................**293**

What Do Those Little Numbers Mean? ........................................293
When My Computer Boots Up, It Spits Out Weird Words .........................295

**Chapter 23: Ten Common Warning Beeps and What They Mean ......297**

What's This BIOS Beep Business? ...............................................297
AMI BIOS Beeps ...............................................................298
Genuine IBM BIOS Beeps ......................................................300
Phoenix BIOS Beeps ...........................................................301

**Chapter 24: Ten Common Error Messages
(and How to Avoid Them)** ...............................................**303**

Insert disk with COMMAND.COM in drive A
    Press any key to continue ................................................303
Invalid media or Track 0 bad disk unusableFormat terminated ...............304
Access denied ................................................................304
Divide Overflow .............................................................304
Drive not ready Abort, Retry, Ignore, Fail? ..................................305
Insufficient memory .........................................................305
Track 0 Bad — Disk Unusable ................................................305
Bad command or file name ...................................................305
Bad or missing filename .....................................................306
General failure .............................................................306
Incorrect DOS version .......................................................306
Insufficient disk space .....................................................306
Internal stack failure, system halted .......................................307
Sector not found ............................................................307

*Index* ...........................................................**309**

*Reader Response Card* ...........................................*Back of Book*

# Introduction

· · · · · · · · · · · · · · · · · · · · · · · · · · · · · · · · · · · · · · · · · · · · · · · · · · · · · · · ·

*Y*ou're no dummy; we both know that. But something about computers makes you feel like a dummy. And that's perfectly understandable. Unlike today's MTV-soaked kids, you didn't start learning about computers while at the day care center. And you haven't spent much time trying to catch up, either.

You haven't missed much, though. Computers are still as boring as they were the day you first saw one. They haven't gotten any friendlier, either. A bank's ATM rewards its users with a $20 bill after they've figured out which keys to press. Computers just *take* your money.

In fact, your computer's probably asking for some more of your cash right now, and that's why you're flipping through this book's Introduction.

Most of today's computer owners face at least one of the following problems:

- ✔ Your new software comes on those small shirt-pocket-sized disks, and your computer only takes the big black ones.

- ✔ Somebody says that you "need more RAM."

- ✔ Even if your software *did* come on the right-sized disks, your hard drive isn't big enough to hold the software.

- ✔ Your computer made three long beeps, and now it won't work anymore.

- ✔ You're wondering why you should pay the repair shop $75 an hour to install a part that only cost half that much.

## About This Book

That's where this book comes in handy. With this book in one hand and a screwdriver in the other, you'll be able to repair your own computer or add new parts to it. Best yet, this book won't force you to learn anything during the process.

Instead, this book is a reference filled with nuggets of information — sort of a miniencyclopedia. For example, if your floppy drive starts acting weird, just flip through to the section dealing with weird-acting floppy drives. There, you'll find simple instructions for jump-starting your floppy drive back into action.

Floppy drive still won't work? Then follow the clearly numbered steps to pull out your old floppy drive and stick in a new one. You won't find any techno-babble blocking the way, either. Instead, you can just jump to the details you need to know now: Which screws do you need to remove? Which cable plugs into which hole? How do you put the computer back together? And what happens if you lose an important screw in the shag carpet somewhere beneath the desk?

Unlike other computer repair books, this book steers clear from headings like "Integrated I/O Circuitry on the Mainboard" or "Procedures for Measuring Capacitor Flow." Who cares?

# How to Use This Book

Suppose that your keyboard's on the fritz. Don't know how a healthy keyboard's supposed to act? Then head to Chapter 3 for a quick rundown. (That's the chapter that explains all the computer stuff everybody thinks you already know.)

Then, when you're ready, flip to Chapter 5, the keyboard chapter, to hear about common keyboard foul-ups, as well as tips on how to make your keyboard work again. In that chapter, you'll find fixes for problems like these:

- When I turn on my computer, the screen says `Keyboard not found -- Press <F1> to continue` or something equally depressing!
- Some of the keys stick after I spilled a Hansen's Natural Raspberry Soda over them!
- My arrow keys don't move the cursor — they make numbers!
- My keyboard doesn't have F11 and F12 keys, and Microsoft Word for Windows uses those!

If your keyboard's truly beyond repair, head for the chapter's "How Do I Install a New Keyboard?" section. There, you'll find out which tools you'll need (if any) and how much money this setback will cost you. Finally, you'll see a list of clearly numbered steps, explaining everything you need to do to get that new keyboard installed and ready for hunting and pecking.

# *Type This Stuff Here*

If you need to type anything into your computer, you'll see the text you need to type displayed like this:

```
C:\> TYPE THIS IN
```

Here, you type the words **TYPE ME IN** after the C:\> thing and then press the Enter key. If the material you're supposed to type is particularly awkward, a description of what you're supposed to type follows so that there's no confusion (well, as little confusion as possible, anyway).

# *Read These Parts*

If you're lucky (and your computer's healthy), you won't have to read very much of this book. But, when something weird happens, this book will help you figure out what went wrong, whether it can be repaired, or whether you'll have to replace it.

Along the way, you'll find helpful comments or warnings explaining the process in more detail.

You'll find tips like this scattered throughout the book. Take a look at them first. In fact, one tip may spare you from having to read more than a paragraph of a computer book — a worthy feat indeed!

# *Don't Read These Parts*

OK, I lied a little bit. I did stick some technobabble in this book. After all, I'm a computer geek myself. (Whenever I sit down in a restaurant, my palmtop computer shoots out the top of my back pocket and clatters on the floor.) Luckily for you, however, all the technical drivel has been neatly cordoned off.

Any particularly odious technical details are isolated and posted with this icon so you can avoid them easily. If a computer nerd drops by to help with your particular problem, just hand the computer nerd this book. With these icons, he or she will know exactly which sections to look for.

# How This Book Is Organized

This book has five major parts. Each part is divided into several chapters. And each chapter covers a major topic, which is divided into specific sections.

The point? Well, this book's indexer sorted all the information with an extra-fine-tooth flea comb, making it easy for you to find the exact section you want, when you want it. Plus, everything's cross-referenced. If you need more information about a subject, you'll know exactly which chapter to head for.

Here are the parts and what they contain:

## Part I: Biting Your Fingernails

You'll find the basics in here. One chapter explains your computer's basic anatomy so that you'll know which parts are *supposed* to be making noise. Another chapter helps you figure out which part of your computer isn't working right. Plus, the very first chapter offers a few ego-boosting tips. Yes, you *can* do it yourself.

## Part II: The PC Parts You Can See (Peripherals)

Here, you'll find "fix it" information on the parts of your PC that are in plain sight: your monitor, for example, as well as your printer, keyboard, and other stuff you have to wipe the dust off of every once in a while. Each chapter starts off with repair tips and — if the thing still won't work right — detailed instructions on how to yank it out and stick in a new one.

## Part III: The Stuff Hiding Inside Your PC

Your PC's more mysterious parts lurk inside its big beige case, hidden from sight. Tilt down the brim of your safari hat as you rummage through the inside of your PC to replace floppy drives, add memory chips, or add fun computer toys like compact disc players.

## Part IV: Telling Your Computer What You've Done

If anybody's a dummy here, it's your computer. Even after you've stuck a new part in its craw, your computer probably won't know that the part is there. This part of the book explains how to tell your computer that it has just received a new part and that it should start groping around for it.

## Part V: The Part of Tens

Some information just drifts away when it's buried deep within a paragraph. That's why these tidbits are stacked up in lists of ten (give or take a few). Here, you'll find lists like "Ten Cheap Fixes to Try First," "Ten Ways to Make Your PC Run Better," "The Ten Easiest Things to Upgrade," and other fun factoids.

# Icons Used in This Book

This book's most exceptional parts are marked by icons — little eye-catching pictures in the margins:

This icon warns of some ugly technical information lying by the side of the road. Feel free to drive right by. The information is probably just a more complex discussion of something already explained in the chapter.

Pounce on this icon whenever you see it. Chances are that it marks a helpful paragraph worthy of a sticky note.

If you've forgotten what you were supposed to remember, keep an eye toward the margins for this icon.

Better be careful when doing stuff marked by this icon. In fact, this icon usually warns you about stuff you *shouldn't* be doing, like squirting WD-40 into your floppy drives.

Sometimes computer parts don't live well together. Computer upgrades that sometimes lead to even *more* repairs are pegged with this icon.

Auto mechanics can find the most helpful sections in their manuals by just looking for the greasiest pages. So, by all means, draw your own icons next to the stuff you've found particularly helpful. Scrawl in some of your own observations, as well.

# *Where to Go from Here*

I'm not going to kid you. You won't be able to replace and/or fix *every* part in your PC. For example, most repair shops don't fix monitors or power supplies. Those items are just too complicated (and dangerous) to mess with.

What this book will do, however, is tell you which parts of your PC you can fix *yourself* (most of them) and which parts are simply over your head. That way, you'll know which repairs should be parceled out to the technoweenies in the shop. You won't have to worry about attempting any repairs that are simply beyond your mortal abilities.

Also, your path will be easier if you're briefly familiar with your PC. For example, you should know how to see a directory of the files on a floppy disk. Don't know? You type this at the A:\> prompt:

```
A:\> DIR
```

That's the word DIR followed by a press of the Enter key. Your computer will display the names of that disk's files. If these concepts seem foreign to you, pick up a copy of this book's great-grandfather, *DOS For Dummies,* 2nd Edition. It's chock-full of introductory PC dance steps.

Ready to go? Then grab this book and a screwdriver. Your computer's ready whenever you are. Good luck.

# Part I
# Biting Your
# Fingernails

# In this part . . .

**E**xcited about electrolytic capacitors?

All agog over Schottky Integrated Circuits?

Then back up and keep reading those two sentences. You won't find any words like that in the *rest* of this book.

# Chapter 1

# Are You Nerdy Enough to Do It Yourself?

## In This Chapter

▶ Computers are difficult to destroy

▶ PCs are easier to fix than cars

▶ Can you save money by upgrading your PC yourself?

▶ PCs aren't as scary after you've fixed one

▶ When should you upgrade?

▶ When *shouldn't* you upgrade?

▶ What happens if parts don't work together?

Here's the secret: if you can open a bag of Cheetos, you can upgrade and repair your PC. You don't need to be a technoweenie with a vacant stare or an extra-large DOS Dude T-shirt.

In fact, upgrading a PC is almost always easier than trying to *use* one. I know a guy who can turn a box of spare parts into a whole PC in less time than it takes to print a 3-column page in WordPerfect.

Still not convinced? Then let this chapter serve as a little confidence booster. Remember, you don't *have* to be a computer wizard to upgrade or repair your PC.

## You Probably Won't Kill Your PC by Accident

Are you afraid that you'll mess something up if you take off your computer's case? Actually, there's very little that can go wrong. As long as you don't leave a dropped screw rolling around in your computer's innards, there's just not much to worry about. (And I'll tell you how to retrieve the dropped screw in Chapter 2.)

Do safety concerns keep you from prodding around inside your PC? Not only is the computer safe from your fingers, but your fingers are safe from your computer. After the beasts are unplugged, they're safer than an unplugged blender. You're not going to get a frizzy new hairstyle by accidentally touching the wrong part. Besides, you can fix a lot of your computer's problems without even taking off the case.

Are you afraid that you may accidentally put the wrong wire in the wrong place? Don't worry about it. Most of the wires in your PC are color coded. It's easy to tell which wire goes where. The computer designers even catered to groggy engineers: most of the cables only fit in their plugs one way — the right way.

If you can change a coffee filter (even one of those expensive, gold-plated coffee filters), you'll be able to change the parts of your PC.

- ✓ The PC was designed to be *modular* — all the parts slip in and out of their own special areas. You can't accidentally install your hard drive where the power supply is supposed to go. Your hard drive simply won't fit. (To be sure, I tried just now.)

- ✓ Although computers suck 110 volts from a wall outlet — the same as any household appliance — they don't actually use that much electricity. A computer's power supply turns 120 volts into 5 or 12 volts, which is less than the amount used by some freebie Radio Shack flashlights. This way, computers are a little less dangerous.

- ✓ If you install a part incorrectly, your PC won't explode; it just won't work. Although a computer that won't work can lead to serious head scratching, it won't lead to any head bandaging. Simply remove the misinstalled part and try installing it again from scratch. Then be careful to follow this book's step-by-step instructions. (And keep an eye out for the trouble-shooting suggestions found in any nearby paragraphs.)

- ✓ When IBM built its first PC ten years ago, the engineers designed it to be thrown together quickly with common parts. It's still like that today. You can install most computer upgrades with just a screwdriver, and other parts just snap in place like expensive Lego blocks.

Just as wicked witches don't like water, computer chips are deathly afraid of static electricity. A little static zap might scare you into dropping your pencil, but that zap can be instant death for a computer chip. Be sure to touch something metal — the edge of a metal desk, a file cabinet, or even your PC's chassis — before touching anything inside your computer.

# Upgrading a PC Is Much Easier Than Working on a Car

Forget about the mechanic's overalls; computers are *much* easier to work on than cars for several reasons. Ninety percent of the time, PCs can be upgraded with the use of a screwdriver from the kitchen's junk drawer. No need for expensive tools, protective gloves, or noisy hydraulic wrenches. You don't even have to grunt, spit, or wipe your hands on your pants (unless you already do that stuff anyway).

Second, computer parts are much easier to find than car parts. Every year, cars use a different kind of bumper or a new air filter. But, with a PC, all the parts are pretty much the same. You can take a mouse off a friend's computer and plug it into your computer without any problem (unless your friend sees you doing it).

There's never any heavy lifting. And you'll never have to roll under your computer, either (unless you're laptopping at the beach).

- ✔ If you have an old car, you're probably stuck buying parts from a hard-to-find garage in New Jersey. But, if you have an old computer, just grab the floppy drive sitting on the store shelf. You don't have to search old IBM heaps for an '87 floppy drive for a TurboChunk 286.

- ✔ There aren't any pipes to drop bolts into, like I did when I foolishly tried to replace the carburetor on my '65 VW van. After watching the tow truck haul my car away, I decided to stick with PCs: Computers don't have any open pipes, they don't use bolts, and they smell a lot better than carburetor cleaner. Plus, there aren't any moving parts to catch your sleeve and drag you perilously close to the whirling gears.

- ✔ Here's one more difference: Car mechanics *repair* stuff. If something inside the engine breaks, the mechanic laboriously takes apart the engine, replaces the bad part with a good one, and laboriously puts the engine back together. But, with PCs, you *replace* stuff. If your PC's video card dies, throw it away and screw in a new one. Much less fuss. And it's cheaper, too.

# Can You Really Save Bundles of Money?

Many people think that they can build their own PC from scratch and save a bundle. But it just doesn't work that way. Nobody can save money on a Corvette by picking up all the parts at the Chevy dealer's parts window and bolting them together. The same holds true for a PC.

Today's computer dealers buy zillions of parts at a bulk rate discount, slap 'em all together in the back room, and stick the finished product in the store window 20 minutes later. Without any bulk discounts on the parts, a self-made computer costs about as much as a brand-new one.

- ✔ If your computer is so old that you want to replace *everything,* go for it. But replace everything by buying a *brand-new computer.* You'll not only save money, and time, but you'll probably get some free software tossed in as well.

- ✔ It's almost always cheaper to *replace* a part than to *repair* it. Most repair shops charge upwards of $75 an hour; a long repair job can cost more than a new part. And many shops don't even bother trying to repair the really scary stuff, like monitors or power supplies. It's cheaper (and easier) for the shops to just sell you new ones.

- ✔ So why bother upgrading your computer at all? Because you'll save cash on repair bills. Plus your computer will be up and running more quickly: it won't be stuck in a back-logged repair shop while you're stuck with no computer. Horrors!

# PCs Aren't as Scary After You've Fixed One

When I was a kid, my mom once took the car into the shop when it made a strange rattling sound while she turned corners. My mom didn't have any idea what could be causing the problem. The car's rattles and pops *all* sounded scary and mysterious to her.

The mechanic couldn't find anything wrong, though, so my mom took him on a test drive. Sure enough, when the car rounded a sharp corner, the rattling noise appeared. The mechanic cocked his ear for a few seconds and then opened the metal ashtray on the dashboard. He removed a round pebble and the sound at the same time.

My mom was embarrassed, of course. And, luckily, the auto shop didn't charge for the fix. But it proves a point: if my mom had known a little bit more about her car, the rattling sound wouldn't have been scary, and she could have saved a trip to the shop.

"So what's your point?" you ask. Well...

- ✔ After you've opened your PC's case and seen what's inside, your PC won't be as mysterious or scary to you. You'll see that it's just a collection of parts, like anything else.

✔ After you've fiddled with a PC, you'll feel more confident about working with your computer and its software. Fiddling with PCs doesn't have to become a hobby, heaven forbid. But you won't be afraid that if you press the wrong key, the monitor will explode like it did on *Star Trek* last week. (And come to think of it, the week before that, too.)

✔ If you're going to be bringing small rocks back from the desert, put them in the glove compartment. They don't rattle as loudly in there.

# When Should You Upgrade?

Your computer will tell you when you need to upgrade. You may have already seen some of the following warning signs.

## When Windows or other programs demand it

Everybody's using Windows, or at least that's what the folks who sell Windows say. And finicky Windows works best on one of those big, new, sporty computers with a fast CPU, a big hard drive, and large smokestacks.

## When you keep waiting for your PC to catch up

You press a button and wait. And wait. Or, if you're using Windows, you click on a button and watch the little hourglass sit on the screen. When you're working faster than your PC, it's time to give the little fellow a boost.

## When you can't afford a new computer

If you're strapped for cash and can't afford a new computer, buy the parts one at a time. For example, add that new hard drive now and add other parts a few months later, when your credit card's not as anemic.

## When your old equipment becomes tired

Is your mouse hopping across the screen? Are the keys on your keyboard stickingggg? Do your disk drives burp on your floppy disks? Is your old hard drive sending you weird messages? If so, chances are that the parts are saying, "Replace me quick, before I pack my bags and take all your reports, spreadsheets, and high-game scores with me."

### When you want a new part in a hurry

Computer repair shops aren't nearly as slow as stereo repair shops. Still, do you really want to wait four days for them to install that hot new video card? Especially when you've got a nagging suspicion you could do it yourself in less than 15 minutes?

Also, if you're buying your parts through the mail to save some bucks, you'd better count on sticking them inside the computer yourself.

## When Shouldn't You Upgrade?

Sometimes, you *shouldn't* work on your computer yourself. Take caution under the following circumstances.

### When a computer part breaks while your computer is under warranty

If your computer is under warranty, let *them* fix the part. In fact, fixing a part yourself may void the warranty on the rest of your computer.

### When the dealer says, "I'll install the part for free, within 15 minutes!"

Fifteen minutes? By all means, take the dealer up on the offer before he or she wises up and starts charging, like all the other dealers.

### On a Friday

Never try to install a new computer part on a Friday afternoon. When you discover that the widget needs a *left* bracket, too, all the shops will be closed, leaving you with a desktop full of detached parts until Monday morning.

## *When you need your computer up and running within 90 minutes*

Just like kitchen remodeling, computer upgrading and repairing take twice as long as you originally thought. Don't try to work on your computer under deadline pressure, or you'll wind up steam-cleaning your ears when your head explodes.

# *Beware of the Chain Reaction*

One upgrade often leads to another. Like quarreling office workers, some *compatible* computer parts refuse to work together.

For example, you buy a new hard drive, install it, and wonder why it doesn't work. Then you discover that your computer has a *controller card,* and it's not compatible with the hard drive you've just installed.

Luckily, controller cards are relatively cheap. However, it's still something to be aware of. When you see the Chain Reaction icon in this book, be aware that you may have to buy yet another part before the upgrade will work.

- ✔ Chain reactions can pop up with just about any part, unfortunately. For example, sometimes you'll have to replace *all* your memory chips instead of just plugging in a few new ones, like you had hoped. Or sometimes buying a new video card means that you'll have to buy a new monitor, too: your old monitor will still work, but it probably won't take advantage of all your new card's whiz-bang features.

- ✔ None of this stuff is *your* fault, though. The same chain reaction would have happened even if you had let the folks at the repair shop upgrade your computer. The only difference is that you'd hear the sorry news over the phone, just like when the mechanic calls the office saying that you need a new radiator when you only took the car in for a new set of shocks. Yep, those are some shocks all right.

- ✔ If a part doesn't work in your computer, there's still hope. You can return computer parts for a refund just as if they were sweaters that didn't fit. If you don't feel like replacing all the incompatible parts, just take back your new part for a refund. As long as you return it within a reasonable amount of time and in good working order, there shouldn't be a problem.

# Chapter 2
# The *Right* Way to Fix Your PC

● ● ● ● ● ● ● ● ● ● ● ● ● ● ● ● ● ● ● ● ● ● ● ● ● ● ● ● ● ● ● ● ● ● ● ● ● ● ● ● ● ● ● ●

## In This Chapter

▶ Ten steps for upgrading your PC

▶ Where you should work on your PC

▶ The tools you need

▶ How to make a System disk

▶ Things to do when working on your PC

▶ Things *not* to do when working on your PC

▶ How to fish out dropped screws

● ● ● ● ● ● ● ● ● ● ● ● ● ● ● ● ● ● ● ● ● ● ● ● ● ● ● ● ● ● ● ● ● ● ● ● ● ● ● ● ● ● ● ●

*W*hen I was a little kid, my sister and I met a guy who lived by the beach and liked to fiddle around with gadgets. One day, he cut the power cord off an old lamp and tied a big nail to the ends of each wire.

Then he stuck a nail in each end of a hot dog and plugged the cord back into the wall. Sure enough, the hot dog cooked. Sizzled, even, and made some sputtering sounds. But we didn't eat the hot dog. In fact, we kind of gave the guy a wide berth after that.

My sister and I knew there was a *right* way to do things and a *wrong* way. This chapter points out the difference between the two when you're working on your computer.

## The Ten Steps for Upgrading Your PC

Those technodrones in the back room will charge you $75 an hour for replacing a part, but they're merely following simple steps they learned at Computer School. Consider these steps the Cliff's Notes of Upgrading (in fact, you'll see them repeated in the handy cheat sheet at the front of this book):

**1. Back up your hard drive so you won't lose any data.**

Whenever you drop a new part into your PC, you run the risk of upsetting its stomach. Your PC probably won't wipe out any information on your hard drive for revenge, but wouldn't you feel like a dweeb if something *did* happen? Make sure that you have a backup copy of everything on your hard drive. Of course, you've been backing up your data every day, so this shouldn't be too much of a chore.

If you're tired of copying everything onto floppy disks, consider buying a *tape backup unit*. It's a little gizmo that records all your information onto computerized cassette tapes. It can even back up your hard drive automatically at the end of each day, so you don't have to remember anything. (Ready to install one? Then head to Chapter 12.)

One simple way to back up your data is to install a second hard drive in your computer. At the end of each day, simply copy all your information from one hard drive to the second. Chances are slim that both hard drives will go on vacation at the same time. If one suddenly leaves, you'll still have your information saved on another. (To add a second hard drive, flip ahead to Chapter 12.)

**2. Read the instructions that came with the part.**

After you tear open the box, look at the installation instructions. Chances are that the instructions booklet has a page in the front labeled "At Least Read This Part." It's designed for people who're too excited about their new computer part to wade through the boring manual.

Next, look for any enclosed computer disks. Find one? Then stick it into your floppy drive and look for a file called README.TXT, README.COM, or something similar. Manufacturers often update their equipment more often than they update their manuals, so they'll stick the most up-to-date information on the floppy disk.

If you find a file that says README.COM, type the following at the prompt and then press Enter:

```
A:\> README
```

The program brings some last-minute information to your screen. If you find a file called README.TXT, you can read it in any word processor, like Windows' Notepad. Don't have Windows handy? Then type this at the prompt:

```
A:\> TYPE README.TXT | MORE
```

(That weird | thing between README.TXT and MORE is on the slash key by the Enter key.) When you press Enter after typing the word **MORE,** your computer brings the information to your screen and pauses thoughtfully at each page. Press the spacebar to advance to the next page.

See anything good? Then write it down. Otherwise, head for the next step.

**3. Exit any programs, turn off your PC, and unplug it from the wall.**

Don't ever turn off your PC while it has a program on the screen. That's like plucking a kid off the merry-go-round before it stops turning — potentially dangerous and certainly hard on the ears.

Make sure that you exit any currently running programs — especially Windows. When you see the C:\> prompt on the screen, you can safely turn off the computer. Just to make sure that nobody trips over it, unplug it from the wall, too.

**4. Clean off the counter space next to your computer.**

Dump the junk mail and shelve any stray floppy disks. You'll need an empty place to set things so you don't have to stack stuff on top of each other.

Don't keep any liquids near your repair area where they can be spilled into your case. A spilled beverage will almost certainly destroy your computer.

**5. Find your tools and put them next to the computer.**

After you start to install that new part, the adrenaline begins to flow. You don't want to lose momentum while hunting for a screwdriver, so make sure that all your tools are within reach. What tools? Check out the "What Tools Do You Need?" section later in this chapter.

**6. Remove your PC's cover.**

This chore's covered thoroughly in the cheat sheet at the front of this book. Normally, you remove the four screws around the bottom sides of the case (two along each side). Sometimes, there's a screw or two in the back as well. If you're lucky, the case slides off like butter on a hot pancake. Other times, it sticks like gum under the table. Check this book's cheat sheet for full details.

**7. Pull out the old item and insert the new.**

You may want to take notes on a scratch pad so you'll remember which wire goes where. Cables and plugs usually only fit one way, but you'll often feel more confident if you draw your own picture.

**8. Plug in your computer and fire up the gizmo to see whether it works.**

What? Plug in the computer and turn it on when the case is *off?* Yes. Just don't touch anything inside the case and you'll be safe. For example, if you're replacing a video card, you can check to make sure that you see stuff on your monitor when you turn on your computer.

If the new part works, head for Step 9. If it doesn't, turn the computer off, unplug it, and start troubleshooting. Perhaps you forgot to connect a cable. Or you may need to flip a switch somewhere, which is described in Chapter 17.

9. **Unplug the computer and put the PC back together.**

   Done? Then check to make sure that you don't have any leftover screws or, even worse, any leftover holes *without* screws. If a forgotten screw is wedged in the wrong place inside the case, your computer may fry like an electrocuted hot dog.

   You'll find tips on fishing out stubborn screws later in this chapter.

10. **Plug the PC back into the wall and give it a final test.**

    The part's installed, the case is back on, and all the cables are plugged back in. Does the computer still work? *Whew.* If not, check the cables to make sure that they're pushed in all the way.

By carefully following these ten steps, you'll avoid problems. The key is to proceed methodically, step by step. Not watching television at the same time can help, too.

# Making a Garage for Your PC

PCs don't need much of a garage. For the most part, your desktop will work fine. Just make sure that it has plenty of elbow room.

If your desktop is too small, consider moving the computer to the dining room table. Actually, the tablecloth can help out: screws won't roll as far when they're dropped. Plus, the extra padding, no matter how slight, will help protect your PC's more sensitive parts when you set them down.

# What Tools Do You Need?

All the tools required to fix a PC can fit into a single pocket protector: a small Phillips screwdriver will handle 90 percent of the operating room chores, although a few other tools occasionally come in handy.

## Small Phillips screwdriver

The Phillips screwdriver should be able to handle a screw that's the size of the one shown in Figure 2-1.

**Figure 2-1:**
Most of the screws holding
your PC together are this size.

## Itty-bitty flathead screwdriver

Printer cables, monitor cables, and mouse tails all plug into the back of your PC. Most cables have tiny screws on the end to keep them from falling off their plugs. You'll need a screwdriver to handle screws the size of the one shown in Figure 2-2.

**Figure 2-2:**
The screws holding your cables to the back of your computer are *really* this tiny.

## Medium Phillips screwdriver

Sometimes an overeager computer nerd will really bear down on the screws that hold on your computer's case. In that case, a slightly larger Phillips screwdriver will give you better leverage. Check out the size of the screws on your PC's case and shop accordingly.

## Paper clip

Many computer parts are designed and built by tiny elves. That's the reason the special switches, called DIP switches, are so small. A bent paper clip helps to move these switches back and forth. You'll often need to *flip a DIP* when adding a new part to your computer. The switches are really as small as they look in Figure 2-3.

**Figure 2-3:**
A bent paper clip comes in handy for flipping tiny switches like these.

The manual bundled with Toshiba's latest CD-ROM drive shows a paper clip being used for the Emergency Eject Procedure that extracts stubborn compact discs.

## Other handy tools

The following items aren't crucial, but feel free to pick them up if you spot them at a garage sale or a Pic 'n Save.

### Small flashlight

Some of the stuff in your computer is jammed in pretty close together. A flashlight can help you read important labels or spot fallen screws.

### Magnetized screwdriver

A magnetized screwdriver makes it easier to grab a fallen screw you've just spotted with the flashlight. Just touch the screw with the end of the screwdriver and gently lift it out when it sticks to the end of the screwdriver.

Anything with a magnet can wipe out any information on your floppy disk. To avoid problems, don't keep your magnetized screwdriver near your work area. Just grab it when you need to fetch a dropped screw and then put it back on the other side of the room.

### Empty egg carton

Most people use a coffee cup to hold screws. But an empty egg carton is more fun because you can put screws from different parts into different depressions.

### Compressed air canister

Your computer's fan constantly sucks in fresh air through your PC's vents. That means it's also sucking in dust, lint, and occasional dried fern leaves. PC repair geeks can instantly tell which PC owners have cats by simply looking at the layers of hair inside a PC's case. A cigarette smoker's computer looks even worse.

PC repair shops and art supply shops sell compressed air in canisters so you can blow all the dust out of the inside of your PC. Adventurous souls can also squirt coworkers in the back of the head when they're not looking.

Don't blow on your PC's innards to remove dust. Although you're blowing air, you're also blowing moisture, which can be even worse for your PC than dust.

Every few months, pull off the dust balls that clog the air vent on the back of your PC. The cooler you can keep your PC, the longer it will last.

### Pencil and paper

Sometimes a pad of paper and a pencil can be handy for writing down part numbers — or angst-ridden poetry when things aren't going according to plan.

### Spare computer parts

A spare parts collection is something you can only build up through time. Repair shops are filled with extra computers and have stacks of parts lying around in boxes. If a part doesn't work in one computer, the repair person pulls out the part and tries it in another. Through the process of elimination, repair shops figure out which parts are bad.

You don't have that many boxes of parts. Yet . . .

# *Making a System Disk*

Any time you're working on a hard drive, you need a *System disk,* also called a *Boot disk.* Whenever you turn on your computer, it looks for hidden "who, what, and where am I?" information stored on your hard drive.

If a floppy disk is sitting in the disk drive when you turn on your computer, it cannot find that hidden information and sends a message like this:

```
Non-System disk or disk error
Replace and press any key when ready
```

Your computer is saying that it couldn't find its hidden information on the floppy disk, so it gave up and stopped working. (The information was on the hard drive, but the computer was too lazy to look there.)

However, you can copy that important *system* information to a regular floppy disk. Then you can use that floppy disk to start up your computer, even if your hard drive is on the fritz.

You'll need a System disk if you're replacing your hard drive (see Chapter 12).

To make a System disk, follow these steps:

1. **Insert a blank disk (or a disk with information you're trying to get rid of) into drive A and close its latch.**

   The latches usually close automatically on the 3½-inch disk drives. Make sure that the disk matches your floppy drive's capacity — either high or low. Finally, only use drive A. Your computer never bothers to look for its hidden information in drive B, no matter how hard you try to make it do so.

2. **At the DOS prompt, type the following and then press Enter:**

   ```
   C:\> FORMAT A: /S
   ```

   That is, type the word **FORMAT**, a space, an A, a colon, a space, a forward slash (found near the right Shift key), and then an S. Got it? Then press Enter.

   Now, twiddle your thumbs. Eventually, the computer says, System transferred, which means it's through. Almost . . .

3. **Then your computer asks you to enter something called a volume label. Type the following at the prompt:**

```
Volume label (11 characters, ENTER for none)? SYSTEM DISK
```

That is, after the question mark, type **SYSTEM,** a space, and **DISK.** Press Enter when you're through and ignore the next few lines of gibberish the computer hurls your way.

4. **When asked to** `Format another (Y/N)?` **press the N key.**

One System disk is enough for today. The computer leaves you at the DOS prompt.

5. **Now type these commands, one after another, and press Enter after each command:**

```
c:\> COPY \DOS\FORMAT.COM A:
c:\> COPY \DOS\FDISK. EXE A:
```

Two important DOS commands are copied to your System disk for safe-keeping. You'll need those two commands if you ever replace your hard drive or add another one, a task tackled in Chapter 12.

6. **Remove the disk and use a felt-tip pen to write *System disk* on the label.**

Now, if your computer refuses to start some cold morning, you'll have a weapon: stick you System disk into drive A and press the Reset button. Hopefully, that will get the computer back on its feet.

If some of your best computer games refuse to run, saying that they need more memory, use your new System disk to boot your computer from drive A. That action sometimes placates the game into running.

Don't copy your AUTOEXEC.BAT or CONFIG.SYS files to your new floppy disk. Those are the files your System disk is designed to avoid.

# *Upgrade Do's and Doughnuts*

Whenever you need to do any of the following things, they'll be mentioned in the appropriate chapter next to a description of what kind of screwdriver you need. But all the upgrade do's and do not's have been collected and placed here for quick retrieval.

## Do upgrade one thing at a time

Even if you've just returned from the computer store with a new hard drive, modem, and monitor, don't try to install them at the same time. Install one part and make sure that it works before going on to the next part.

If you install all three parts at the same time and your computer doesn't work when you turn it on, there's no way of knowing which one is gagging your computer.

## Do watch out for static

You'll hear this one several times because it's that important. Static electricity can destroy computer parts. That's why computer parts come packaged in those weird, silvery bags that reflect light like the visor on John Armstrong's helmet. That high-tech plastic stuff will absorb any stray static before it zaps the part inside.

To make sure that you don't zap a computer part with static electricity, you need to discharge yourself — no matter how gross it sounds — before starting to work on your computer. Just touch a piece of bare metal, like the metal edge of your desk, to ground yourself. It's also important to ground yourself each time you move your feet, especially when standing on carpet or after you've moved the cat back out of the way.

## Do hang on to your old boxes and manuals

When you're wrapping up your computer for a move down the street, nothing works better than its old boxes. I keep mine on the top shelf in the garage, just in case I'll be moving. Don't bother hanging onto the smaller boxes, though, like the ones that come with a video card or mouse.

Hang on to *all* your old manuals, even if you don't understand a word they say. Sometimes a new part will start arguing with an older part, and the manuals often have hints on which switch to flip to break up the fight. (You'll find even more hints in Chapter 17.)

## Don't force parts together

Everything in your PC is designed to fit into place smoothly and without too much of a fight. If something doesn't fit right, stop, scratch your head, and try again using a slightly different tactic.

When trying to plug your monitor's cord into the back of your computer, for example, look closely at the end of the cord and then scrutinize the plug where it's supposed to fit. See how the pins are shaped a certain way? See how the plug's shape differs on one side? Turn the plug until it lines up with its socket and push slowly but firmly. Sometimes it helps if you jiggle it back and forth slightly. Ask your spouse to tickle you gently.

Stuff inside the case that plugs directly onto your motherboard seems to take the most force. Anything that plugs into the outside of your PC, however, should slip on pretty easily. It also slips off pretty easily, so the cables have little screws to hold everything in place firmly.

## Don't bend stuff that comes on cards

Many of your computer's internal organs are mounted on fiberglass boards. That's the reason there's a warning coming up right now:

Don't bend these boards, no matter how tempting. Bending the board can break the circuits subtly enough to damage the card. Worse yet, the cracks will be too small to see, so you won't know what went wrong.

If you hear little crackling sounds while you're doing something with a board — plugging it into a socket or plugging something into it — you're pushing the wrong way.

## Don't use head-cleaning disks

Many new computer owners get head-cleaning disks from well-meaning relatives the following Christmas. Head-cleaning disks look like a regular floppy disk with rice paper inside. Head-cleaning disks are supposed to clean any dirt and oxide deposits from the heads on your floppy drives.

Unfortunately, they often do more harm than good. If your floppy drive isn't working, try a head-cleaning disk to see whether it fixes the problem. But don't use head-cleaning disks on a regular basis.

## Don't rush yourself

Give yourself plenty of time. If you rush yourself or get nervous, you're much more likely to break something, which can cause even more nervousness.

## Don't open up monitors or power supplies

There's nothing inside monitors or power supplies that you can repair. Also, the power supply stores up voltage, even when it's not plugged in.

Don't open your power supply. It has electricity inside that can really zap you.

# How to Fish Out Dropped Screws

When a screw falls into the inner reaches of your PC, it usually lands in a spot inaccessible to human fingers. These steps will almost always call it back home:

1. Is it in plain sight? Try grabbing it with some long tweezers. If that doesn't work, wrap some tape, sticky-side out, around the end of a pencil or chopstick. With a few deft pokes, you may be able to snag it. A magnetized screwdriver can come in handy here, as well. (Don't leave the magnetized screwdriver near your floppy disks, though; the magnets can wipe out the information on them.)

2. If you don't see the runaway screw, gently tilt the computer to one side and then the other. Hopefully, the screw will roll out in plain sight. If you can hear it roll, you'll often discover what it's hiding behind.

3. Still can't find it? Pick up the computer's case with both hands, gently turn it upside down, and tilt it from side to side. The screw should fall out.

4. If you still can't find the screw, and it's not making any noise, check the floor beneath the computer. Sometimes screws hide in the carpet, where only bare feet can find them.

# Chapter 3
# Where Does This Piece Go? (Basic Computer Anatomy)

● ● ● ● ● ● ● ● ● ● ● ● ● ● ● ● ● ● ● ● ● ● ● ● ● ● ● ● ● ● ● ● ● ● ● ● ● ● ● ● ● ● ● ● ● ● ● ● ● ●

## In This Chapter

▶ The types of PCs

▶ Your PC: the case, keyboards, mice, scanners, modems, monitors, and printers

▶ Where all the cables plug in

▶ Your PC's innards: the motherboard, memory, disk drives, cards, and the power supply

● ● ● ● ● ● ● ● ● ● ● ● ● ● ● ● ● ● ● ● ● ● ● ● ● ● ● ● ● ● ● ● ● ● ● ● ● ● ● ● ● ● ● ● ● ● ● ● ● ●

*T*his chapter merely points out where your PC's parts live and what they're supposed to do. There's nothing "hands on" in here and nothing thought-provoking enough to share with your spouse over dinner. Instead, treat this chapter like a map to Disneyland — something to keep handy in your back pocket but to pull out for reference when you're looking for the nearest drinking fountain.

Oh, and just like when you visit Disneyland, you'll find yourself visiting different sections of this chapter after you start reading it: if you see a confusing word that's presented in ***bold italics,*** like ***CPU*** or ***motherboard,*** the term is more fully explained later in the chapter.

# The Types of PCs

You've probably heard the term *PC* or *IBM compatible.* You've also probably heard computers called by numbers such as 286, 386, or 8088, to name a few. This naming system can confuse newcomers because there are several models of PCs.

Unlike in the car industry, where new models get fun, imaginative names like *Charisma* or *Entourage,* in the computer industry PCs usually just get slapped with a number — the number of the main chip or ***CPU*** that makes them run.

Here's a rundown of the different PC models so you'll know which one you've been tapping on and how you can give it a little more zip.

## Original IBM PC (1981)

The PC that started the whole craze more than a decade ago isn't worth much today, even to antique dealers (see Figure 3-1). A Model T Ford still gets a raised eyebrow of respect in Sunday parades, but the original IBM PC is worth less than a Brady Bunch lunch box.

**Identifying characteristics:** The original IBM PC has big black *floppy disk drives,* which are almost 4 inches tall. It has no reset button and *IBM* letters across the front. It's heavy — and probably dusty, too. The original IBM PC has space for no more than five *cards.* It has an 8088 *CPU.*

**Why you should care:** This computer is too old for any serious upgrading. Some new parts simply won't fit inside its *case;* other new parts balk at interacting with the machine's older parts. You can repair its broken parts but only with parts that are just as slow. This guy may be able to balance your checkbook but only if you already have the software. Most of today's software won't run on an old IBM original.

**Upgradability:** One guy made a lamp out of his.

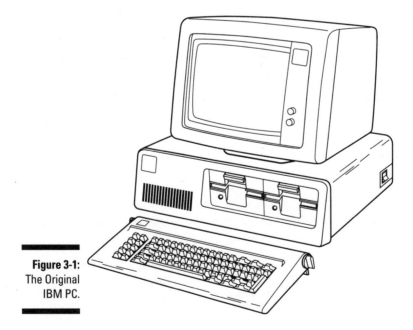

**Figure 3-1:**
The Original
IBM PC.

# IBM XT (early 1980s)

IBM dumped its original IBM PC for the flashier XT model, which introduced the **reset** button. When an XT computer froze, owners could simply push the reset button instead of trying to find the On/Off switch buried beneath cables protruding from their PC's rear.

**Identifying characteristics:** It has an 8086 or 8088 *CPU* and **slots** for eight 8-bit **cards.** But who wants to get technical? Just call the XT model a real slug.

**Why you should care:** Like its prototype, the original IBM PC, this computer is still a weakling. It can't run Windows 3.1, and it's too old to accept most of today's new parts. Like the original PC, it's repairable but don't bother trying to upgrade it. Buy a new computer.

**Upgradability:** You can't even reuse the case from this model; the case is the wrong size for most of today's parts. Make this computer into a lamp for the *other* side of the couch.

# IBM AT (mid-1980s)

The IBM AT is the *XT*'s replacement. This powerful guy finally added a little oomph to the desktop. In fact, all future computers copied this model. Today's computers are sometimes called AT-class computers, to separate them from the anemic XTs and PCs they replace.

**Identifying characteristics:** The IBM AT is up to five times faster than the XT; this computer's 286 *CPU* set the standard for computers to come.

**Why you should care:** This computer can do most of the things that today's powerhouse computers can do but slower — especially if you're trying to run Windows.

**Upgradability:** If you're ready to spend a little time fiddling around inside the case, you can add a new *motherboard* to bring this computer up to 386 status. You'll also have to add a new *power supply* to bring the AT back to life.

# 386 class (late 1980s)

The 386 class of computer (see Figure 3-2) includes the 486 (1989) and 586 (1993), which is known as the *Pentium*.

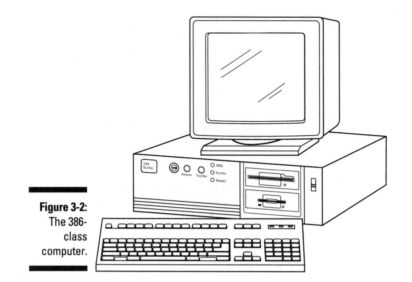

**Figure 3-2:**
The 386-
class
computer.

The chip designers finally got it right with the 386 chip used for these *CPU*s. In fact, that *CPU* spawned a whole new class of computers, simply called the *386 class.* This group includes the 386, the 486, and even the 586 (often called the *Pentium* by marketing whizzes).

These 386-class computers don't squirm as much when you try to upgrade them. You can stick new parts into them without causing a chain reaction of replacements.

**Identifying characteristics:** If your computer is less than three years old, chances are that it's a 386. Many of these computers say *386* on the front label of the case — *ZankMeister386 Turbo* or something similar.

**Why you should care:** You should care because you're typing on the current industry workhorse; most upgrade parts are aimed at the 386.

**Upgradability:** The easiest machines to upgrade, these guys can handle almost anything you throw at them. Most common upgrades include bigger *hard drives,* more *memory,* and faster video *cards.* Some people put wheels on the *case* so they can roll them around like TV carts.

## PS/2 (1987)

IBM, upset that so many other companies were making bucks off its computer design, decided to change the design. IBM added something called Micro Channel Architecture (also known as MCA for the nerds who like to sling letters around).

**Why you should care:** Watch out because these guys differ from *normal* computers. Most important, they use special MCA versions of **cards,** like video cards or internal **modems.** Also, PS/2s have smaller **mouse ports** that can't use the plug on most mice cables (although any old mouse will work, after you buy a cable adapter). When it comes to finding replacement parts for your PS/2, your best bet is to haul your old part to the shop and say, "I need another one of these."

**Upgradability:** Here's the bad news: you can upgrade a PS/2 pretty easily, but the PS/2-compatible parts cost more than their generic counterparts.

IBM pulled a fast one; not all PS/2s use that MCA stuff anymore. The only way you'll know for sure is to pull out the manual and peek: does it say MCA or *ISA?*

## A look at laptops

Like a spouse, laptops are quite resistant to change. Upgrades are not only difficult but expensive — almost every part must come directly from the laptop manufacturer. Nothing else will fit. Extra **memory,** internal **modems,** and bigger **hard drives** are available but only if you want to pay the price.

So you think that PCMCIA stuff is too expensive to read about? Actually, laptop manufacturers finally settled on a standard. They built little credit-card-sized slots into the laptops and let people stick little credit-card-sized gizmos called PCMCIA cards inside them. Today, you can buy extra memory or even modems on those little PCMCIA cards. They'll slide right into the side of the laptop like an ATM card. They're whoppingly expensive right now, but the prices are dropping quickly.

Keep your laptop's lid closed if you take it bungee jumping; otherwise, the screen can snap off at the hinge during the crucial bounce-back point.

## PCjr

IBM tried to make a *home-sized* computer for the home market, but nobody bought it. Rumor has it that several thousand PCjrs are sitting in a warehouse somewhere back east. The PCjr is not standard with a *real* PC. Leave any PCjrs (yours included) sitting on the shelf with the 8-track players at Salvation Army.

# The Case

The guts of your PC live inside the case, which is almost always beige. However, some executives buy stylish black cases to match their leather chairs. Like everything else about PCs, cases come in several styles.

## Big

The lumbering old *XT* computer came in a big case to house all its big parts. Now, just as television sets have shrunk to fit in the dashboards of taxi cabs, computers have shrunk, too. Nobody sells those big cases anymore, and some newer parts don't fit in them, either.

## Little (also called small footprint)

These newer, smaller cases don't eat up as much room on your desktop as the big, *XT*-style cases. But they still hold as many computer parts because today's parts have shrunk along with the cases.

## Tower

Macho young men like to put big tires on their pickup trucks and stand around with their arms folded. Macho young computer nerds like to put their PCs in a *tower case* — a regular computer case that's been turned on its side. Tower cases take up less space on your desk. They're also a little roomier, so you can jam a few extra goodies inside.

## Can I just turn my regular case on its side?

Most of the newer computers can be propped up sideways. Some stores even sell cheap little *tower props* to keep your PC pointing skyward. But some of the older computers don't like working sideways.

Older hard drives never knew that people would try such weirdness, so they sometimes have trouble spitting your data back out if kept on their side. If you're really keen on the sideways idea, give it a try. But back up your hard drive first and be on the lookout for any error messages in the weeks ahead.

In fact, some people recommend that you do the following steps if you're going to try the sideways thing:

1. Back up all your data.

2. With the PC on its side, reformat your hard drive.

3. Copy all your data back to your hard drive.

# Case Lights and Buttons

Like a car's dashboard, the front of your computer's case comes with lights and buttons (but no coffee cup holder, unfortunately). Figure 3-3 shows the various lights and buttons.

## Power light

Some power lights have a picture of a little light bulb next to them; others simply say *Power.* Either way, the light comes on when you turn on your PC. (And the light is off when the computer is off.)

## Power switch

The power switch used to be mounted on the back of a PC's case, where nobody could reach it. A few years later, some savvy engineers moved the power switch to the PC's side, which was one step better. About three years ago, a core group of designers broke new ground by mounting the switch on the computer's front, within easy reach. (However, some people still prefer the rear-mounted switch where three-year-old Larissa can't flip it back and forth while her father's trying to pay the bills.)

The power switch is rarely labeled On or Off. Instead, the little line means On, and the little circle means Off. The most educated people just listen to their PCs: the humming sound means on, and silence means off.

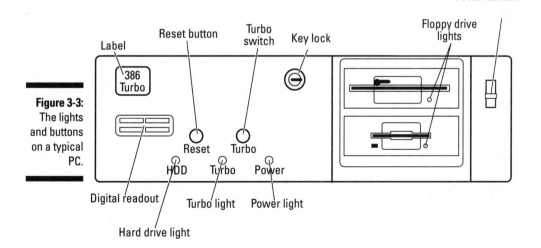

**Figure 3-3:**
The lights
and buttons
on a typical
PC.

## Turbo buttons and exhaust emission trivia

Fast computers are a good thing. That is, until you start losing to Rashtar because his ship can shoot faster than yours. So frustrated computer engineers added a Turbo switch to let their computers run slowly for games. Normally, your PC runs as fast as possible. But when you push the Turbo button, the little light goes off and the computer slows down.

Some computers don't have a mechanical Turbo switch. Instead, you press some awkward key combination, like Ctrl and Alt and a hyphen. You may have to pull out your manual to see which direction you'll need to contort your fingers.

If your computer seems to be running slowly, make sure that the Turbo switch is set to the normal, fast speed.

## Reset button

One of the most often used buttons, the reset button gets the attention of a PC that's frozen solid. Unfortunately, when your PC comes back to life, it drops everything it was working on. That means you'll lose any work you hadn't saved to a file. Only push the reset button as a last resort.

## Floppy drive lights

*Floppy drives* are those slots in front of your computer that eat floppy disks. Almost all floppy drives have a little green or yellow light on the front. The little light turns on when your computer reads or writes any information to the disk, making it easier to tell whether the drive's working.

Don't ever remove a floppy disk from its drive while the little light is still on, or some of your data may vanish.

## Hard drive light

Like their floppy cousins, *hard drives* also flip on their little light when sending information to or from your computer's brain. Sometimes that light is labeled with letters like *HDD*; other computers use a little picture that looks like a can of beans.

If your hard drive's light isn't working, it's an easy fix. Head for Chapter 12 to learn which wires fell off and need to be reattached. (Floppy drive lights can't be repaired as easily, if at all.)

## Digital readout

The fanciest computers these days flash little numbers and letters in a display on the front of the computer's case. Sometimes the display says how fast the computer's running, and other times it shows a user-written message, like "Ookie is Good." Digital readout is simply a frill, though, just like the fancy red bookmarks that come stitched into the Book Classics of the Month Club titles. A digital readout doesn't make your computer work any better.

## Key and lock

The key doesn't start the computer. It doesn't even open a secret storage area in the case where you can find stashed snack foods. The key just disables the keyboard so nobody can poke through your computer while you're at lunch. Don't feel bad if yours disappeared a few months after you bought your computer. Most people lose their keys.

# Those Port Things

The front of a computer is pleasant and clean. A few sculptured air vents may add to the motif. The rear of a computer is an ugly conglomeration of twisted cables, plugs, and dust. You'll probably have to pull the PC away from the wall before you can see which cable protrudes from which hole.

Some people call these holes *ports*. Others call them *plugs* or even *jacks*. Either way, your PC's rear should look something like the one in Figure 3-4.

Most computers have a few empty ports on the back. They don't all need cables in them for your computer to work.

All the cables that plug into the back of your PC will only fit one way. If a cable doesn't seem to fit right, try turning it gently, back and forth, until it slips in.

The following sections show you what these plugs look like and examine what they're *doing* back there, anyway.

## Power cord

The power cord goes into one of the biggest holes in the back of your computer. (The power cord is usually the thickest cord coming out of your computer.) It looks like the picture in Figure 3-5.

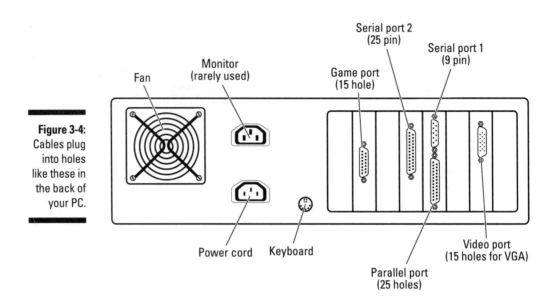

**Figure 3-4:**
Cables plug
into holes
like these in
the back of
your PC.

What's the other inverted power plug for? Most computers have a second plug next to the power plug that looks the same — only inverted, like the one in Figure 3-6. Years ago, that's where monitors used to plug in to get their power. Today, almost all monitors plug into the wall, but the little plug remains to befuddle the curious.

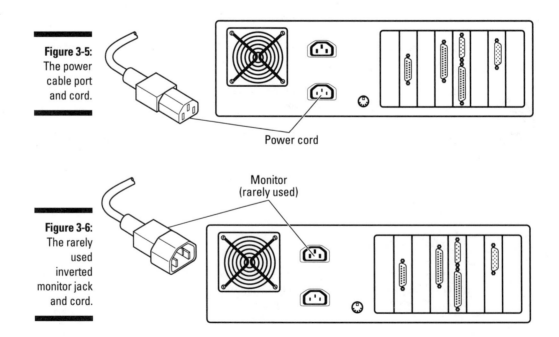

**Figure 3-5:**
The power
cable port
and cord.

Power cord

**Figure 3-6:**
The rarely
used
inverted
monitor jack
and cord.

Monitor
(rarely used)

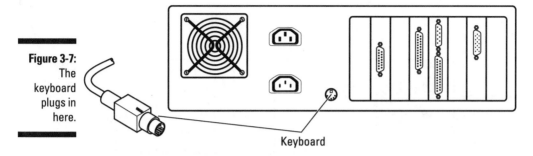

**Figure 3-7:**
The keyboard plugs in here.

Keyboard

## Keyboard cord

Your curly **keyboard** cord plugs into a little round hole in the back of your computer (see Figure 3-7). The plug is usually located near the middle about an inch up from the bottom. (An occasional renegade computer will have the keyboard hole on the side or even the front.)

Look carefully for a little raised plastic line or bump on one side of the keyboard plug. That little bump faces up, toward the top of the case, when you're plugging in the keyboard.

## Serial port

Here's where things get a little wacko. If your computer has one serial port, it's almost always shaped like the one in Figure 3-8.

If your computer has a second serial port, it's almost always shaped like the one in Figure 3-9.

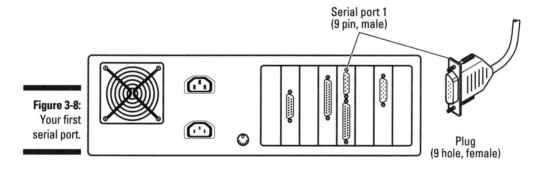

Serial port 1
(9 pin, male)

**Figure 3-8:**
Your first serial port.

Plug
(9 hole, female)

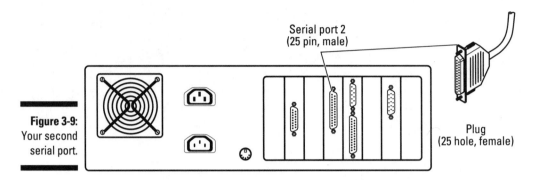

**Figure 3-9:**
Your second
serial port.

Serial port 2
(25 pin, male)

Plug
(25 hole, female)

Serial ports are where you plug in cables connected to gizmos that feed the computer information — gizmos like *modems, scanners,* and even *mice.* Serial ports are very popular; dozens of gizmos want to use them. (Your computer can only listen to two serial ports at the same time, however, creating a bit of madness that's covered in Chapter 17.)

Some manuals refer to serial ports as COM ports. Manuals over the deep end call them RS-232 ports or even RS-232c ports. Nobody will guffaw if you just call yours a serial port, though.

Some gizmos inside your computer can use a serial port without physically plugging into one. Internal modems are notorious for this practice and, there-fore, cause much confusion and gnashing of teeth. In fact, to receive an Ameri-can Dental Association endorsement, this book added a special "COM port" section in Chapter 17.

The serial ports on some older computers may vary. Luckily, you can find inexpensive adapters at Radio Shack and most computer stores.

## *Parallel port*

Plug the cable from your ***printer*** into the thing that looks like Figure 3-10. The end of the cable that looks like a grim robot's mouth plugs into your printer, and the end with little protruding pins plugs into your parallel port.

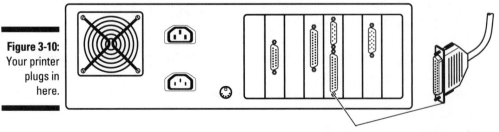

**Figure 3-10:**
Your printer
plugs in
here.

Parallel port
(25 hole, female)

Printer cable
(25 pin, male)

## Is your parallel port bi?

For years, parallel ports simply shoveled informa- tion to the printer. But now, bidirectional parallel ports are the rage. For example, Kingston Tech- nologies sells a portable hard drive. It plugs into your parallel port and appears as drive D on your screen. You can copy information back and forth from it like a regular hard drive. Some little palmtop and laptop computers can send information back and forth through a parallel port, too.

Some computers, including a few models from Toshiba, don't have bidirectional parallel ports. If you're only going to be using your parallel port for sending information to your printer, that's no prob- lem. But if you plug something into your parallel port that's supposed to send information to your computer, it may not work.

## *Game port*

Sized midway between a parallel port and a serial port, a game port is where you plug in the joystick (see Figure 3-11). The card that houses your serial and parallel port usually has a game port tossed in as well.

You don't need two game ports to plug in two joysticks. Just buy a cheap Y adapter cable, usually sold at the same place you've been buying computer games.

Be aware that many *sound cards* come with game ports as well. In fact, the two game ports will probably argue over who gets priority until you disable one of them. (Jump to the "Jumpers" section in Chapter 17.)

Also, most sound cards let your game port double as a *MIDI* port. By plugging a weird boxy thing into your game port, you can plug in music synthesizers, drum machines, and other things that let you sound like David Bowie on his *Heroes* album.

Not even David Bowie cares that MIDI stands for Musical Instrument Digital Interface.

Game port
(15 hole, female)

**Figure 3-11:**
Plug
joysticks
into this
thing.

Joystick cable
(15 pin, male)

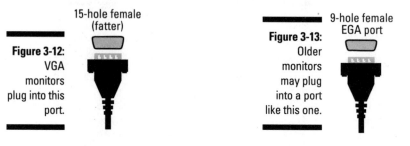

**Figure 3-12:** VGA monitors plug into this port.

15-hole female (fatter)

**Figure 3-13:** Older monitors may plug into a port like this one.

9-hole female EGA port

## Video port

Although it looks like a fat serial port, a video port is a plug for your ***monitor.*** Nothing but your monitor will fit (unless you use a hammer). The most popular video port, called ***VGA,*** looks like the one in Figure 3-12. Older monitors may plug into ports like the one in Figure 3-13.

## Other ports

Other unidentified ports might peek from the back of your computer. Some may be for networks, letting your computer socialize with other computers. Others can be for ***sound cards*** or ***compact disc drives.*** You may even spot a plain old phone jack that is resting on the end of an internal modem.

The old IBM PCs had a second port identical to the keyboard port: computer nerds would plug a tape recorder cord in there to store their files because floppy drives were too expensive.

# Keyboards

Keyboards come in zillions of different brands but three basic flavors:

**The old *XT*-style keyboard:** One of the oldest keyboards, this 83-key antique doesn't have any little lights on it, making it harder to tell whether you've pressed your Caps Lock key.

**The *AT*-style (standard) keyboard:** The designers at IBM added little lights to this newer keyboard, shown in Figure 3-14. They also tossed in a separate numeric keypad on the right side. Some eccentric engineer also added an 84th key, called SysRq, that has never done anything but confuse people. IBM meant to use it for something revolutionary but then forgot which department had come up with the idea. Nobody has used the key since.

**Figure 3-14:**
A standard
AT keyboard
(84 key).

**The 101-key (enhanced) keyboard:** Also known as the extended keyboard, the keyboard in Figure 3-15 not only has a separate numeric keypad, but it also has a second set of cursor-control keys sitting between the keypad and the rest of the letters.

✔ You can use either an *AT*-style keyboard or an Enhanced Keyboard with your new AT or 386-class computer. But don't try to reuse your old *XT* keyboard — those guys used different types of wiring.

The old XT-style keyboards don't work with anything but XTs. But here's a secret: many manufacturers sell one keyboard that can work with both. Check the bottom of your keyboard, and you might find a little switch. Flip the switch to the X side to use it with an XT computer or flip the switch to the A side to use it with the AT-style computer.

✔ Some expensive keyboards have a *trackball* built in: by whirling around the little ball, you can make an arrow scoot across your screen. When the arrow points to the right button on the screen, click the little button next to the trackball. The button on the screen will be selected, just as if you'd pushed it with an electronic finger. It's quick, sanitary, and saves you the cost of a mouse.

**Figure 3-15:**
An AT
Enhanced
Keyboard
(101 key).

Don't bang on your keyboard. You're not using an old typewriter anymore. Just a tap will do the trick and your keyboard will last a little longer.

That weird little ridge along the top of most keyboards isn't just there to look sporty. It's designed so you can prop a book against it, leaning it back toward your monitor. That makes copying stuff out of books a lot easier.

Looking for more ridges? Check out the F and J keys. You'll find little lumps on them, which makes it easier to reposition your fingers if you're typing in the dark.

# Mice, Scanners, and Modems

Referred to as *input devices* by computer scientists, gizmos like mice, scanners, and modems feed information to your computer. The information may be the motion of your hand, as with a mouse, or the newspaper picture you're scanning for your club newsletter.

## Mice

Like all things attached to PCs, mice come in several different breeds, described next:

**Serial mouse:** The tail from a serial mouse plugs into one of your **serial ports.**

**Bus mouse:** The tail from a bus mouse, in contrast, plugs onto the mouse's own **card.** You'll need to take the **case** off your computer to stick the bus mouse's card inside.

**PS/2 style:** Usually found on IBM's PS/2 series of computers, the tail on this mouse plugs into a tiny round port with seven holes.

**Exotic species:** A few other types of mice have hit the scene. For example, cordless (tailless) mice come in handy for people who're tired of knocking papers off their desk with their mouse cord. Cordless mice are not only more expensive than their tailed counterparts, but they eat up batteries, too.

- The latest breed of mice uses feet rather than balls. When a normal mouse ball rolls around, it gathers dust, which rolls up into the mouse's guts. The little optomechanical feet on Honeywell's footed mouse don't roll, so they don't flip dust and hairs into any vital organs.

- Some people prefer **trackballs,** described in the "Keyboards" section. Others think that trackballs are as awkward as dental floss, especially the tiny ones that clip to the sides of laptops.

## Who really cares how many buttons a mouse has?

Although mice come in two- and three-button models, very few software packages require a three-button mouse. In Windows, you'll only use one button, unless you're doing weird color changes in the Paint program. In IBM's OS/2 software, you'll need to use both buttons.

Actually, the three-button mouse seems to be a dying breed, so don't feel cheated if your mouse has only two buttons. (Just don't try to use a Macintosh mouse. It only has one button, and it won't even work with Windows.)

## *Scanners*

Handheld scanners look like *mice* with anvil heads, as you see in Figure 3-16.

When you slide a scanner over letters or pictures, the scanner sends a copy of the image onto your computer screen, where it can be saved as a file (much to the consternation of copyright attorneys around the world). The latest, full-page scanners look a little bit like fax machines.

Like *bus mice,* scanners usually come with their own *cards.* The expensive scanners can read in color pictures. The cheap ones can only handle black-and-white pictures.

The latest breed of scanners has Optical Character Recognition (OCR). That simply means that when you slide the scanner over a page of text, the scanner "types" the text into your computer as letters and words and not as a picture of the text.

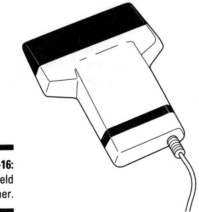

**Figure 3-16:**
A handheld
scanner.

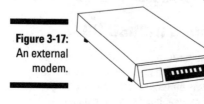

**Figure 3-17:**
An external
modem.

## *Modems*

These little boxes let your computer connect to the telephone line, so you can call up other computers, meet friends from around the world, and swap biscuit recipes. You can also grab the news, weather, stock reports, and weird stories about weird people doing weird things. Modems are the 90s equivalent of the 50s short-wave radio, but you don't need a towering network of nerdy antennas that embarrass your neighbors.

Like *mice* and *scanners,* external modems plug into *serial ports,* where they're easy to reach and use. An external modem is shown in Figure 3-17.

Internal modems live inside your computer on little *cards,* where they're hidden from view, but they cause more trouble. Actually, internal modems are easy to install but notoriously difficult to set up, especially if your computer's already hooked up to a mouse or a scanner. (Chapter 17 is waiting for you.)

The newest modems can send faxes of information that's already inside your computer. That makes it easy to fax party fliers you've created in your word processor, but impossible to send that newspaper clipping you know Jerry would get a kick out of.

## *Monitors*

A computer monitor may look like a TV, but it's nowhere near as repairable. In fact, you'll buy a new monitor after you hear how much money the shop wants to fix the old one. Monitors come in several styles, with the most expensive being the biggest, clearest, and most colorful.

Here are the basic types of monitors:

**Hercules, Color Graphics Adapter (CGA), Enhanced Graphics Adapter (EGA):** These are the older types of monitors you want to upgrade because everything on them looks so grainy. Plus, the colors are pretty awful, especially after you've seen a better quality monitor in the store.

**Video Graphics Array (VGA):** The current industry workhorse, this type of monitor works very well with Windows. It usually needs a *16-bit card* that requires a *16-bit slot,* so this type won't always work in an *XT.*

**Super Video Graphics Array (SVGA):** This type of monitor packs more colors and images onto the same size screen and is starting to replace the VGA monitor as the norm.

**Extended Graphics Adapter (XGA), 8514/A:** This expensive monitor is mostly for high-end (expensive) graphics work.

*Beware:* Your monitor only displays what your computer's *video card* has sent. The two work as a team. That's why it's best to buy your monitor and video card at the same time to make sure that they'll work well together.

No, a TV set won't work as a monitor anymore. They both use different technology, as you can see for yourself if you press your nose against the TV screen and then against your monitor. Some fancy cards let you watch TV on a computer monitor, though. However, the bad news is that they cost more than a real TV set of the same size. These cards are mostly for people who want screen shots of Gilligan's Island for their Windows wallpaper.

Because software slings a lot of graphics onto the screen, accelerator cards are the rage today. The computer's brain, the *CPU,* was designed to crunch numbers, not to paint pictures of lilies. So accelerator cards come with built-in *graphics chips* that relieve the CPU of its most intensive graphics chores. Windows, Prodigy, and other colorful software run much faster with an accelerator card.

# Printers

Printers take the information from your screen and stick it on paper. They accomplish this feat in a wide variety of ways. Several types of printers use different methods, as described next:

**Dot matrix:** One of the noisiest printers, dot-matrix printers create images by pressing tiny dots against the paper. They're inexpensive, and it shows. Many people are dumping dot-matrix printers when they break and buying an inkjet or laser printer instead.

**Daisywheel:** The noisiest by far, these printers work like a typewriter, pushing little letters and numbers against a ribbon to leave images on the page. A dying breed, they're found most often in thrift shops. Upgrades? You can just replace the ribbon and add little *wheels* to get different styles of letters.

**Figure 3-18:**
A laser
printer.

**Inkjet:** Popular for its low price and high quality, inkjet printers squirt ink onto a page, which leads to a surprisingly high-quality image. They're not upgradable, but you need to replace the cartridge every once in a while.

**Laser:** Laser printers, like the one in Figure 3-18, are currently the most popular. They use the same technology as copy machines — *good* copy machines. There's not much to upgrade here, although some laser printers let you put more memory into them. With more memory, they can print more graphics on a single page. Eventually, you'll have to replace their toner cartridge (which costs more than an inkjet's cartridge).

You'll find tips for changing ribbons and cartridges in Chapter 8.

The Kauffman Machine Shop in Olathe, Kansas, sells a $20,000 printer that transfers pictures from your computer's screen into colored icing on a cake. It can also decorate cookies and cupcakes.

# The Motherboard

Some people call a motherboard a *system board,* but they're the same thing — a sheet of khaki green fiberglass that lines the inside bottom of your computer's **case.** A motherboard with its parts labeled is shown in Figure 3-19.

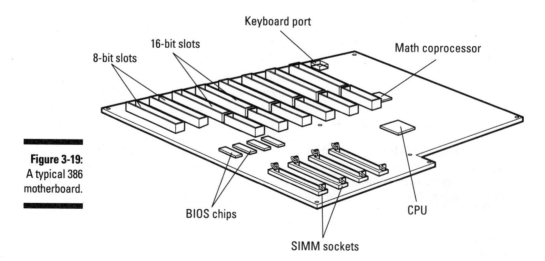

Keyboard port

16-bit slots

8-bit slots

Math coprocessor

**Figure 3-19:**
A typical 386
motherboard.

BIOS chips

CPU

SIMM sockets

By itself, a motherboard is like an empty plate. The important stuff lives on top of the motherboard. The motherboard then acts as a roadway of sorts, pushing information back and forth between all the following residents.

## Central processing unit (CPU)

Your computer's brain is its CPU (pronounced *See Pee You*) — a little chip that shovels information back and forth between all your computer's parts. Like the one in Figure 3-20, a CPU is a tiny little thing, ranging from the size of a Wheat Thin to a Triscuit.

Even though CPUs are tiny, they're one of the most expensive parts of your computer, costing hundreds of dollars. That's why computers are named after the type of CPU they contain: a 286, 386, 486, or 586 (also call the Pentium).

Actually, CPUs get two numbers. The first is the design number (386, 486, and so on), which measures power or how big a shovelful of information the CPU can move around. The second number is the chip's megahertz (25 MHz, 33 MHz, and so on), which measures its speed or how fast it can sling information around. The design number is more important, though. For example, a 25 MHz 486 will be faster than a 33 MHz 386.

> ✔ Some CPUs even get letters: a 386SX is a slightly retarded (and much cheaper) version of the 386DX (or a plain old 386). A 486SX is a slower version of a plain old 486. And a chip ending in SL means that it has some power-saving features, usually cherished by laptop users.

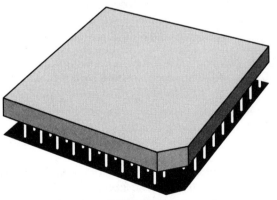

**Figure 3-20:**
A 286 CPU.

68-pin package (80286 microprocessor)

✔ For the most part, CPUs come bundled with the motherboard. You can't upgrade your 286 by sticking a 486 CPU into it. The chip won't fit in the little hole, and the motherboard can't handle the chip's extra power.

✔ The oldest PCs, like IBM's original PC and XT, came with an 8088 or 8086 CPU. These toddlers will never grow up. Leave them on the doorstep of a thrift shop and take a tax deduction. You can't upgrade them and nobody wants to buy them.

Here are some trivial CPU death facts: most chips are rated by the number of "million hours" they're supposed to last. (One million hours is about 114 years, by the way.) When chips die, it's because of dust particles that fell into the chip while it was being cooked up on the manufacturing line. With so many tiny wires and electrical passages packed into a little chip, a single dust particle is like a tree falling across a freeway. There's no highway patrolman to stop traffic and pull the tree off the road, so the chip just stops working.

## Math coprocessor

A chip like the *CPU,* a math coprocessor acts as a calculator of sorts. It pipes up with quick answers to math questions like that wiseguy in Mrs. Jackson's class. By listening to the math coprocessor's answers, the CPU can work more quickly.

Coprocessors are optional because they only speed up math problems: most people don't calculate logarithms very often. If you're doing a lot of math work, like running spreadsheets or creating engineering drawings, a coprocessor may help out. Otherwise, don't bother. (A coprocessor won't speed up Windows unless you're running spreadsheets; then it will quicken up Excel and accelerate Quicken.)

If you have a 486DX chip, you already have a math coprocessor; it's built in to the chip. The 486SX lacks the coprocessor; you'll have to add one to speed up your math homework.

## BIOS

If the *CPU* can be described as the computer's brain, then the BIOS can be called its nervous system. Short for Basic Input/Output System, the BIOS handles computing chores in the background, kind of like our nervous system keeps us breathing, even when we forget to.

The BIOS handles the bare grunt work of a PC: how *floppy disks* grab data or what happens when you press a key on the *keyboard.*

- The BIOS comes written on special little chips called **ROM** chips that live on the motherboard of all IBM-compatible computers. When you first turn on your computer, you'll see which company's bunch of nerds wrote your computer's BIOS and in what year. For example, one of my computers says, "386-BIOS (C)1988 American Megatrends Inc." when it starts. That means the American Megatrends company wrote my computer's BIOS in 1988.

- Why should you care? Well, an older BIOS sometimes can't handle a newer product (or vice versa). That means you need to buy new BIOS chips (often difficult to locate), or you can bite the bullet and buy a new motherboard.

## Expansion slots and cards

A motherboard has little parking spaces called *slots*. The slots are for little computer gadgets that come on *cards*. Together, they make most upgrades a breeze: pop off the computer's **case,** slide a card into a slot, fasten down the card with a single screw, and stick the case back on.

Cards look like miniature motherboards — daughterboards, so to speak. Something so simple had to have a problem, so here it is: cards come in two sizes, 8-bit or 16-bit, as shown in Figure 3-21 and Figure 3-22.

An 8-bit card has one little protruding thing from its bottom that matches up with the single slot it fits into.

A 16-bit card has two little things protruding from its bottom that match up with the two little slots it fits into.

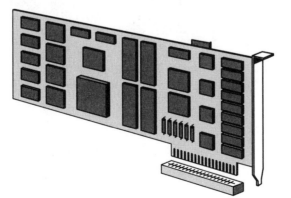

**Figure 3-21:**
An 8-bit card and its 8-bit slot.

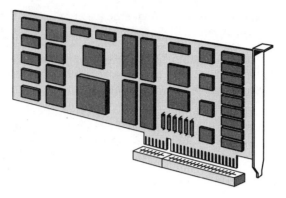

**Figure 3-22:**
A 16-bit card and its 16-bit slot.

✔ Before you go card shopping, peek inside your computer's case to see whether it uses 8-bit or 16-bit slots. Most *386-class* computers come with a mixture of 16- and 8-bit slots.

The bigger 16-bit slots still work with the smaller 8-bit cards. The small 8-bit slots can't handle any 16-bit cards, though (although some 16-bit VGA cards can run in 8-bit mode when plugged into an 8-bit slot).

✔ One last detail — some people refer to those slots as your computer's *expansion bus.*

Some 386 computers have slots in odd places, and nothing seems to fit into them. Those are 32-bit slots, designed especially for the manu-facturer's own particular brand of card. Some manufacturers let you stick their expensive memory cards into the slots. Others let you stick in little CPU upgrade cards. Those cards are very expensive, however. Most users ignore their 32-bit slots.

Your computer's row of parking space slots is called an *expansion bus.* It's called a bus because it's really a roadway of sorts for carrying information back and forth between the cards and your CPU. The 16-bit cards and slots have a bigger roadway, so they can carry more information back and forth than the smaller 8-bit cards and slots.

✔ Some folks refer to cards as *boards,* but they're the same thing: little goodies that slide inside your computer to make it more fun.

## More gibberish about ISA, EISA, and HEE-HAW

Your computer's little slots not only come in two sizes (that 8-or 16-bit stuff) but in three different types:

ISA: Chances are, your computer uses ISA (Industry Standard Architecture) cards. Just about every card you can find works in an ISA type of computer.

MCA: If you bought an *IBM PS/2,* you probably have MCA (Micro Channel Architecture) slots. Those slots aren't compatible with the ISA cards that everybody else uses, and they cost more. Don't feel too bad, though. The MCA slots have a better design, with fewer complications when you're installing new cards.

EISA: Finally, some people shelled out the extra bucks for EISA (Enhanced Industry-Standard Architecture) slots. Designed by jealous computer companies after IBM came out with its MCA stuff, EISA hasn't really caught on. Specially designed EISA cards were supposed to solve some ISA problems, but only a few companies make EISA cards, and most of them are for boring network stuff. The good news? EISA can run ISA cards, so people who bought EISA computers aren't mad.

## *What cards does your computer have?*

Get this: Most of those **ports** you've been plugging cables into at the back of your computer are *really* cards. They're the *tail ends* of cards, as you'll see when you open your computer case for the first time.

In fact, your computer probably came with these three cards inside:

**I/O card:** This is a fancy name for the card with your **serial port** and **parallel port.** Some companies toss in a **game port,** as well.

**Video card:** Your monitor plugs into this one. This card tells it what to put on the screen.

**Controller card:** You might not know that you have this one because it's hidden inside the **case.** Cables from this card connect to your **floppy drives** and your **hard drive.**

**Other cards:** Any other cards you spot may be for internal **modems, compact disc players, sound cards, scanners,** and a variety of other toys.

One last thing: Some cards are starting to do double-duty. For example, Intel's SatisFAXtion 400 internal modem lets you plug a scanner into it, too. Orchid's Fahrenheit video card comes with built-in sound card circuitry that lets you record sounds. Sometimes these double-duty cards can be a life-saver when you've run out of slots for all your cards.

## Complete, utter gibberish

For years, people would stick their new gadgets into their computer's slots, where their computers could find and play with them. But the slot system wasn't the quickest way to move data around. So some companies started taking stuff that normally came on cards — video cards, serial and parallel ports, and hard drive controllers — and building it right onto the motherboard itself.

That way the data not only moves faster, but it frees up some slots for more exciting stuff like sound cards and CD-ROM drives.

The latest news is called VL-bus. Some companies are putting special super-fast VL-bus slots on their computers' motherboards. Will it become a new standard, like ISA, EISA, or MCA? Who knows? The key players are still arm-wrestling over patents and other geekish corporate stuff.

## *Battery*

Believe it or not, your PC has a battery, just like your smoke detector. It sits on the *motherboard* and usually lasts about three years. Most batteries are easy to replace. You'll know that yours has died if your computer keeps asking you what time it is or if it forgets what type of *hard drive* you own and subsequently won't let you use it. You'll find the sorry symptoms (and battery replacement instructions) in Chapter 9.

## *Memory (random-access memory, or RAM)*

If you've talked to people about your computer problems, you've probably seen them rub their jaw, narrow their eye, and say, "Sounds like you might need more memory." Adding more memory is one of the most popular upgrades today. It's also one of the easiest upgrades, depending on the friendliness of your computer.

When your computer's *CPU* is telling all your computer's parts what to do, it doesn't have a scratch pad for taking notes. So the CPU stores its information in your computer's memory. The more memory the computer has to work with, the more complicated stuff it can do.

If you're using Windows, you can probably use more memory.

Memory comes on *chips*, just like your CPU. Just as CPUs are rated by their power and speed, memory chips are rated by their storage and speed.

Although all the memory serves the same purpose, it comes in three different packages:

**DIP:** This is the old-style chip. DIP stands for dual in-line package, but everybody just calls it DIP. (This DIP is no relation to DIP switches, which are little rows of switches you can flip on or off.) DIPs look like antennaless cockroaches, as shown in Figure 3-23. These chips plug into sockets on the motherboard, where they lie down in neat little rows like graves.

**SIMM:** DIPs worked fine for years, except for two things: People kept breaking off the DIPs' little legs when trying to push them into their sockets. Plus, because they lie flat, DIPs hogged up too much room. So some spry engineer took a leftover strip of fiberglass from a motherboard, fastened the little DIPs onto it, and called it a SIMM (single in-line memory module). You can see both types of memory in Figure 3-23.

SIMMs slide into their own tiny slots. Because the DIPs are hanging sideways from the SIMM, they take up less room. Confused between a SIMM's slots and **expansion slots?** They're actually very different: the SIMM's slots are tiny things; expansion slots are huge in comparison, as shown in Figure 3-19. There's no way to get slapped by accidentally putting the wrong one in the wrong place.

SIMMS come in several varieties. Some have three DIP chips on them; others have nine. Don't mix varieties if you can help it.

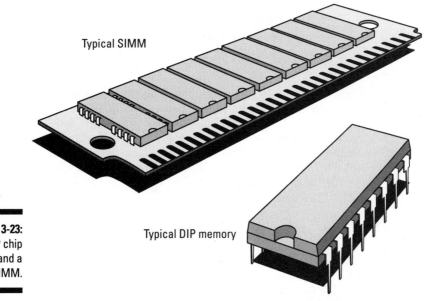

Typical SIMM

**Figure 3-23:**
A DIP chip
and a
SIMM.

Typical DIP memory

Some programs, notably IBM's OS/2, run into problems when a computer's SIMMs aren't all the same type. If your SIMMS don't all run at the same speed, OS/2 can burp indiscriminately and cause sporadic crashes that can't be traced to anything in particular. Also, OS/2 tends to have problems if some of your SIMMs use nine chips and others use three. To be on the safe side, try to keep your SIMMs running at the same speed and with the same number of DIP chips (three or nine).

### SIPs

A SIP is pretty much like a SIMM: a tiny little card with a bunch of DIPs on it. But whereas a SIMM has a long flat edge that pushes into a slot, a SIP has a bunch of little prongs that push into a bunch of little holes. It looks kind of like a cat's flea comb.

If you're not sure what kind of memory you have, pluck out a chip, put it in a Ziploc baggie, and bring it to the memory chip store. The person in the T-shirt behind the counter can then sell you some more of the same kind.

The price of chips moves up and down faster than pork belly futures. You'd be surprised how much money you can save by watching the prices and waiting for the right moment.

### Memory on expansion boards

What's an owner to do if the computer's motherboard can't hold any more memory? Some people add a memory expansion *card.* Packed with memory chips, this card pops into a *slot* just like a *video card.*

The computer can grab for its memory there just as if the memory chips were sitting on the traditional spot in the motherboard.

Here's yet more memory stuff to remember: the memory chips on your *motherboard* have life goals that are different from the ones on your *printer* or video card. You can't swap memory chips from your printer to your video card or from your computer to your printer. The chips won't fit.

# All those other little parts on the motherboard

Who cares about all those other little chips sitting on the motherboard, like the 8253 Programmable Interval Timer (U34)? Very few people, that's for sure. So ignore the rest of the little lumpy things sitting on your motherboard.

## Rambling about DRAM, SRAM, RAM, and ROM

For the most part, you're not breaking any computer etiquette rules when you say, "I need some more RAM for my computer." But here are the nerdy distinctions:

SRAM (static random-access memory) is very fast and very expensive. Little snippets of SRAM live in a special place on your motherboard. Whenever the CPU dishes out information to a computer part, it sends a copy of that information to the SRAM. If any computer parts ask for the same information, the CPU just grabs it from the SRAM and dishes it out again, saving time.

DRAM (dynamic random-access memory) is a little slower than SRAM but a little cheaper. When

people say that you need more RAM, they're talking about DRAM.

RAM, mentioned by itself, almost always means DRAM, described in the preceding paragraph.

ROM (read-only memory) differs from all the preceding types of memory. Normally, a computer moves information in and out of RAM as it works. But a ROM chip holds onto information and doesn't ever let go. For example, your computer's *BIOS* comes on ROM. Because your computer's BIOS doesn't normally change, it's stored permanently on a ROM chip. ROM chips are not only a convenient way to store information, but they're a safer way, too: your computer can't accidentally erase the information.

Even if those other little chips break, you won't be able to fix them or even tell which one's broken. Leave that job to the folks in the shop, who'll hook them up to expensive instruments with flashing lights and probe around while wolfing down mouthfuls of Atomic Fire Ball candies.

# Disk Drives

Computers use memory chips for doing immediate work: running programs or putting pictures on the screen. But when you're done working and want to save the fruits of your labors, you'll be putting your data on disks. They come in two basic flavors: floppy disks and hard disks.

## Floppy drives

Remember back in the old days of wide-spaced parking lots when you could easily back a car in and out of your parking space? Unfortunately, shop owners figured that they could cram twice as many cars in the same-sized lot by making each parking space a little smaller.

Computer engineers did the same thing with floppy disks and floppy drives. The older floppy drives, like the one shown in Figure 3-24, are called *full-height drives.* The newer one shown in Figure 3-25 is half the size, so it's called a *half-height drive.*

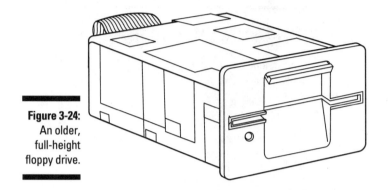

**Figure 3-24:**
An older,
full-height
floppy drive.

But, although half-height drives take up half the size, they're more than twice as filling — they're *high-density drives.* That means they can pack your data onto disks more tightly, allowing the disks to hold more information. (Luckily, if you've stored any information on low-density floppies, the high-density drives can still read them.)

Table 3-1 shows the amount of information the low- and high-density drives can hold.

| Table 3-1 | Floppy Drive Sizes and Capacities |
|---|---|
| *Drive Size* | *Storage Room* |
| 5¼-inch, low-density | 360K |
| 3½-inch, low-density | 720K |
| 5¼-inch, high-density | 1.2MB |
| 3½-inch, high-density | 1.44MB |

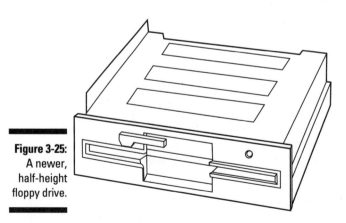

**Figure 3-25:**
A newer,
half-height
floppy drive.

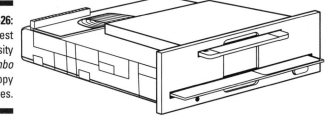

**Figure 3-26:**
The latest
high-density
*combo*
floppy
drives.

## Combo drives

The latest drives, like the one shown in Figure 3-26, pack two high-density floppy drives into a single package.

Instead of buying two drives, you can buy a single combo drive. Most people drool over them because they're so much smaller. The space where that second drive lived can now be rented out to another toy, like a **CD-ROM drive,** **tape-backup unit,** or computerized yogurt maker.

## Hard drives (hard disks)

Hard drives live inside your computer where they can't fall in the crack behind the wall and your desk. Hard drives hold hundreds of floppy disks' worth of information, making them quite annoying when they finally wear out (often in about three years). Whether it's called a *hard disk* or a *hard drive*, it's just that big can of information that becomes your C:\> drive.

## I don't wanna read about dead floppy drives!

Floppy drives die the quickest when people smoke around them or use the cheapest disks they can find. You know how bad your jacket smells the next morning after you've been at the Blue Bayou the night before? Those same smoke particles coat the disk drive's little heads, which read information off the disks. The cheapest floppy disks are made of cheap materials, which can coat the disk drive's heads with a substance known technically as *gunk*.

Keep your computer in the nonsmoking section and don't feel so bad about spending an extra dollar or two for a box of disks. Your floppy drive will thank you for it.

The hard drive has a friend inside your computer: a ***drive controller card.*** Like any other card, it plugs into a ***slot.*** The card grabs information from your computer's ***CPU*** and routes it through cables to your drives.

Hard drives come in several types, described next:

**IDE:** Currently the most popular type of drive, IDE stands for Integrated Drive Electronics. These drives are called integrated because they also have a lot of the electronics that used to live on the controller card. In fact, many IDE drives don't need a controller: They'll plug right into special slots built in to the latest motherboards.

If your motherboard doesn't have a special slot, you can still use an IDE drive by buying an IDE controller card. It's cheaper than the average controller. Unfortunately, it's not as compatible with older hard drives.

**MFM and RLL:** These older hard drives, known as Modified Frequency Modulation and Run-Length Limited drives, are probably the ones you'll be replacing with the sexier new IDE drives.

The problem? Well, you can't mix IDE drives with these older drives: the two drives don't get along because they each like different kinds of controllers.

So you can use all IDE drives or use all MFM/RLL drives. Just don't try to mix the two.

**SCSI:** Pronounced *scuzzy,* SCSI stands for Small Computer System Interface. SCSI drives, like MFM and RLL drives, use a controller card. And they're the most expensive option right now. But people like SCSI drives because they can chain stuff together.

For example, after installing the SCSI ***card,*** you can run its cable to your SCSI hard drive. From there, you can run the cable to your compact disc player, where it can head over to a tape-backup unit or yet another SCSI toy, provided that all the parts get along with each other.

Most ***compact disc drives*** use SCSI cards.

## *Other data storage tanks*

The following sections describe cards that have strayed from the traditional hard drive path but mostly for good reasons.

## Compact disk drives

Compact disk drives are fun because compact discs are so versatile: they hold great gobs of information, so compact disk drives let you listen to music CDs, watch movies, read encyclopedias, or watch special multimedia CDs, which combine sound and pictures to create multifun.

✔ Compact disc (CD) drives can only *play* stuff — not record stuff. You can't store your own information on them; compact discs come with the information already in place.

✔ CD drives, like modems, can be mounted inside your computer like a floppy drive or outside your computer in their own little case. If your computer doesn't have room for the internal CD drive, the external drive works just as well. (You'll need a spare power outlet to plug its power cord into the wall, though, unlike with the internal drive.)

✔ Most CD drives come with audio jacks in the back. You can't just plug in speakers, though; the sound needs to run through an amplifier before you can hear it. To combat this nonsense, some people hook their players up to *sound cards;* others hook their players to their home stereo system. Others forget about the speakers and simply use headphones, which don't need amplifiers.

✔ Most compact disc drives require a SCSI card. Some drives come with the card, and sometimes you have to pay extra for the card. You'd better check the side of the box to find out.

✔ Many *sound cards* come with a built-in SCSI port. Make sure that the SCSI port is compatible with the drive you're after, though. (A few sound cards aren't 100 percent compatible with all drives.)

✔ Compact disc players can move data around faster than a floppy drive but slower than a hard drive. When shopping, look for something called *access time*. An access time of 600 ms (milliseconds) is slower than an access time of 200 ms.

## Detachable hard drives

Detachable hard drives don't fit inside your computer. Instead, they come inside a little box. The box's cable then plugs into your computer's *parallel port* (the same place your printer cable lives). After you install a software driver (described in Chapter 17), you'll see your new drive D on the screen. It works just like any old hard drive after that, but you can carry it around from computer to computer, making it great for backups.

## Weird technical words on the CD drive box

Compact disc manufacturers all started sticking information on discs in different, incompatible ways. Instead of reaching a consensus, they just made compact disc players that support all the different standards. Here's a rundown of the weird words you might see:

**MPC:** Drives with this label can handle multimedia discs with pictures and sound. The criteria for an MPC label is pretty weak, though, so your MPC drive may still work pretty slowly.

**CD-I:** Short for Compact Disc-Interactive, CD-I is an important standard for both data and hardware. Most drives support CD-I.

**ISO-9660/High Sierra:** Almost all CDs adhere to this standard. which makes sure that they store information in ways that DOS computers can recognize.

**Kodak Photo CD:** When you take your pictures to be developed, some developers can stick the pictures on a compact disc, too. Kodak Photo CD-compatible drives can display these pictures on your computer's monitor. Look for a multisession drive, which lets you stick all your pictures on the same disc; single session drives make you use a new disc for each roll of film.

**WORM:** Short for write-once read-many, this expensive drive lets you write information to a disk but only once. WORMs are mostly found in large offices.

Compact disc technology changes so fast that you'll probably need to read the newsstand computer magazines to keep up with the latest formats and details.

### Hard cards

Just about every computer part comes on a *card* these days, and hard drives are no exception. For example, Quantum's Hard Card looks like a slightly flattened hard disk that has been glued to a card. Slide the card into an expansion slot and then install the driver (described in Chapter 17), and you'll have a new hard drive. Best yet, Quantum promises that its hard card won't argue with any other drives you may have installed.

## The Power Supply

PCs would be whisper quiet if it weren't for power supplies. Power supplies suck in the 110 volts from the standard American wall outlet and turn the 110 volts into the 5 or 12 volts your computer prefers. This simple task heats up the power supplies, however, so they cool off with a noisy, whirling fan.

The fan also sucks any hot air out of your computer's case and blows it out the hole in the back. In fact, if you keep your computer too close to the wall and don't move it for several years, the fan will leave a round black dust mark on the wall.

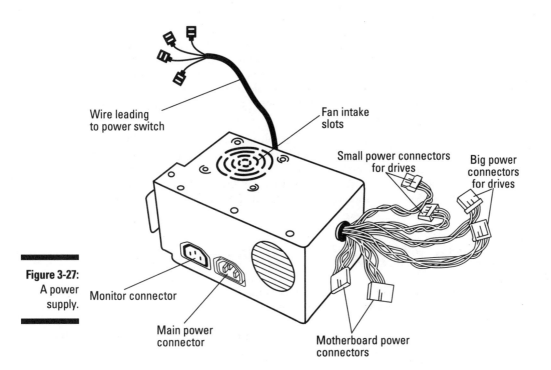

**Figure 3-27:**
A power
supply.

Wire leading
to power switch

Fan intake
slots

Small power connectors
for drives

Big power
connectors
for drives

Monitor connector

Main power
connector

Motherboard power
connectors

Extra fans are available as add ons. They can be a lifesaver if your computer is
failing due to head buildup, which can happen if your motherboard has a ***math
coprocessor*** or a speedy ***486 chip*** on it.

For some reason, power supplies seem to die faster than most computer parts.
Luckily, they're one of the easiest parts to replace. They vary in size, but a
typical power supply and its wires appear in Figure 3-27.

Power supplies vary in size. Your best bet is to remove your old power supply
and take it to the store so you can get another one that's the same size.

Don't ever open up the power supply to try to fix it. Doing so can cause serious
bodily harm, even if the computer's turned off and unplugged.

  ✔ After finding a power supply that's the right size, check its wattage. Older,
    XT computers can get away with the cheaper, 130-watt models. If you're
    using a 386 or 486 computer, though, buy a 200-watt model. That goes
    double true if your computer also supplies power to a lot of internal toys:
    internal modems, tape-backup drives, compact disc players, and other
    power-eating devices.

✔ If you live in an older area where the power fluctuates a lot, consider buying a surge suppressor. Basically, it plugs into the wall and conditions the power before it enters your computer. Many power strips come with a surge suppressor built in. They wear out, though, so for extra protection, replace power strips every six months or so. But most higher priced power strips have indicator lights to let you know when the suppressor has worn out.

✔ An Uninterrupted Power Supply goes one step further: if the power dies suddenly, it kicks in, keeping your computer up and running. Most Uninterrupted Power Supplies only last for 5 to 15 minutes, but that's usually plenty of time to shut down your computer, grab a soda, and feel good about your foresight while waiting for the lights to come back on.

# How Do I Know Which Parts I Have?

It's not always easy to figure out which parts are inside your computer. All computers really *do* look the same.

Your best bet is to look around for your old manuals. They often have a hint as to which parts live inside your PC's case.

Sometimes your sales receipt can be a better gauge, however. Dealers occasionally hand out the wrong manual, but they're usually a little better about putting the right part on the receipt.

If you picked up your computer at a garage sale, or it's a hand-me-down from the office, you may have to do a little exploring on your own.

Take off the computer's case (an occasionally laborious process described in the cheat sheet at the front of the book) and start looking at the parts described and pictured in this chapter. You'll find a product name and number stamped on the most important ones.

If you have DOS 6.0 or Windows 3.1, you're in luck! Type the following at any prompt and press Enter:

```
C:\> MSD
```

MSD stands for Microsoft Diagnostics, and it's a program Microsoft has been tossing in with some of its products for free. When you type **MSD,** the program probes the depths of your computer and reveals any pertinent information, including the amount of memory, ports, disk drives, claws, and tongue length. On my computer, MSD brings up the screen shown in Figure 3-28.

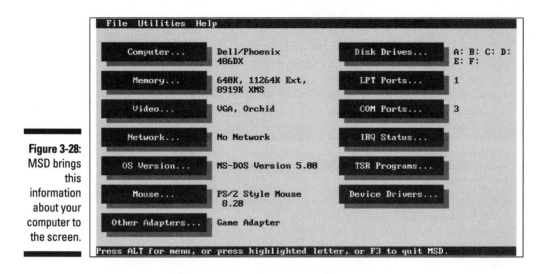

For example, MSD found my computer's three COM ports as well as the printer port. For more detailed information about any subject, click on its box. Some of the information will be technical glop that doesn't make any sense, but you'll find some worthwhile information poking up from the swamp.

Computers often boast of their CPU when first turned on. Watch carefully when any words start flashing by. Your computer usually displays the name of its video card first and then its BIOS, which often contains the CPU number.

Some computers come with a diagnostic disk. If you haven't lost yours yet, put it into your floppy drive and run the program. The diagnostic disk can often identify what stuff's hiding inside your computer's case.

# Chapter 4
# Figuring Out What's Broken

## In This Chapter

▶ Figuring out what's wrong with a computer

▶ Finding any recent changes

▶ Spotting clues when your PC is first turned on

▶ Listening for warning signals

▶ Using diagnostics programs

▶ Buying replacement parts

▶ Calling technical support

When PCs aren't casting you in the role of the anguished user, they're making you play the detective in The Case of the Broken Part. Your computer's dead: who dunnit?

At the PC repair shop, nerdy technodetectives wield expensive curly-wired probes that make accusatory blip sounds when they uncover the guilty part. You're merely armed with a cheap screwdriver.

If you already know what your computer needs — a bigger hard drive, for example, or a better monitor — head for that particular chapter. No need to stop here.

But if you're still searching for the culprit, this part of the book will help you figure out which part of your computer has gone bad. After you've fingered the culprit, head for the chapter that describes that part for more specific advice.

## It Doesn't Work Anymore!

PCs don't die very often. Unlike a car, PCs don't have many moving parts, leaving much less to wear out. When computers do start to cause problems, usually just one small piece has gone bad, spoiling the rest of the experience. (Kind of like finding gum under the table of a fancy restaurant.)

The biggest problem isn't fixing the problem. It's simply *finding* the problem. Is the software acting up? Your disk drive? Both? Or is it some complicated mystery part you've never heard of before?

Before you whip out your screwdriver, give the tricks in the following sections one final shot.

## Make sure that the computer is plugged in and turned on

This one sounds so obvious that many people overlook it. However, a vacuum cleaner or stray foot can inadvertently knock a power cord out of place. Give it one last check for the Gipper.

## Make sure that the cables are fastened securely

Make sure that the PC's power cord nestles snugly between the back of your computer and the wall outlet. While you're rummaging around beneath the desk on your hands and knees, check the monitor's power cord as well. Finally, check the monitor's second cord — the one that runs to the back of your PC. Some monitor cords can come loose on both ends — from the back of the monitor as well as from the back of your PC.

## Turn the computer off, wait 30 seconds, and turn it back on again

This sounds odd, but if it works, who cares? Turning the computer off and waiting a few seconds before turning it back on has solved many of my PC problems. In fact, this trick even fixed my laser printer a couple of times, too. Be sure to wait 30 seconds before turning the computer back on, though.

Flipping a computer off and on quickly can send damaging shocks to its sensitive internal organs.

Does your monitor say something like

```
Non-System disk or disk error
Replace and press any key when ready
```

This message usually means you've turned on your computer with a floppy disk sitting in drive A. Push the disk drive's eject button, press your spacebar (or any other handy key), and wish that all your problems were this easy to fix.

If none of these quick fixes work, move on to the next section.

# Narrowing Down the Problem

Technogeeks talk up a storm in the locker room, but it's just talk. There *isn't* an easy way to figure out why your computer has gone kaput. It doesn't take much at all to send a PC running in circles. Maybe your software can't find a crucial piece of itself. Or maybe some tiny computer part buried deep inside the case simply gave up under pressure.

The only way to find a cure is to keep narrowing down the problem. Does the computer only act weird when a certain program is running? Or does it just act up when trying to print the eighth page? Do you hear a funny whine from inside the case?

When confronted with a real head-scratcher, ask yourself the following questions.

## Have you added new software lately?

Sometimes new software not only doesn't work right, but it keeps everything else on your computer from working right, too. No easy solutions here. Your best bet is to reinstall the suspect software. This time, however, answer some of the installation questions differently.

## Dealing with your AUTOEXEC.BAT and CONFIG.SYS files

When you flick your PC's switch on, your PC looks for two important files. They're called AUTOEXEC.BAT and CONFIG.SYS. Many programs add their own stuff to these files — things like the program's location on your hard drive and how the program should be treated. Sometimes, however, one program's additions upset those left by another program.

How do you combat the problem? Well, the best way is to copy those two important files to a floppy disk before installing a new program. Then, if something goes dreadfully wrong, you can delete the new program and copy AUTOEXEC.BAT and CONFIG.SYS back onto your hard drive.

Of course, this advice comes after the fact, so it probably isn't helpful. But it will be next time.

Note that some programs will save your old AUTOEXEC.BAT and CONFIG.SYS by renaming them when the program is installed. Check your manual.

## Have you discovered a weird file that didn't do anything and deleted it?

Some of the most important files on your PC have the weirdest names. Unfortunately, there's no easy way to tell the truly important files from the truly technoid trash.

If an adventurous urge caused you to delete a useless file and now your software doesn't work, you have two choices:

**Choice 1:** Beg a computer guru to figure out what you've done wrong.

**Choice 2:** Reinstall the software that's not working right.

## Have you moved any files or directories around? Changed any of their names?

When a program installs itself, it often tells the computer where it's living on your hard drive. If you subsequently move that program from C:\FISH to C:\FISH\TUNA, for example, your computer may not be able to find it again.

Windows programs are notorious for this, leading to big trouble if you move files around, change a directory's location, or simply change some names. The fix? Try to remember which files or directories you moved and move them back. Change the filenames back to their originals, too. If the program still doesn't work, your best bet is to delete the programs that aren't working and reinstall them.

It's bad luck to delete unidentified files because they often turn out to be important. Don't delete a file unless you have a compelling reason. If in doubt, grab a computer guru the next time one shuffles down the hall. A guru can usually spot a wolf in sheep's clothing.

## Have you changed the computer's location on your desktop?

Did you pull your computer out from the wall a few inches to plug in the joystick? Did the janitor move the desk slightly to clean beneath it? Cables often fall off or loosen themselves when the computer's case is moved, even just a few inches here and there.

If a *swivel-mounted* monitor swivels too far in one direction, the monitor's cables can often come loose. Leave a little slack in the cables so they won't get yanked around. Often, loose cables don't dangle or give other visible warning signs. When in doubt, give them all a little push inward for good measure.

# Trying a Different Part

Here's where repair shops have you beat. If you don't think that your hard drive is working right, you can only flap your neck wattles in exasperation. At the repair shop, the nerds will pull out your computer's hard drive and stick it inside another computer to see whether it works.

If it works in that other computer, your hard drive must be OK. Something else inside your computer was making it act weird. Or, if your hard drive *doesn't* work, the nerds will sell you a new hard drive.

Even if you don't have a "test-drive" computer, you can try some of the same tricks. If your floppy drive is acting up, try using a different floppy disk. (Maybe the disk was bad.) Computer doesn't get any power? Try another wall socket.

By combining part swapping with other clues, you'll continue to narrow down your PC's problem.

# Watching the Screen When You Turn On Your PC

Whenever you turn on your PC, it sits still for a while, flashes some words and numbers on the screen, and then belches out a beep or two before letting you get some work out of it.

Those aren't idle yawns and stretches. Your computer's using that time to examine itself. It is trying to figure out what you've been able to afford to attach to it and whether everything is working up to snuff.

This series of wake-up checks is called the *power-on self test,* dubbed POST by the acronym-happy engineers. By watching and listening to your computer during its POST, you can often pick up a clue as to what's bothering it.

- ✔ When you find a cockroach in your slippers, you shriek. When the computer finds something it doesn't like, it beeps. This may sound like something straight out of a Captain Crunch commercial, but it's true. Listen to the number of beeps when you turn on your computer, and you'll know which of your computer's parts are acting up. (You'll hear more on this musical weirdness in the next section.)

- ✔ Sometimes your PC will display a cryptic code on your screen when it's first turned on. It never says anything really helpful, like `The mouse doesn't work`. Instead, it says something like `Error Code 1105`, making you flip to Chapter 22 to find out what your computer is complaining about this time.

- ✔ Most POST errors happen after you've installed something on a *card* that the computer didn't like. (If the word *card* has you stumped, head for Chapter 3 for a quick refresher.)

- ✔ When your computer's battery dies, your exhausted computer probably won't be able to find your hard drive. The POST message may say, `ERROR Code 161`. That's usually a pretty simple fix. You'll find the explanation in Chapter 9.

- ✔ The POST makes sure that your keyboard is plugged in; that's the reason that your keyboard's lights flash when you first turn on your computer. The lights on your disk drives flash, too, as your computer checks to see whether they're *really* there.

- ✔ The most visible part of the POST comes with the *memory check*. Your PC first counts all its memory and then checks to make sure that all the memory works. If you have a *lot* of memory, you'll be drumming your fingers on the table as your computer adds it all up on the screen for you.

CHAIN REACTION

## Cures for quarreling cards

If you have recently replaced or added a new card, then your POST may alert you to a potential problem or, worse yet, a chain reaction of replacements. Card problems leave four possible fixes:

1. Fiddle with the buttons on the new card so it won't interfere with the old card (see Chapter 17).

2. Fiddle with the buttons on the *old* card so it won't interfere with the new card.

3. Buy a different brand of card.

4. Replace the older card that's conflicting with your new card. (Unfortunately, doing so leads to the chain reaction talked about in the book's Introduction.)

# Listen to the Beeps, Luke!

That single beep you hear a few seconds after you first turn on your computer is a happy beep. It means that the computer has found all its parts, given them a little kick, and decided that they're all working as they should.

If you hear more than a single beep, though, your computer is trying to tell you some bad news. See, the PC designers figured that if PCs were so smart, they should be able to tell their users what's wrong with them. But because computers speak a bizarre language of numbers, the beep is the best they could do.

By counting the number of beeps and looking them up in Chapter 23, you can figure out what your computer is trying to tell you.

- POST messages and beeps sound serious and look befuddling. But they're not always that bad. Sometimes just a loose cable can start your PC beeping and weeping.

- Even if you've bought a sound card, don't expect more elaborate beeps. Your PC's beeps will sound the same, no matter how much your sound card cost.

- By combining your computer's beep clues with any accompanying error message, you'll know which chapter to scurry toward for more information.

# Calling In Doctor Software

In the old days, people bought software for PCs that *worked.* Then some sly programmer made millions by designing software for computers that *didn't* work. Today, some of the most popular software merely helps you figure out why your PC has suddenly stopped walking the dog.

For example, many new PCs come bundled with a disk that says *diagnostic* or *DIAG* somewhere on its label. If you're lucky, that disk contains a helpful program designed to help you figure out what's wrong with your PC.

If you can find your PC's diagnostic disk, stick it into drive A and push your computer's reset button. The diagnostic program will try to take over, scrutinizing your system and offering clues as to what's ailing the beast.

- Microsoft tossed in a helpful diagnostic program with Windows 3.1 and MS-DOS 6. Type **MSD** at any `C:\>` prompt. The program will leap into action, letting you know what parts are attached to your computer. For example, the program lets you know whether your computer knows that you've just added a new mouse. Best yet, the program is free.

- If you didn't get a diagnostic disk with your computer, head for the Utilities aisle of your local software store. The Norton Utilities program, for example, offers stealth-like information similar to Microsoft's MSD program. Other Norton programs can salvage the wreckage from damaged hard disks and other disasters.

- Some utility and diagnostic programs are better left for the computer gurus, however. Some of these programs dish out information that's detailed down to your PC's bare ribs. Then they delve into complicated technical specifics, like bone composition, blood type, and DNA composition. A lot of the information these programs dish out won't make much sense at all. Still, the programs might be worth a try in some desperate cases.

# Buying Replacement Parts

After you've fingered the bad part, it's time to decide how to replace it. Should you replace the bad part with a part of the same brand and model? Or should you buy something a little better? Only you can decide. Keep the following points in mind, though:

- Avoid the cheapest parts. They're made of shoddy material that is put together cheaply. Feel free to avoid some of the most expensive stuff, too. You'll be paying for the name, the advertising, and the fancy package. Shoot for somewhere in between.

- Try to buy from friendly dealers. If your new part doesn't work, can you take it back? If you're having trouble installing it or getting it to work, can somebody tell you over the phone which buttons to push?

- Mail-order parts work well for computer geeks who know exactly what they want and how to put the parts together after they get them. If that's not you, you're probably best off shopping at the friendly local computer store.

- Most parts come with a standard one-year warranty covering parts and labor. Watch out for the ones that don't.

> ✔ Some places charge a 15 percent restocking fee if you return a product because you didn't like it or it didn't work right in your computer. Avoid these places.
>
> ✔ Check out some of the newer, upgradable computer parts. For example, U.S. Robotics' latest modem comes with a special socket inside. When modems become faster, you can plug the new, speedy miracle chip into that socket. Voila! Your six-month-old modem is instantly transformed into state-of-the-art stuff.

# Calling Technical Support

There comes a time when you should just plain give up. You've installed a new part, and it won't work. You've fiddled with the part's switches, you've fiddled with the software, and still the part just sits there looking expensive.

Stay calm. Think of a flock of brilliant-green parrots flying toward you, bringing luscious chunks of pineapple and the latest hot movie rental.

Then start rooting through the part's packaging for a little piece of paper with the technical support number. It's often on the same paper with the warranty information. Found the number? Then collect the following information before you call.

## The part's serial number

Usually printed on a small sticker, the serial number often lurks on the side of the box or somewhere on the product itself.

## Information about your computer

The nerds on the phone will try to blame the part's failure on some other company. So write down the names of all the other gizmos installed in your computer — the video card, sound card, mouse, and anything else you can think of.

## The version of the operating system

Do you know what version of DOS or Windows you're using? For DOS, type **VER** at the C:\> prompt and press Enter. Or, while in the Windows Program Manager, press Alt, H, and A. A little box will pop up, listing the version number near the top.

# A copy of your CONFIG.SYS and AUTOEXEC.BAT files

These two files contain lines of gibberish that your computer likes to wallow in. If you're in the Windows Program Manager, press Alt, F, and R. When the little box comes up, type **SYSEDIT** and press Enter. A little program will appear, looking like Notepad with four heads. See those two files — CONFIG.SYS and AUTOEXEC.BAT — lurking in there? Send them to your printer with the Print command, just like you would in any other Windows program.

If you're in DOS, type these two lines:

```
PRINT C:\AUTOEXEC.BAT
PRINT C:\CONFIG.SYS
```

You have to press Enter twice after typing the first line; then just press Enter once after the second line. In a few minutes, your printer will spit those two files onto a piece of paper.

Done? Now load a favorite computer game and call the technical support number. You'll probably be on hold for many moons and be routed through several departments.

Hopefully, a helpful person will answer and explain why the part's not working or tell you where to send the part for a refund.

Whenever you find helpful people on technical support lines, *ask for their names and write them in a safe place.* Ask whether they have their own phone numbers as well. Sometimes, using this information will keep you from waiting on hold the next time you need to call.

If your modem's finally working, rummage around in the box's paperwork for the modem company's technical support BBS. You can call the BBS and type in your questions. Chances are that either a techie or a passing stranger will leave you an answer. Modem people are mysteriously helpful sometimes.

# The 5th Wave
## By Rich Tennant

"It's Kevin from 'PC Fix-It', only they're trying to change their image, so I'm supposed to say it's 'Menlo Park Jones' from 'Raiders of the DOS Ark'."

# Part II
## The PC Parts You Can See (Peripherals)

"IT STARTED OUT AS A KIT, AND WHILE I WAS WAITING FOR PARTS, THEY MERGED WITH A VACUUM CLEANER COMPANY."

## In this part . . .

This part of the book deals with the parts of the PC you can see — the parts that aren't hiding from you inside the computer's case.

Here, keyboards, mice, modems, monitors, and printers all get their due. In each chapter, you'll find a list of the part's symptoms. Next to each symptom, you'll find the fix — be it a software tweak, a flip of a switch, or a gentle, fatherly discussion.

And, if none of those fixes do the trick, you'll find explicit instructions for ripping the darn thing out, throwing it away, and installing a replacement that'll work twice as well.

# Chapter 5
# The Sticky Keyboard

*In This Chapter*

▶ Helping your computer find your keyboard

▶ Removing a spilled beverage from the keys

▶ Stopping arrow keys from making numbers

▶ Working with the F11 and F12 keys

▶ Changing to a Dvorak keyboard

▶ Using keyboards with different plugs

▶ Fixing keyboards that just beep

▶ Installing a new keyboard

*T*alk about moving parts — most keyboards have more than 100 of 'em, each moving up and down hundreds of times during the day.

Keyboards don't die very often, but when they start to go, they're easy to diagnose. A few keys will start to stickkkk or stop working at all. And when the water glass hits the keyboard, every key will stop working at the same time.

This chapter starts with a list of sick keyboard symptoms that are followed by a quick fix. If you discover that your tired old keyboard is ready for retirement, however, head for the "How Do I Install a New Keyboard?" section at the end of the chapter.

## When I Turn On My Computer, the Screen Says `Keyboard Not Found, Press <F1> to Continue` or Something Equally Depressing!

Chances are that your keyboard's cord isn't plugged all the way into its socket. (And pressing F1 won't do anything, no matter what your computer says.)

Fumble around in the back of your computer until you find the keyboard's cable. Push it into its socket a little harder.

After you've fastened the keyboard's cable more securely, you'll probably have to push your computer's reset button. Some computers only look for their keyboards once — and that's when they're first turned on. The reset button forces the computer to take a second look.

Also, make sure that nothing's sitting on any of the keys, like the corner of a book or magazine. If any of your keys are pressed when the computer is first turned on, the computer thinks that the keyboard is broken.

Still doesn't work? Look for a tiny switch on the bottom of your keyboard and try flicking it the other way. Maybe some nerdy jokester flipped the switch while you weren't looking. (Not all keyboards have this switch, though, so just shrug your shoulders in bewilderment if yours doesn't.)

If your keyboard still doesn't work, check to see whether something gross may have been spilled on it (see the following section).

# Some of the Keys Stick After I Spilled a Hansen's Natural Raspberry Soda over Them!

Your keyboard is probably a goner. But here's the Emergency Keyboard Preservation Procedure: save your work if possible, turn off your computer, and unplug the keyboard.

With a sponge, wipe off all the spilled stuff you can find. Then sit there and feel foolish for the 24 hours or so it will take for the keyboard to dry.

If you've only spilled water, your keyboard may still work the next day. But if you've spilled anything containing sugar — soda pop, coffee, margaritas, Tang — you've probably coated the inside of your keyboard with sticky gunk. The gunk will attract dust and grime. Your keyboard will start a slow decline within a few months and die sooner or later, depending on the tragedy level of the spill.

> ✔ If you have a lot of spare time, pry off all the keycaps one by one. Start in one corner and work your way across. (Don't bother trying to take off the spacebar because it has too many gizmos holding it on.) When the keys are off, sponge off any stray gunk, dry off the moisture, and try to put all the keycaps back in their right locations. (Figures 3-14 and 3-15 in Chapter 3 might help.)

✔ Some people report success and, sometimes, odd stares by immediately taking their wet keyboard to the gas station and squirting it with air from the tire pump to loosen debris. Other people (including me) have successfully used a hair dryer.

✔ Still others claim that you can remove the six screws along the keyboard's bottom and pull out the little board that contains the keys. Then, when no one is looking, rinse the gunk off the keys in the sink with hot tap water.

If you've spilled something more gross than water on your laptop's keyboard, don't take it apart and don't rinse it off in the sink under tap water. Take the keyboard to the nearest repair shop to be cleaned professionally and keep your fingers crossed. You won't be typing with them again for a few days anyway.

Wait at least 24 hours before giving up on your keyboard. Many wet keyboards can be salvaged but only after they are completely dry.

If none of these treatments resurrect your drenched keyboard — even after it has had 24 hours to dry out — it's probably shot.

# My Arrow Keys Don't Move the Cursor — They Make Numbers!

Look for a key labeled Num Lock or something similar. Press it once. The little Num Lock light on your keyboard should go out, and your arrow keys should go back to normal.

# All the Letters and Numbers Wore off My Keys!

If your rapidly moving fingers wore the letters off, you've probably already memorized all the locations. Still want labels? Then either buy a new keyboard, salvage the keycaps from a friend's dead keyboard, or look in the back pages of computer magazines for a mail-order company that sells new keycaps. Magic markers don't work. They just turn your fingertips black.

# My Keyboard Doesn't Have F11 and F12 Keys, and Microsoft Word for Windows Uses Those!

If your keyboard doesn't have F11 and F12 keys, you're using an older 83- or 84-key keyboard. Microsoft Word for Windows prefers the more expensive (naturally) 101-key keyboard. Buy a 101-key keyboard and try to find a place in the garage to store your old keyboard. (Very few stores take trade-ins.)

Actually, very few programs use the F11 and F12 keys. The programs that do use them usually don't make those keys do anything very exciting.

Besides, a mouse almost always works faster than function keys.

# How Can I Change to a Dvorak Keyboard?

The Dvorak keyboard strays from the standard key arrangement — the one that spells *QWERTY* along the top row. Instead, the Dvorak keyboard uses a new layout that has been specially calibrated for speed and finger efficiency.

Nobody wants the agony of learning how to type all over again. So only a few diehards use the Dvorak keyboard. If you want to be a diehard, head for the software stores and ask for a *Dvorak keyboard layout program*.

Windows 3.1 has the Dvorak program built in. Head for the Control Panel and double-click on the International icon. There, buried under the Keyboard Layout drop-down list (shown in Figure 5-1) is the US-Dvorak option. You'll still have to move around all your keycaps yourself, though.

Although the Dvorak layout sounds as promising as solar energy, make sure that you learn the QWERTY layout, too. Otherwise, you'll be hunting and pecking at typewriters and terminals in airports, libraries, offices, and just about every other place in the civilized world.

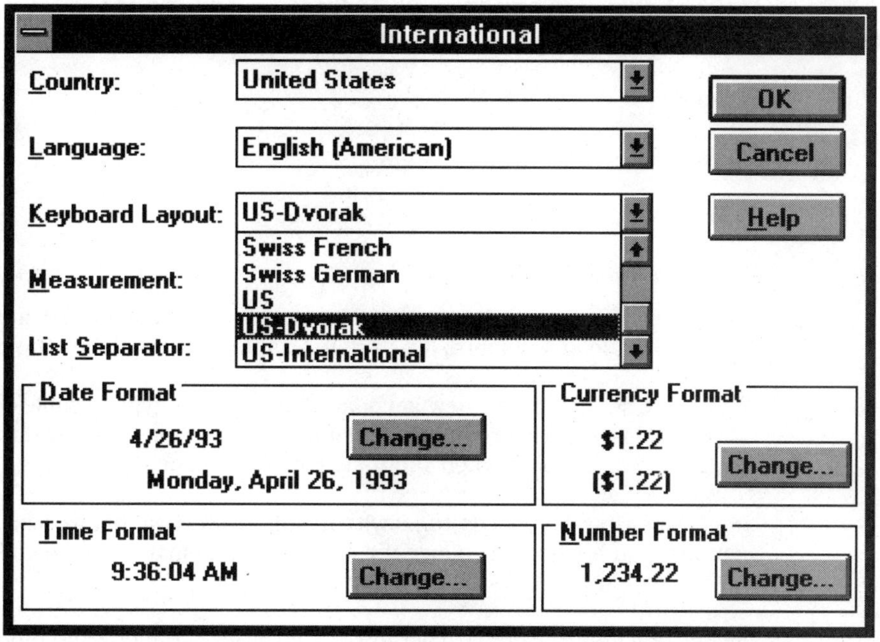

| International | | |
|---|---|---|
| Country: | United States ▼ | OK |
| Language: | English (American) ▼ | Cancel |
| Keyboard Layout: | US-Dvorak ▼ | Help |
| Measurement: | Swiss French ▲ | |
| | Swiss German | |
| | US | |
| | US-Dvorak | |
| List Separator: | US-International ▼ | |

**Date Format**

4/26/93    Change...

Monday, April 26, 1993

**Time Format**

9:36:04 AM    Change...

**Currency Format**

$1.22    Change...

($1.22)

**Number Format**

1,234.22    Change...

Figure 5-1: With Windows 3.1, you can change your keyboard layout to the Dvorak layout.

# *Every Time I Press a Key, the Computer Beeps at Me!*

Are you in a program possibly filling out some boring form? Some computers beep frantically if they want *letters* and you're typing *numbers* or vice versa. Other times, they'll beep if you're trying to squeeze some more letters or numbers into a box that's already full.

Can your computer be frozen solid? A frozen computer beeps every time you press a key.

The reason is that your keyboard stores about 20 characters in a special place called a *keyboard buffer*. If the computer doesn't wake up from its icy slumber, the buffer fills up as you pound the keyboard in exasperation. When the buffer's finally full, each character that didn't make it inside will beep in protest.

That's bad news. Your only solution is to hold down your Ctrl, Alt, and Delete keys at the same time and restart your computer. Unfortunately, you'll lose all the work you haven't had time to save.

If the Ctrl-Alt-Delete thing doesn't work, push the reset button on your computer's front. You'll lose all your unsaved work that way, but at least you'll get your computer's attention when it starts up again.

# How Do I Install a New Keyboard?

**IQ level:** 70

**Tools you need:** One hand

**Cost:** $25 - $120

**Things to watch out for:**

If you don't know the difference between an XT's 84-key keyboard and an AT's 101-key Enhanced Keyboard, flip back to Chapter 3 so you'll buy the right one.

Also, make sure that your new keyboard has the same type of cable connector as your old keyboard, or it won't plug into the same hole. It never hurts to bring along the old keyboard when shopping for the new one.

Some expensive keyboards come with a built-in *trackball* that works like a built-in mouse. Others let you change the keys around to match your own keyboard tastes. Let your pocketbook be your guide.

Finally, don't buy a keyboard without taking it out of the box and typing nonsense words on it with your own fingers. You'll be working closely with that keyboard for years to come, so don't pick one that's too hard or too spongy.

To install a new keyboard, perform the following steps:

1. **Save any work you have on the screen, exit your program, and turn off your computer.**

   Don't ever unplug or plug in your keyboard cable while the PC is turned on. Something dreadful is supposed to happen. Besides, the computer only recognizes the keyboard when it's first turned on anyway.

2. **Remove your old keyboard by pulling the cable's plug from its socket on the back of your computer.**

   When unplugging a cord, pull on the plug, not the cord. The cord lasts a little longer that way.

3. **Carefully insert the new keyboard's plug into the socket.**

   The plug only fits one way. If the plug has a little plastic lump or ridge on its outside edge, that edge faces up. If there's no lump, try to match up the plug's little pins with the socket's little holes. Then gently push the plug into the socket and turn it back and forth slowly until it begins to slip into the holes. Got it? Then push firmly until it's all the way in.

   Does your keyboard have a PS/2 connector? It's a small little plug, about the size of a back molar. A PS/2 connector doesn't fit in the standard-sized hole, which is about the size of your thumb. You can buy a converter at most computer shops for about $5.

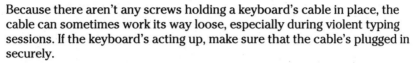

Unlike most computer cables, a keyboard's cable doesn't have tiny screws to hold it tightly in place. Just push it in, and friction holds it in place.

Because there aren't any screws holding a keyboard's cable in place, the cable can sometimes work its way loose, especially during violent typing sessions. If the keyboard's acting up, make sure that the cable's plugged in securely.

4. **Turn your computer back on.**

One of the first things a computer does when waking up is reach for its keyboard. If the computer doesn't complain, it found the new keyboard and decided that it was appropriate. Hurrah!

# Chapter 6
# Of Mice and Modems

*In This Chapter*

▶ Cleaning the mouse ball

▶ Fixing "jerky" mouse pointers

▶ Deciding between a bus and a serial mouse

▶ Loading a mouse driver

▶ Using an optical mouse

▶ Figuring out modem language

▶ Turning off call waiting

▶ Installing a mouse

▶ Installing an external modem

**M**ice and modems don't look alike, cost alike, or work alike. However, they plug into the same little port in the back of your computer. In fact, they often fight over who gets to use that same little port.

This chapter tells you how to referee the fights and tend to the injured. And don't forget that weird words like *cards* and *serial ports* are deciphered in Chapter 3.

## My Mouse's Arrow or Cursor Is Starting to Jerk Around

If you haven't installed any new software or hardware recently, your mouse is probably just dirty. (If you *have* installed new software or hardware, head for the "How Do I Install or Replace a Serial Mouse?" section later in this chapter.) Mouse balls must be cleaned by hand every so often. It's a pretty simple procedure:

1. **Turn the mouse upside down and look at the little square or round plastic plate that holds the ball in place.**

   You'll usually find an arrow indicating which way to turn a round plate or which way to push a square plate.

**2. Remove the plastic plate holding the ball in place, turn the mouse right side up, and let the mouse ball fall into your hand.**

Two things will fall out: the plate holding the ball in place and the ball itself.

**3. Set the plate aside and pick all the hairs and crud off the mouse ball. Remove any other dirt and debris from the mouse's ball cavity, too.**

If you have a Q-tip and some rubbing alcohol handy, wipe any crud off the little rollers inside the mouse's ball cavity. The rollers are usually white or silver thingies that rub against the mouse ball. Roll the little rollers around with your finger to make sure that there's no stubborn crud that you can't see hiding on the sides. Make sure that the crud falls *outside* the mouse and not back into the mouse's guts.

If there's some stubborn grunge on the mouse ball, some mild soap and warm water should melt it off. Never use alcohol on the mouse ball; that can damage the rubber. Also, make sure that the ball is dry before popping it back inside the mouse.

Mouse balls give off a very disappointing bounce. Don't waste too much time trying to play with them.

**4. Drop the mouse ball back inside the mouse and put the plate back on. Turn or push the plate until the mouse ball is locked in place.**

This cleaning chore cures most jerky mouse cursor problems. The mouse ball will stay as clean as your desk. Computer users with cats or shaggy beards may have to pluck stray hairs from their mouse ball every month or so.

# My Computer Says That It Can't Find My Mouse

Are you sure that the mouse is plugged in? Grope around until you're sure that the plug on the end of its cable fits snugly into the little socket on the back of your computer. Plugged in tight? Then the problem could be something like the following:

Ever had a soggy bit of lettuce mulch stuck between your teeth after lunch, but you didn't know that it was there until you got home and looked in the mirror? Computers are the same way. Even though a mouse may be plugged into the case, the computer doesn't necessarily know that the mouse is there.

Before the computer can fiddle with your mouse, the computer needs to read a piece of software known as a *driver*. (Drivers are confusing enough to warrant their own section in Chapter 15.)

Here's what may be happening: When you turn on your computer, it finds the mouse's special *driver* software. The driver tells the computer where to look for the mouse. But when the computer turns its head and looks, the mouse isn't there.

The cure? Head for Chapter 15 to see how to edit two of your computer's weirdest files, called AUTOEXEC.BAT and CONFIG.SYS. Then look for the word *mouse* mentioned in one of those files. The line that contains the word *mouse* is the one that whispers to your computer about your mouse *driver*.

The line may look something like the following:

```
C:\MOUSE\MOUSE 1
```

Do you see the number 1 at the end of that line? Try changing it to the number 2. Or, if it's the number 2, try changing it to the number 1.

Then save the files and reboot your computer.

If you're lucky, your computer will discover that the mouse had been there all along. If you're not lucky, stay in Chapter 15. It's built for people with driver problems. In fact, if your computer doesn't mention your mouse at all when it's first turned on, the computer may not even be finding the little driver, much less the entire mouse.

# I Installed a Modem (or Scanner or Sound Card or Weird Network Thing), and Now My Mouse Cursor Jerks Around or Disappears

Mice and modems usually squirt information into the computer through something called a *serial port* (also known as a *COM port*). Unfortunately, sometimes a mouse and modem will try to squirt through the same port at the same time. When stuck with two conflicting sources of information, your poor computer feels as lost as a character in a Franz Kafka novel.

It boils down to this: you need to make sure that all your devices get a serial port all to themselves. This stuff gets pretty grueling, so head for Chapter 17 to see how to break up fights over a COM port.

A serial port is sometimes called a COM port, which is short for *communications* port. Your computer uses the serial port to communicate with other computer parts by moving messages back and forth.

# My Cordless Mouse Sometimes Acts Weird

Cordless mice need fresh batteries every so often. If your cordless mouse is acting funny, try replacing the batteries. Some batteries fit in the mouse's receiving unit; others slip into the bottom of the mouse itself.

An *infrared* cordless mouse needs a clean line of sight between itself and its *receiving unit,* the thing that actually plugs into the back of your computer. But because that clean line of sight is going to be the only clean spot on your desk, that's the first place you'll tend to set down books and junk mail. Try moving your books and junk mail out of the way, and the mouse will probably calm down.

# My Friend's Mouse Won't Work on My Computer

Chances are that the mouse needs different *drivers* — software that translates your mouse's movements into something the computer can relate to. Ask for the software that came with your friend's mouse and run its installation program.

Also, some mice are *optical,* which means that they don't have balls like normal mice; instead, they use little sensors that read a special reflective pad with little lines on it. Without that special pad, the mouse won't work. In fact, if you have an optical mouse, you're forever stuck with that special optical pad. You can't use the free one that a computer magazine sent you for subscribing.

OK, so somebody already broke the rules. Honeywell's optical mouse doesn't need a special reflective pad. In fact, it doesn't need any pad at all. Because there's no ball, there's nothing to clean. Finally, the mouse even works upside down, making it suitable for outer-space computing. The laptop aboard the Space Shuttle Discovery uses Microsoft's Ballpoint *trackball.* However, the trackball clips to the laptop's edge so it won't float around in the aisles.

# After Installing a Modem and a Mouse, I Don't Have a Serial Port Left for My Other Gizmos!

This problem is rough enough to send you to Chapter 17. Serial ports can quickly turn into a complicated, odorous problem. Your computer can only use two serial ports at the same time, and yet dozens of computer gadgets want to grab one of them.

One quick solution may be to buy a *bus* mouse, described in the very next section.

# Which Is Better — a Bus Mouse or a Serial Mouse?

At first glance, neither. Both mice scoot the little arrow across the screen in the same way. You won't be able to tell any difference by the mouse's look or feel.

**Serial mouse:** The cable from a serial mouse plugs into your computer's serial port — one of those protruding outlets along the back of your computer's case. Simple and easy.

**Bus mouse:** In the bus mouse's box, you'll find two things: the mouse and a special card to stick inside your computer. After you've installed the card, you'll see its little *mouse port* protruding from the back of your computer. The cord from the bus mouse plugs in there.

Why bother with such hardship? The answer is that you may not have any serial ports left. For example, some computers have only one serial port, and the modem's cable might be already hogging it. Other computers have two serial ports, but the modem grabs one and some other toy hogs the other. By installing a bus mouse, you don't have to worry about filling up your coveted serial ports with a mouse.

# Why Is All This COM and Serial Port Stuff So Difficult?

It's really pretty easy — unless you already have a bunch of toys plugged into your computer. Like a nursing mother, a computer has a limited number of resources. If you try to install more than two gizmos, one gizmo will have problems talking to your PC.

If you're only installing a mouse and a modem, you'll probably do fine. But if you try to install a third guy — a scanner, a network card, or even a sound card — the potential for problems will increase.

It all boils down to the fact that your PC was designed more than a decade ago when nobody could afford more than two toys. Now, with cheap toys everywhere, the PC's antique design is coming back to haunt people.

# How Do I Install or Replace a Serial Mouse?

**IQ level:** 80 - 110, depending on your computer's setup

**Tools you need:** A screwdriver

**Cost:** Anywhere from $10 - $120

**Things to watch out for:**

If you are going to replace a serial mouse, you'll need to look out for a few things. Make sure that your mouse box says *Microsoft mode, Microsoft compatible,* or just plain *Microsoft mouse* somewhere on the package. Most programs prefer that kind of mouse.

 Some mice can work in two modes: Microsoft mode and some other weird mode. Increase your chances of success by installing them to work under Microsoft mode. Then, whenever a new program asks what type of mouse you're using, answer Microsoft.

Mice come with their own software and attached cord. There's nothing extra to buy. Finally, serial mice can be bought dirt cheap — often as low as $10. The ones with the better warranties, better parts, and bigger ad campaigns can cost a lot more.

To replace or add a serial mouse, follow these steps:

1. **Look at the back of your computer and look at the serial ports section of Chapter 3 to see where you're going to plug in your mouse. Then follow the instructions for that port.**

   **Your old mouse port:** If you're just replacing a dead mouse, take its corpse to the software store and buy another one just like it. That way it'll be sure to plug into the same hole and all will be well.

   **Small serial port:** You're in luck! The plug on the cable of just about every serial mouse sold today will fit without a problem.

   This smaller port is usually called COM1. The software will ask you about it later.

   **Big serial port:** Because this port is probably too big for the mouse cable plug, ask the salesperson for a 9-pin to 25-pin adapter. Some people call it a DB25 female/DB9 female connector. Whatever it's called, it costs about $5 and lets a serial mouse's small plug fit into a computer's big serial port.

   This larger port is usually called COM2. The software will want to know later.

   **Small, round PS/2-style port:** You'll have to be a little more careful here. You can buy a PS/2-style mouse and plug it right in. If you can't find a PS/2-style mouse, buy a plain old serial mouse and a PS/2-style mouse adapter. The adapter, also called a 9-pin to 6-pin PS/2-style adapter, costs about five bucks.

   If you have a PS/2-style mouse port, by all means use it. By using this port, you can free up one of your serial ports for other computer gadgets.

   **No empty port at all:** If you don't have *any* serial ports at all, head to the software store and ask for an *I/O card*. (Installation instructions are in Chapter 14.)

   If your computer only has *one* serial port and your modem is using it, head back to the computer store and ask for a second serial port for your I/O card. The second serial port will be one of the big serial ports, described earlier.

   If you have *two* serial ports, but a modem is in one and a network cord is in the other, sidestep this serial port stuff altogether by buying a *bus mouse*. It comes with a *card* that has its own port and is covered in Chapter 14.

2. **Turn off your computer.**

   Be sure to exit any of your currently running programs first.

3. **Push the plug on the end of the mouse's tail into the port on the back of your computer.**

Push the plug until it fits tightly. If it's not fitting correctly, you're probably trying to push it in the wrong port. (You may need one of the adapters described in Step 1.) After the cable is firmly connected, use your tiny screwdriver to screw it in place. Some plugs have protruding thumb screws, making them easier to screw in.

4. **Run the mouse's installation program.**

Somewhere in your mouse's box, you should find a floppy disk. Stick the floppy disk into drive A or drive B, close the latch, type **A:** or **B:**, and press Enter. Then type the word **INSTALL** or **SETUP** and press Enter to start things rolling.

Some installation programs can figure out for themselves where you've plugged in your mouse and handle everything automatically. Others interview you like a job applicant. The programs make you tell them whether the mouse is connected to COM1 or COM2. If the program asks, answer with the COM port you remembered from Step 1.

The program will probably want to add some information to your AUTOEXEC.BAT or CONFIG.SYS file. Feel free to let it continue. You'll find more information on those two files in Chapter 15. And if you're stuck at that weird COM port stuff, head for Chapter 17.

You'll probably have to tell Windows about your new mouse, as covered in Chapter 16.

Finally, you'll probably need to reboot your computer before the mouse will take effect. When the installation program is through, press Ctrl-Alt-Delete to give birth to your newly activated mouse.

# Who Can Understand What All That Modem Stuff Means?

Nobody, really, but here's enough information so you can fake it, like everybody else:

The only thing that really counts with modems is how fast they can spew information back and forth over the telephone lines. You'll find the rundown in Table 6-1.

| Table 6-1 | Funny Modem Words |
|---|---|
| *This Funny Word* | *Means This* |
| 300 baud or bps | These older modems are rowboats among cruise ships. They're slow relics to be avoided. |
| 1200 baud or bps | These guys are four times faster than the 300 bps guys but still woefully slow and out of date. |
| 2400 baud or bps | These are the current standard, but they're slowly giving way to the 9600 modems. |
| 9600 baud or bps | Now we're talking. These modems are four times faster than the 2400 bps modems they're replacing. The price is dropping, and more people are buying them. |
| | A 9600 bps modem considerably speeds up the Prodigy on-line service. |
| 14,400 baud or bps | Compunerds who want only the speediest and most expensive computer toys buy these. |
| MNP4, MNP5, V.42, V.42bis | These numbers refer to complicated things like being able to compress data before sending it so that it moves a little more quickly. |

Note that the higher the modem's bps number, the faster the modem can move data around and the more it will cost.

The speediest modems can still talk to the slower ones. For example, a 9600 bps modem can still talk to a 2400 bps modem, 1200 bps modem, and 300 bps modem. It has to slow down to the lower bps speed, but it still works.

# Don't bother with bps and baud banter

Modem speed is measured in bps (bits per second)—the number of bits of information a modem can throw across a telephone line in one second. Some people measure modem speed in *baud rate*, a term that only engineers really understand.

Here's where things get sticky. A 300 or 1200 bps modem is also a 300 or 1200 baud modem. But modems of 2400 bps or faster don't have a baud rate of 2400 or faster. The terms *bps* and *baud* don't stay the same past speeds of 2400 bps.

So, if you casually mention that your modem works at 2400 baud or 9600 baud, the nerds will laugh at you.

Forget about the word *baud* and always use the term *bps*. Then you won't have to see the orange stuff between the nerds' teeth when they start laughing.

Actually, using the word *baud* when you mean *bps* is a pretty common mistake. So, if you see the word *baud* in a magazine advertisement, just remember that it really means *bps*.

# My Modem Hangs Up Whenever Anybody Calls Me

Some popular people have *call waiting* installed on their phone line. When the person is talking on the phone and somebody else calls, the phone makes a little *beep* sound. The person then interrupts the conversation to say, "Can you hold on a second? I have another call."

But your modem is even ruder than that. If your modem is talking to another modem and that call waiting beep blasts into the discussion, your modem will simply hang up.

The solution? Dial the four characters **\*70,** before dialing the other modem's number if you have a push-button phone line. That's an asterisk, the number 7, the number zero, and a comma.

For example, instead of dialing **555-1212**, dial **\*70,555-1212** in order to turn off your call waiting on a push-button line. That funky little code tells the phone company to turn off call waiting for your next call. Incoming callers get busy signals. Then, when that call is finished, your call waiting is automatically turned back on.

**If you have a pulse phone, dial 1170**.

It's hard to remember to turn off call waiting before each call, so you can tell your modem software to do it automatically. Look for a "dialing command" area in the software. It's usually set up to say ATDT. Change it to **ATDT\*70,** and call waiting is turned off automatically before each call.

# How Do I Install or Replace an External Modem?

**IQ level:** 80 - 110, depending on your computer's setup

**Tools you need:** One hand

**Cost:** Anywhere from $25 - $800

**Things to watch out for:**

First, buy the fastest modem you can afford. You can find cheap, slow ones for under $30. The faster ones can cost 30 times as much.

Modems are as easy as mice to install. The hard part is trying to make them do something useful. A mouse's software is pretty much automatic; it works in the background. A modem's software forces you to make all the complicated decisions, even when you're not in that kind of a mood.

Also, mice need special *drivers.* Modems don't. However, modems need cables. Unlike mice, they don't come with any attached.

Finally, internal modems come on *cards,* so they're covered in Chapter 14.

To install an external modem, follow these steps:

1. **Look at the back of your computer and then look at the serial ports section of Chapter 3 to see where you're going to plug in your modem. Then follow the instructions for that port listed.**

   **Replacing your old modem:** Pull the cable off the back of your old modem and plug it into the back of your new modem. Then jump to Step 3.

   **Small serial port:** A small serial port has 9 little pins in it. Most external modems have big female serial ports on them. The female ports have 25 little holes in them. So, to connect them, your cable needs to have a 9-pin female plug on one end and a 25-pin male plug on the other.

   This smaller port is usually called COM1. Your modem software will want to know in a few minutes.

   **Big serial port:** For this, you'll need a cable with a 25-pin female plug on one end and a 25-pin male plug on the other end.

   This larger serial port is usually called COM2. Modem software always wants to know these things.

   Having trouble remembering all that male/female pin adapter stuff? Grab a piece of paper and draw a picture of the port on the back of your modem and the one on the back of your computer. Then bring that paper to the computer store when shopping. Don't bother counting all the pins or holes. There will be either 9 or 25.

   **No empty port at all:** If you don't have any serial ports at all, head to the software store and ask for an *I/O card.* (Installation instructions are in Chapter 14.)

   If your computer only has *one* serial port and your mouse is already using it, head back to the computer store and ask for a second serial port for your I/O card. It'll be one of the big serial ports described earlier. Or buy an internal modem, described in the next paragraph.

If you have two serial ports and both are being used, sidestep this serial port stuff altogether by buying an *internal modem*. It comes on a *card*, so it's covered in Chapter 14.

2. **Connect your cable between the end of your modem and the port on the back of your computer.**

   The cable should fit perfectly at either end. If not, keep perusing Step 1 until you've found a cable that fits right. Sometimes it helps to draw a picture. When you've finally plugged the cable in, use your little screwdriver to fasten the two little screws that hold it in place. The more expensive cables have thumb screws that make screwing them in easier.

3. **Plug the phone line into the back of the modem.**

   If your modem has a single phone jack in the back, plug one end of the phone cord into there and plug the cord's other end into the phone's wall jack.

   However, if your modem has two phone jacks, the procedure is a little harder. One phone jack is for the phone line cord, and the other is for you to plug a desk phone into. You must put the right cord into the right jack, or the modem won't work.

   If you're lucky, the two phone jacks are labeled. The one that says *phone* is for you to plug your desk phone's cord into. The one that's labeled *line* is for the cord that runs to the phone jack in your wall.

   If the two jacks *aren't* labeled, you'll have to dig out the manual while cursing under your breath the whole while. Turn the modem upside down first, though. Sometimes you'll see helpful pictures or labels on its bottom.

   If the two jacks aren't labeled, and you can't find the manual, just guess at which line plugs into which jack. If the modem or your phone doesn't work, just swap the two plugs. (Having them wrong at first will not harm anything.)

4. **Plug the modem's AC adapter into the wall and plug the other end into the modem. Then turn the modem's power switch to on.**

   Mice suck their power right from the serial port, so they don't need batteries or power cords. Modems aren't so self-contained. Almost all of them need an AC adapter. Then they need to be turned on. (These are two things that can go wrong.)

   A company named Practical Peripherals sells some tiny modems that don't need batteries or an AC adapter. Like mice, they suck their power right from the computer's serial port. They're great for laptops.

### 5. Run your modem software.

Modems usually don't need complicated *drivers,* like mice do. No, a modem's communications software is complicated enough. You'll find it on a disk somewhere inside the box.

When you type **SETUP** or **INSTALL,** the software will take over and start asking you questions. You did remember which COM port you plugged your modem into, didn't you?

The software also will ask your modem's speed, so keep that information handy as well. (It's listed on the box.)

If your modem software complains about IRQ conflicts or COM port problems, sigh sadly. (Sigh.) Then troop to Chapter 17 for help with all the IRQ stuff.

Finally, modems are notoriously cranky partners for computing. If you'd like to know how to force your modem into behaving, check out *Modems For Dummies,* published by IDG Books Worldwide. It's filled with valuable tips and convincing weapons.

# Chapter 7
# Tweaking the Monitor

## In This Chapter

▶ Fixing monitors that won't turn on

▶ Finding missing cursors

▶ Cleaning dust off the screen

▶ Matching monitors with video cards

▶ Buying an accelerator card

▶ Understanding video vocabulary

▶ Adjusting a monitor's screen

▶ Adjusting a laptop's screen

▶ Preventing burn-in

▶ Installing a new monitor

*M*ost computer terms sound dreadfully ho-hum: High density. Device driver. Video adapter. Yawn.

But the engineers had just returned from a horror flick when they started coming up with monitor terms: Electron gun! Cathode ray! Electromagnetic radiation! Zounds!

This chapter talks about the thing everybody stares at and puts sticky notes on — the computer monitor. Plus, you'll hear a few digestible tidbits about your *video card,* the gizmo inside your computer that bosses your monitor around.

## The Screen Has Dust All over It

Monitors not only attract your attention, but they also attract dust. Thick, furry layers of dust. And it's attracted on a weekly basis.

Do not clean your monitor while it is turned on! The static charge that builds up on the surface can wipe out a few little parts in your computer. Wait 3 to 5 minutes after the monitor is shut off before cleaning it.

Computer salespeople brush dust off quickly with a single swipe of their sleeve. Don't have a beige sports coat? A soft cloth and a little glass cleaner will do the trick. There's really only one thing to remember:

Spray the Windex onto the *cloth,* not the monitor itself. A monitor won't blow up if its screen gets wet, but the Windex can drip down the screen's front and make the parts inside soggy.

And don't spray Windex into the monitor's top or side vents, even if you like the burning smell.

## It Doesn't Turn On!

Are you *sure* that your monitor is plugged in? Actually, your monitor has four plugs you need to check:

1. **Check to make sure that the power cord is plugged securely into the wall or power strip.**

2. **Wiggle the connection where the monitor's cord plugs into the back of your computer.**

3. **Check the back of your monitor.**

   Sometimes the video cord can come loose from its connection. Give the cord a few little wiggles just to make sure that it's plugged in tight.

4. **Check the back of your computer.**

   Maybe your monitor is plugged into that extra plug at the back of the computer. If it is, you must turn on your computer, too. Then your monitor will come on with the computer.

You know how some outlets are wired to wall switches? For example, you flip a wall switch by the door, and a lamp turns on from across the room. Don't plug your monitor (or your computer) into one of those switched outlets. If you use one of those outlets, you may find yourself scratching your head, wondering why the monitor doesn't always work.

## What Do All Those Funny Video Words Mean?

Video cards and monitors are full of technical buzzwords. But you don't need to know what the buzzwords mean. Instead, just trust your eyes.

Believe it or not, the best way to buy a monitor and a card is to head for the computer store and play Windows Solitaire on a bunch of different monitors. When you decide which monitor looks best, buy it along with the video card that's powering it.

Some salespeople may gab about *dot pitch* this and *vertical sync* that. But don't buy a monitor and card unless you've seen it in action. All the technical specifications in the world don't mean anything compared with what you see with your own eyeballs.

If you're still curious about what those video buzzwords mean, though, check out Table 7-1.

| Table 7-1 | Awful Monitor Terms | | |
|---|---|---|---|
| **This Word** | **Describes This** | **and Means This** | **So?** |
| Pixel (PIX-el) | Monitor | A single little *dot* on your monitor. | Computer pictures are merely collections of thousands of little dots. |
| Resolution | Monitor, card | Pixel dots are stacked across your monitor in a grid, like tiny bottles in a wine rack. *Resolution* describes the number of rows and columns your monitor and card can display. | Common resolutions are 640 rows by 480 columns, 800 rows by 600 columns, or 1,024 rows by 768 columns. Bigger rows and columns mean you can pack more information onto the screen. (they also mean a bigger price tag.) |
| Color | Card | The number of colors you can see on the screen. | Here, the card is the limiting factor. Most of the newer monitors can display *any* amount of colors. |
| Mode | Card, monitor | A combination of resolution and color. | Most cards and monitors can usually display several different *modes*. For example, you can run Windows in 640-by-480 resolution with 256 colors. Or you can switch to 800-by-600 resolution with 16 colors. |

*(continued)*

| Table 7-1 | Awful Monitor Terms *(continued)* | | |
|---|---|---|---|
| *This Word* | *Describes This* | *and Means This* | *So?* |
| Mode | | | There's no right or wrong mode. Use your personal preference. |
| Dot pitch | Monitor | The distance between the little pixel dots on the monitor. The smaller the dot pitch, the clearer the picture is. | *Tip:* Don't buy any monitors with more than .28 dot pitch, or the picture will look hazy. |
| Digital | Monitor | An old-technology way to display pictures. | These monitors don't work with newer cards, like VGA, Super VGA, and other newcomers. |
| | | | *Tip:* Check to see whether an old monitor has a *digital/analog* switch. If so, it may still work with some of the newer cards. |
| Analog | Monitor | The new-technology way of displaying pictures. | Today's video cards all require analog monitors. |
| Multiscan, Multifrequency, or Multisync | Monitor | These friendly monitors can switch back and forth to work with a wide variety of video cards. | Being the easiest monitors to please, they're also the most expensive. |
| Bandwidth | Monitor, card | The speed at which your card can send information to your monitor. The faster, the better. It's measured in megahertz, and 70 MHz is about right. | A monitor must be capable of accepting information as fast as the card can send it. That's why multi-scanning monitors are popular; they can accept information at many different bandwidths. |

*(continued)*

| This Word | Describes This | and Means This | So? |
|-----------|----------------|----------------|-----|
| Refresh rate | Monitor, card | How fast your monitor and card can *repaint* the picture. | Bigger numbers mean less flicker on the screen. |
| Accelerator | Card | These cards have a special chip that helps your computer put pictures on the screen more quickly. | *Tip:* For an easy way to work faster in Windows and other graphics programs, replace your old card with an accelerator card. |
| Memory | Card | The amount of random-access memory (RAM) chips on your video card. Some cards can be upgraded by adding more memory chips. The higher the card's resolution, the more memory it needs.<br><br>High-resolution images with lots of colors can require 1MB or more of memory. | Don't confuse video memory with your computer's memory. Video memory lives on the video card. Your computer's memory lives on the motherboard. They can never visit each other's houses.<br><br>*Tip:* Don't buy a video card with a small amount of memory, thinking that you'll add more later. That action only leads to problems. |
| Driver | Card | A piece of soft-ware that trans-lates a program's numbers into pictures that can be drooled over. | If you're going to use Windows or OS/2, make sure that the card has a Windows or an OS/2 *driver*.<br><br>*Tip:* Windows comes with drivers for most popular video cards. OS/2 doesn't. |
| Interlaced, noninterlaced | Monitor | Technical stuff that's much too awful to bother with. | Just remember that a noninterlaced display has less flicker and is easier on your eyes. |

# I Bought an Expensive New Monitor, but My Screen Still Looks Ugly

A television merely displays pictures that come through the air waves, like the Movie of the Week. Even with cable television, you're stuck with whatever's coming over the wire.

It's the same with computer monitors. They only display what is being sent by your computer's video card, which lives inside your computer's case.

Upgrading your computer's display can get expensive — fast. The expense quickly adds up because you usually need a new video card as well as a new monitor.

Basically, card and monitor shopping boils down to these simple "make sures":

✓ Make sure that your video card and your monitor match in resolution — the number of little rows and columns they can display. The most popular resolutions are 640 by 480 and 800 by 600.

✓ VGA monitors rarely work with CGA or EGA cards. If you upgrade your old CGA or EGA monitor, make sure that you buy a new video card, too.

✓ VGA cards rarely work with CGA or EGA monitors. If you upgrade your card to VGA, make sure that you buy a new monitor, too.

✓ A VGA monitor still works with a newer, SuperVGA card but only in VGA mode. A VGA monitor can't show any of the SuperVGA card's super-duper video modes.

✓ The term "spit roasted" sounds pretty unhygenic, if you stop to think about it.

## The monitor's screen looks washed out

Just like a television set, a monitor comes with a row of fiddling knobs. Although most people just kind of spin 'em around and squint until things look better, there really is an official way to fine-tune your monitor's picture.

Here's the scoop:

1. **Locate your monitor's brightness and contrast knobs.**

   The knobs usually live along the monitor's right edge where they irritate left-handers. Or the knobs are somewhere beneath the monitor's front edge where they are often concealed behind a little fold-down plate.

   The knobs aren't always labeled, unfortunately, but they almost always have little symbols next to them, like in Figure 7-1.

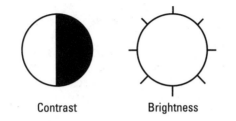

**Figure 7-1:**
These sun and moon symbols usually appear next to the brightness and contrast knobs.

Contrast          Brightness

2. **Open a word processor and put some text on the screen.**

   With characters on-screen, turn the monitor's brightness knob all the way clockwise, which turns the brightness up all the way. A light-colored border will glow along the edges of the screen.

3. **Turn the contrast knob back and forth until the letters on-screen look sharp.**

   Look for a clear difference between the dim and bright areas. You may have to fiddle for a bit until it looks just right. Also, try moving your desk lamp around until you've found the best picture.

4. **Turn down the brightness until the light-colored glow around the screen's border merges into the blackness.**

   Your screen should be at its best. You may need to repeat the trick after your monitor has warmed up or after a well-meaning coworker fiddles with the knobs.

## The colors look awful in one of my programs

You can adjust a monitor's brightness and contrast. But, unlike with a television, you can't fiddle with the colors. You're spared from the bother of rectifying green newscasters.

Instead, you can change the colors from within your program. Look for the program's *setup screen* or *control panel*. Chances are that the setup screen or control panel will let you change the colors to something more pleasing.

If you're using a laptop, check to see whether the program supports *LCD* or *monochrome* colors. Those settings look best on laptops that don't have color screens.

Flip to Chapter 16 to see how to change your colors in Windows from the traditional boring blue to the more exciting Black Leather Jacket or Emerald City.

# How Do I Know That My Old Monitor Will Work with My New Video Card?

If your old monitor is VGA, your new card will probably work with it. However, the VGA monitor probably won't be able to display all the new colors and resolutions the new card has to offer.

The only way to tell whether your old monitor and your new card can work together is to get technical. You'll have to find the old monitor's manual and make sure that your monitor can match your new card's *resolution* and *refresh rates.* You'll find those weird words explained in Table 7-1.

Or you can just plug your monitor in, turn it on, and have a look-see.

## My computer doesn't have a video card!

Some of the newer computers don't have a video card. The video stuff is built right onto the computer's motherboard. This fancy stuff is called *local bus* video.

With local bus video, a computer can often toss pictures onto the screen more quickly. Unfortunately, that built-in video leaves you with a problem when you want to upgrade: you need to turn off the built-in video before your computer will start using your newly installed card.

You'll have to pull out your computer's manual for this one. With some computers, you need to move a *jumper,* which is described in Chapter 17. Other computers make you run a Setup program that came with the computer.

Still, some computers are smart enough to know that you've put your own card in and that they should turn off their own card. Imagine that — a smart computer!

## Should I buy an accelerator card?

For years, people bought new video cards to make their pictures look more realistic on-screen. That little green parrot would look more and more like it flew right out of *National Geographic.*

But as the video quality improved, the computer had to slow down. Tossing all those hundreds of thousands of colored dots onto the screen takes a lot of muscle.

So somebody invented a *graphics accelerator chip*. Instead of straining to toss dots onto the screen, the computer just tosses the chore to the graphics accelerator chip. The chip takes over all the rough graphics, and the computer goes back to doing more traditional computer-oriented stuff.

These accelerator cards come with the accelerator chip built in, so you merely have to install the card.

- ✔ If you use Windows and you're in the market for a new video card, buy an accelerator card. Windows will really zoom.

- ✔ Even if you don't use Windows, an accelerator card will toss stuff onto your screen more quickly. The difference won't be quite as noticeable, though.

# *I Bought a Fancy New Card and Monitor, but All My Programs Look the Same!*

That's because very few programs support the fancy new cards on the shelf today. In fact, most programs merely support VGA graphics, which is the same stuff that's been around since 1987.

Windows, along with some computer games, can support the fancier, more expensive graphics cards. But most DOS programs that just display words and numbers don't look any different.

Most video cards come with some color pictures and a viewer on a floppy disk. You can look at those pictures when you want to see what your expensive new monitor can do.

# *My Cursor Disappeared!*

Some programs are not only rude but spiteful. When you give up on an awkward program and return to the C:\> thing, you discover that the program has left you a final insult. The program has stolen your little blinking cursor. There's simply nothing there.

Crashed programs often take the cursor down with them, too. Neither of these cursor kidnappings is your fault.

You can retrieve your cursor in two ways, depending on your mood. First, you can load another program and then immediately exit it. Your cursor will probably reappear when the program ends. (Loading and exiting Windows is almost always a sure-fire cure.)

You can also cure the cursor kidnapping by just rebooting your computer. To reboot, save your work. Then press the Ctrl, Alt, and Delete keys at the same time.

# My Monitor Makes Weird Noises!

Almost all monitors make little *popping* sounds when first turned on or while warming up. That's nothing to worry about. But they're never supposed to whine, buzz, or make threatening sounds like they're about to blow up.

Monitors are normally one of the quietest parts of your PC. If yours ever starts making noise, something is wrong. If those noises are ever accompanied by an odd smell or even smoke, turn off your monitor immediately.

If your monitor is slowly turning into an old creaker, it may pick up a few odd sounds toward the end. Better start saving the cash for a new one.

But, if you've just installed a new video card and the monitor's screaming, the card's trying to make the monitor do something cruel and unnatural. Chances are that the two aren't compatible. Try fiddling with the card's software to make it run in a different video mode.

- ✔ Even if you've had the card and monitor for a great deal of time, changing the card's video mode can make the monitor squeal. Avoid the video mode. Only power supply fans are allowed to squeal.

- ✔ If the monitor only squeals in one program, then that program is probably forcing the monitor to display a mode it just can't handle. Color televisions can cheerfully display old black-and-white movies, but monitors can burn themselves out if they're not built for the mode they're receiving. Head for that program's setup area and choose a different video mode or video resolution.

# I Don't Want My Screen to Burn In

Have you ever seen an old monitor that looks like it's running WordPerfect even when it's turned off? That permanent, leftover image is known as *screen burn-in*.

When constantly displaying the same program, older monochrome monitors would develop screen burn-in. The program's lines would permanently burn themselves into the monitor.

To prevent the burn-in, some wizened computer guru invented a *screen blanker.* After nobody touches a computer's keyboard for a few minutes, the computer assumes that the owner has wandered off and the computer blanks the screen.

Color monitors don't have much of a burn-in problem. But some wizened, whacky, and now wealthy computer guru invented a colorful *screen saver*. Instead of blanking the screen while the owner is away, the computer displays a fish tank complete with animated fish (or flying toasters or other colorful images).

- Windows comes with a screen blanker built in. It's rolled around in Chapter 16.

- Some people like screen blankers because prying eyes can't read their screens when they're in the lunch room getting coffee.

- Most people just use screen blankers because they're fun, though. Besides, you never have to scrub the algae off the insides of the on-screen aquarium.

# My Laptop's Screen Looks Weird

Most laptop screens are temperature sensitive. Whenever I charge the battery in my laptop, for example, the battery heats up and warms the bottom corner of the screen. Then, when I turn on my laptop, that bottom corner looks weird until it cools down.

Also, check your program's setup screen. Most programs let you change the colors. Keep cycling through them all until you find the one that is most readable.

# How Do I Install a New Monitor?

**IQ level:** 70

**Tools you need:** A screwdriver

**Cost:** Anywhere from $150 - $3,000

**Things to watch out for:**

Be sure to match your monitor with your video card. Like Bill and Hillary, your monitor and video card work as a team.

If you're installing a video card at the same time, flip to Chapter 14 first. There you'll find all the card-installing instructions. When the card is in, head back here.

Unless you're installing a new card while adding a new monitor, your new monitor's screen won't look much different from your old monitor's screen.

Finally, don't shudder too violently when looking at that $150 to $3,000 price range listed. The cheapest monitors are black and white, and the most expensive ones are huge, colorful appliances that can display two full-size pages on the screen at the same time.

Chances are that your monitor will fall somewhere between $200 and $500, depending on its level of video oomph.

To install a new monitor, perform the following steps:

1. **Turn off your computer and unplug your old monitor.**

   Save your work and exit any programs. Then, after turning off your computer, unplug your old monitor's power cord from the wall. Then unplug the monitor's video cable from its little port on the back of your computer's case. You may need a tiny screwdriver to loosen the tiny screws.

   Remember what little port the monitor cable plugged into. You'll need to plug your new monitor's cable in there.

2. **Remove the old monitor from your desktop.**

   You can either store the old monitor next to the electric wok in your garage's Old Appliance Graveyard or try to sell it to a friend or stranger.

3. **Remove the new monitor from the box.**

   Monitors are packaged pretty securely, so you'll have to remove a lot of Styrofoam balls and plastic wrap. The cable is wrapped up in its own little package as well.

4. **Place the monitor on your desk and plug it in the video port, as shown in Figure 7-2.**

   Plug the monitor's cable into the back of your computer. Make sure that the cable is fastened securely on the monitor's end as well.

   If the cable is not fitting right, then you've either bought the wrong monitor or are trying to plug it into the wrong card.

   Do you have one of those cool *swivel* stands? Then be sure to leave a little slack on the cables. Otherwise, one little angle adjustment can pull the cables loose.

15 - hole female
(fatter)

**Figure 7-2:**
Most
monitors
plug into a
port like this.

Plug the monitor's power cord into the wall or a power strip — if you've finally given up and bought a power strip. Or, if your monitor's power cord plugs in the back of your computer, plug it in there.

**5. Turn on your monitor and then turn on your computer.**

Can you see words on the screen as the computer spews its opening remarks? If so, you're done. Hurrah! If it doesn't work, however, keep going through some of the fixes you skimmed in this chapter. The monitor should be pretty easy to fix.

# Chapter 8
# Printers (Those Paper Wasters)

. . . . . . . . . . . . . . . . . . . . . . . . . . . . . . . . . . . . . . . . . . . .

## In This Chapter

▶ Troubleshooting the printer

▶ Curing blotchy pages

▶ Fixing spacing problems

▶ Understanding fonts

▶ Fixing paper jams

▶ Understanding printer terms

. . . . . . . . . . . . . . . . . . . . . . . . . . . . . . . . . . . . . . . . . . . .

*M*ost newly installed programs grovel around inside your computer. After some electronic poking and prodding, the programs can figure out for themselves what stuff is hiding in there. But even the smartest programs can't figure out what's on the end of your printer cable.

Windows makes this process a little easier. When you install Windows, it asks you for your printer's brand name. Then Windows kindly spreads the printer's name to any Windows programs that ask.

Even without Windows, printers are getting easier to use every day. The only problem is those odd days. You know, when the margins just don't look right, the letter to the phone company looks like some weird weather map, or the printer won't even turn on.

When your printed pages look funny — or the paper won't even come out of the printer — this is the chapter to peruse.

## My Printer Doesn't Print Anything

Are you *sure* that the printer is plugged in and turned on?

Then check to see whether the printer's little *power* light is beaming merrily. If not, plug a lamp into the outlet to make sure that the outlet works. If the lamp works in the outlet where your printer doesn't, the printer is most likely suffering from a blown power supply. You'll have to take your printer to the repair shop and hope that the repair folks can fix it within two weeks. If the power light is on, though, keep reading.

- ✔ Does the printer have paper? Is the paper jammed somewhere? Some printers have a little readout that announces *paper jam* when the paper is stuck. With other printers, you'll have to ogle the paper supply yourself.

- ✔ Is the printer cable plugged firmly into its ports? Be sure that you check the port on the computer and the port on the printer.

- ✔ Do you have a *switch box* that lets two computers connect to one printer? Check to make sure that it is switched to the right printer. While you're there, give the cables a tug to make sure that they're firmly attached.

- ✔ Also, try printing from a different program. Maybe your program is messing up, and the printer is perfectly innocent. If the program is messing up, it probably doesn't know what brand of printer you have bought. Head to the "When I try to print something, I get Greek" section later in this chapter.

 Laser printers are *supposed* to heat up. That's why you shouldn't put pillow-cases or covers on laser printers when they're running. If you don't allow for plenty of air ventilation, your laser printer may overheat. When you're not using your laser printer, however, put the cover on to keep dust and dead flies out of it.

## *The Page Looks Blotchy*

Sometimes the page looks, well, blotchy. You'll see big patches of black here and there or big empty white spots. Those patches and spots usually mean that it's time for a trip to the repair shop. Your laser printer needs to be poked, prodded, cleaned, and billed by a professional.

**Black streaks:** These usually mean that you'll need a new drum — a big, expensive thingy inside the laser printer. Sometimes, the repair shop can just clean the drum to bring it back to normal, though.

**Faded print:** You probably need a new toner cartridge. But, before you buy a new one, try this tip:

 When your print looks faded, your printer is probably running out of toner. Open the lid to the laser printer and look for a big, black plastic thing. Pull it straight out and then gently rock it back and forth. Don't turn the cartridge upside down unless you want to make an incredible mess. Then slide the cartridge back in the same way. This procedure usually lets your laser printer squeeze out a few dozen extra pages.

**Creased paper:** Keep paper stored in a dry place and not the bottom corner of the garage or under the coffee maker. Moist paper can crease as it runs through a laser printer.

Also, all that laser stuff really heats up a laser printer. If you're running some preprinted letterhead through it, the ink on the letterhead may smear.

# Everything's Double-Spaced or Everything's Printing on the Same Line

After a printer puts a single line of text on the paper, the printer needs to drop down a line and start printing the next line. But should the printer do so automatically? Or should the printer wait until the computer says so?

This awful bit of computerized politeness can really mess things up. If your printer and computer *both* drop down a line, everything turns out double-spaced. But, if neither of them speaks up, all your text prints out on the same line, over and over.

The solution? If your lines are always double-spaced or all the text prints on the same line, flip the printer's *line feed* switch.

- After flipping the line feed switch, you'll need to turn your printer off, wait ten seconds, and turn it back on again. Printers only look at their switches when they're first turned on.

- If only one of your programs has this problem, *don't* flip the printer's line feed switch. Flipping the switch will make the printer act weird with all your other programs. Instead, tell that renegade program to reverse its line feed setting. You'll find that setting in the program's setup area or installation program.

- Some printers change their line feeds with a *DIP* switch. A DIP switch is the size of two ants standing side by side. You'll need a little paper clip to flick the DIP switch the other way. (That delicate procedure is covered in Chapter 17.) The switch is usually near the back.

- If your stuff is printing OK, ignore the line feed switch. Otherwise, your stuff won't print OK.

# *How Do I Install a New Toner Cartridge?*

Laser printers need black stuff to put on the page. That black stuff is called *toner,* and it comes inside *cartridges.* When your pages start to look blotchy or faint, you probably need a new cartridge.

Various printers work differently, but here's the general rundown:

1. **Turn off the printer and open its top.**

   Laser printers usually have a hood-release type of latch that lets their top pop up. You may need to remove the paper tray first.

   If your laser printer has been turned on, let it cool off for 15 minutes. Laser printers get hot enough inside to brand a pig. The parts that seem hot *are* hot, and they can hurt your fingers.

2. **Pull out the old cartridge.**

   The cartridge usually slides straight out. While the cartridge is out, wipe away any dust or dirt you see inside the printer. The printer's manual will tell you the most appropriate places to clean. A little rubbing alcohol on a soft rag usually works well. Check your printer's manual to make sure that alcohol won't damage any parts inside.

3. **Slide in the new cartridge.**

   Before sliding in the new cartridge, gently rock it back and forth to evenly distribute the toner that is lurking inside. Don't turn the cartridge upside down or completely on one end.

   When the new cartridge snaps in place, close the printer's top and turn it back on. You may need to put the paper cartridge back on.

   ✔ New toner cartridges are sometimes blotchy for the first few pages, so don't print any résumés right off the bat.

   ✔ Some toner cartridges have a protective plastic strip that must be removed before they're installed. Better check the instructions book on this one.

   ✔ If you run into trouble, take the printer to the repair shop. The printer probably needs a good cleaning anyway.

# *I Dunno What All This Printer Stuff Means*

Like monitors, printers have picked up some pretty weird terms over the years. There's nothing really violent sounding, unless *laser* counts. The terms are all just dreadfully boring — unless, of course, the terms are placed in a table that's pleasing to the eye, like Table 8-1.

| Table 8-1 | Boring Printer Words |
|---|---|
| *The Boring Term* | *What It Means* |
| Emulation or printer mode | Some printers pretend that they are *other* printers so they can work with more varieties of software. The most commonly copied printers are IBM Graphics, HP LaserJet, PostScript, and Epson. All these printers are described next. |
| IBM Graphics | IBM's first few printers hit it big, so most competing printers copied them. Most can copy the IBM Graphics printer. |
| Epson | When in doubt about what kind of dot-matrix printer you have, choose Epson. Just about every printer copies Epson, so just about every printer will work in Epson mode. |
| Hewlett-Packard LaserJet | One of the most popular laser printers. This printer is also copied a lot. |
| | *Tip:* For sure-fire results, set your laser printer to LaserJet mode and choose LaserJet from your program's printer menu. |
| PostScript | A weird *programming language* for printers. This language excites artsy, graphics people who put peacock feathers on their desks. PostScript printers can handle high-end, professional-quality graphics and great gobs of fancy fonts. |
| | *Tip:* If you have a PostScript printer, set it to PostScript mode. Choose PostScript from your program's printer menu. |
| Page description language (pdl) | The way a program explains a page to the printer. For example, PostScript and LaserJet use their own pdl. |
| Pages per minute (ppm) | The number of pages a laser printer can squirt out in one minute. That's the *same* page, though. If you print several different pages, the pages won't come out nearly as fast. |

*(continued)*

| **Table 8-1** | **Boring Printer Words (continued)** |
|---|---|
| *The Boring Term* | *What It Means* |
| Dots per inch (dpi) | The number of dots a laser printer can pack into one square inch. The more dots per inch, the better your printed stuff will look. |
| Driver | This little piece of software translates the stuff on your screen into the stuff you'll see on the page. Most software asks for the name of your printer before it lets you print anything. That way, the software can use the right driver. |
| | Because most printers mimic the most popular printers, choose the driver for the printer that your printer mimics. It's probably IBM Graphics, Hewlett-Packard's LaserJet, PostScript, or Epson. |
| Point size | The size of a single letter. This word uses a bigger point size than this word. |
| Typeface | This describes a letter's distinctive style. `Courier` is a different typeface than TimesRoman. |
| Font | A typeface of a certain size and characteristic. For example, TimesRoman is a typeface, but **TimesRoman Bold** is a font within that typeface family. |
| Pitch | The amount of space between letters. |
| Line feed | Flip this switch only if everything is always double-spaced. Or flip this switch if everything is printing on the same line, over and over. Otherwise, ignore it. Note that some dot-matrix printers let you push this button to advance the paper one line at a time. |
| Form feed | On some printers, selecting this button brings up the top of the next piece of paper so it is ready for printing. |
| Toner cartridge | The plastic box inside a laser printer that holds black powder, known as *toner*. The printer heats the toner to make letters appear on the paper. |
| Skip perforation | Does your dot-matrix printer keep printing over the perforation where you tear the paper into pieces? Or does your printer skip the perforation and leave an inch or so between each page? If so, this toggle switch lets you choose to skip or not skip. |
| | *Tip:* After changing a printer's settings, you often need to turn your printer off and then turn it on again. (Turn your printer on and off slowly, though. Electric stuff doesn't like quick flicks.) |

# When I try to print something, I get Greek!

When you see Greek rather than English (or, for you overseas readers, English rather than Greek), chances are that your printer is working right.

It's your *software* that's messing up. The software thinks that you have a different kind of printer on the end of the cable. For example, Figure 8-1 shows what Microsoft Word for Windows prints when it thinks that there's a PostScript printer on the line but there's really a Hewlett-Packard LaserJet.

```
%!PS-Adobe-3.0
%%Creator: Windows PSCRIPT
%%Title: Microsoft Word - CHAP08.DOC
%%BoundingBox: 13 15 595 778
%%DocumentNeededResources: (atend)
%%DocumentSuppliedResources: (atend)
%%Pages: (atend)
%%BeginResource: procset Win35Dict 3 1
/Win35Dict 290 dict def Win35Dict begin/bd{bind def}bind def/in{72
mul}bd/ed{exch def}bd/ld{load def}bd/tr/translate ld/gs/gsave ld/gr
/grestore ld/M/moveto ld/L/lineto ld/rmt/rmoveto ld/rlt/rlineto ld
/rct/rcurveto ld/st/stroke ld/n/newpath ld/sm/setmatrix ld/cm/currentmatrix
ld/cp/closepath ld/ARC/arcn ld/TR{65536 div}bd/lj/setlinejoin ld/lc
/setlinecap ld/ml/setmiterlimit ld/sl/setlinewidth ld/scignore false
def/sc{scignore{pop pop pop}{0 index 2 index eq 2 index 4 index eq
and{pop pop 255 div setgray}{3{255 div 3 1 roll}repeat setrgbcolor}ifelse}ifelse
/FC{bR bG bB sc}bd/fC{/bB ed/bG ed/bR ed}bd/HC{hR hG hB sc}bd/hC{
/hB ed/hG ed/hR ed}bd/PC{pR pG pB sc}bd/pC{/pB ed/pG ed/pR ed}bd/sM
matrix def/PenW 1 def/iPen 5 def/mxF matrix def/mxE matrix def/mxUE
matrix def/mxUF matrix def/fBE false def/iDevRes 72 0 matrix defaultmatrix
dtransform dup mul exch dup mul add sqrt def/fPP false def/SS{fPP{
/SV save def}{gs}ifelse}bd/RS{fPP{SV restore}{gr}ifelse}bd/EJ{gsave
showpage grestore}bd/#C{userdict begin/#copies ed end}bd/FEbuf 2 string
def/FEglyph(G  )def/FE{1 exch{dup 16 FEbuf cvrs FEglyph exch 1 exch
putinterval 1 index exch FEglyph cvn put}for}bd/SM{/iRes ed/cyP ed
/cxPg ed/cyM ed/cxM ed 72 100 div dup scale dup 0 ne{90 eq{cyM exch
0 eq{cxM exch tr -90 rotate -1 1 scale}{cxM cxPg add exch tr +90 rotate}ifelse}{
cyM sub exch 0 ne{cxM exch tr -90 rotate}{cxM cxPg add exch tr -90
rotate 1 -1 scale}ifelse}ifelse}{pop cyP cyM sub exch 0 ne{cxM cxPg
add exch tr 180 rotate}{cxM exch tr 1 -1 scale}ifelse}ifelse 100 iRes
div dup scale 0 0 transform .25 add round .25 add round
.25 sub exch itransform translate}bd/SJ{1 index 0 eq{pop pop/fBE false
def}{1 index/Break ed div/dxBreak ed/fBE true def}ifelse}bd/ANSIVec[
16#0/grave 16#1/acute 16#2/circumflex 16#3/tilde 16#4/macron 16#5/breve
16#6/dotaccent 16#7/dieresis 16#8/ring 16#A/cedilla 16#A/hungarumlaut
16#B/ogonek 16#C/caron 16#D/dotlessi 16#27/quotesingle 16#60/grave
16#7C/bar 16#82/quotesinglbase 16#83/florin 16#84/quotedblbase 16#85
/ellipsis 16#86/dagger 16#87/daggerdbl 16#89/perthousand 16#8A/Scaron
16#8B/guilsinglleft 16#8C/OE 16#91/quoteleft 16#92/quoteright 16#93
/quotedblleft 16#94/quotedblright 16#95/bullet 16#96/endash 16#97
/emdash 16#99/trademark 16#9A/scaron 16#9B/guilsinglright 16#9C/oe
16#9F/Ydieresis 16#A0/space 16#A4/currency 16#A6/brokenbar 16#A7/section
16#A8/dieresis 16#A9/copyright 16#AA/ordfeminine 16#AB/guillemotleft
16#AC/logicalnot 16#AD/hyphen 16#AE/registered 16#AF/macron 16#B0/degree
16#B1/plusminus 16#B2/twosuperior 16#B3/threesuperior 16#B4/acute 16#B5
/mu 16#B6/paragraph 16#B7/periodcentered 16#B8/cedilla 16#B9/onesuperior
16#BA/ordmasculine 16#BB/guillemotright 16#BC/onequarter 16#BD/onehalf
16#BE/threequarters 16#BF/questiondown 16#C0/Agrave 16#C1/Aacute 16#C2
/Acircumflex 16#C3/Atilde 16#C4/Adieresis 16#C5/Aring 16#C6/AE 16#C7
/Ccedilla 16#C8/Egrave 16#C9/Eacute 16#CA/Ecircumflex 16#CB/Edieresis
16#CC/Igrave 16#CD/Iacute 16#CE/Icircumflex 16#CF/Idieresis 16#D0/Eth
16#D1/Ntilde 16#D2/Ograve 16#D3/Oacute 16#D4/Ocircumflex 16#D5/Otilde
16#D6/Odieresis 16#D7/multiply 16#D8/Oslash 16#D9/Ugrave 16#DA/Uacute
16#DB/Ucircumflex 16#DC/Udieresis 16#DD/Yacute 16#DE/Thorn 16#DF/germandbls
16#E0/agrave 16#E1/aacute 16#E2/acircumflex 16#E3/atilde 16#E4/adieresis
16#E5/aring 16#E6/ae 16#E7/ccedilla 16#E8/egrave 16#E9/eacute 16#EA
/ecircumflex 16#EB/edieresis 16#EC/igrave 16#ED/iacute 16#EE/icircumflex
16#EF/idieresis 16#F0/eth 16#F1/ntilde 16#F2/ograve 16#F3/oacute 16#F4
/ocircumflex 16#F5/otilde 16#F6/odieresis 16#F7/divide 16#F8/oslash
16#F9/ugrave 16#FA/uacute 16#FB/ucircumflex 16#FC/udieresis 16#FD/yacute
```

**Figure 8-1:** This garbage appears when Word for Windows prints in PostScript format to a LaserJet printer.

You can reuse your scrap paper. Turn it upside down before sticking it in your printer tray. You don't want to use scrap paper for important stuff but use it for stuff you're not going to be showing other people.

Instead of having Greek come out of your printer, the opposite — having nothing print — can be equally annoying. When Word for Windows prints in LaserJet format to PostScript, nothing comes out of the printer at all.

The problem is that the software is using the wrong *driver.* You need to head for the program's Print Setup menu and then choose the driver that's right for your printer.

> ✔ If you're using a DOS program, you may need to reinstall the program but tell it the name of the right printer this time.
>
> ✔ Some printers come with drivers for Windows; Windows already comes with drivers for most printers, though.

If your printer can switch between PostScript or LaserJet emulation, try to make sure that it's set to the right mode before you start printing on it. Nobody can *always* remember, but you can at least try.

## The paper keeps jamming in my laser printer!

Sounds like you need to get your printer cleaned by a professional. In the meantime, open the laser printer's top and carefully remove the offending sheet of paper.

Grab hold of the paper stack, hold it loosely with both hands, and flick the edges as if they were one of those little flip-page cartoons. This process loosens up the paper and makes it flow through the feeder easier. I also blow gently against the edge to separate the pages.

Keep cats away from laser printers. My friend's cat peed in hers, and it cost her $500 to repair.

Don't run labels through your laser printer — unless the label's box says that it's OK. The heat inside the printer can make the labels fall off inside the printer. The labels gum up everything, which makes you feel just awful.

## My printer says that it has 35 built-in fonts — where?

A printer company's marketing department often plays on the confusion between *typeface* and *font.*

A typeface is a family of letters. Helvetica is a typeface, for example. Courier is a typeface, too.

A font describes a particular *breed* of typeface. Helvetica Bold is a font and so is Helvetica Italic.

Your printer considers Helvetica, Helvetica Bold, and Helvetica Italic to be three different fonts. That's why the term "35 built-in fonts" is pretty boring after you see what the letters really look like.

## How can I add PostScript to my LaserJet?

The easiest way to add PostScript to your printer is to buy a PostScript cartridge and stick it into your LaserJet.

The hardest way to add PostScript to your printer is to buy a special card that sits inside your computer and translates your information into PostScript. (This addition adds speed to your printing; it is faster than the cartridge add on.)

The in-between way is to buy a PostScript translation program. The program translates stuff back and forth to PostScript. All that translating can take some time, however. Translating considerably slows down the printing process.

# Can I Upgrade My Laser Printer?

Like computers, laser printers often have secret compartments where you can add gizmos. Here's the rundown:

**Cartridge:** Many printers work like Atari's old computer game systems: you can stick different cartridges in them to make them do different things. You can add different fonts, for example, or add PostScript if you're serious about printing high-quality stuff.

**Memory:** Text doesn't take much oomph to print. But, if you start adding graphics to a page — pictures, fancy borders, or pie charts — the printer is going to need a lot of memory to handle it all. Many printers let you stick little memory modules inside them so that they can print fancier pages faster.

The memory that goes inside your printer isn't the same kind of memory that goes inside your computer. You can't swap them back and forth. (You can't grab any of the memory off your video card, either.)

Unfortunately, you'll have to buy most of these *add-in* gizmos from the printer's company. They're rarely interchangeable among different brands of printers.

# Why Is My Printer Cable So Short?

It's short because parallel ports are wimpy. They lack the tongue muscles to spit data over a long distance, so the cables are usually only six feet long. Expensive cables may add a few feet, but generally your printer needs to sit pretty close to your computer.

# How Can Two Computers Share One Printer?

Most folks solve the problem of two computers and one printer with an *A/B switch box*. The printer plugs into the box's printer port. One computer plugs into the box's *A* port, and the other computer plugs into its *B* port.

When you want to print from one computer, flip the switch to A. When you want to print from the other computer, flip the switch to B.

It's a pretty simple arrangement, actually. The only problem occurs when you forget to switch the A/B switch box to your computer. Everybody does it. Some folks even brag about forgetting to switch the box.

The newer A/B switch boxes can automatically detect which printer is trying to print and route the incoming page to the appropriate printer. These boxes cost a little more (OK, a *lot* more), but they can prevent a lot of crankiness.

# My Laser Printer Smells Funny

Laser printers contribute to the Earth's ozone layer. Unfortunately, laser printers release the ozone right next to your desk and not 12 to 15 miles into the Earth's atmosphere.

Laser printers come with an ozone filter to absorb the dangerous gas before it reaches your nostrils. The filter can wear out, however. Check your printer's manual to see how often it should be replaced. Sometimes you can replace the old one yourself; other printers make you head for a repair shop.

# Can I Save Money by Refilling My Cartridges and Ribbons?

Some people say that recycling is a great way to save money and protect the environment. Other people say that a botched refill can ruin a printer. There's no clear-cut answer.

Let your own experience be your guide. If you do decide to refill your cartridge or ribbon, however, don't try to do it yourself. Let the repair shop handle the job. A qualified repair person is a better judge of whether or not your cartridge should be refilled.

Inkjet cartridges can be refilled, as well. Check the backs of computer magazines for mail-order outfits that sell the kits. Make sure that you're using the specially formulated inkjet cartridge ink, though.

# How Do I Install a New Printer?

**IQ level:** 70

**Tools you need:** One hand and a screwdriver

**Cost:** Anywhere from $150 - $2,500

**Things to watch out for:**

When shopping for a laser printer, compare printouts from several different printers. Laser printers use several different printing mechanisms, each with its own advantage and disadvantage. For example, one printer may be better for dark graphics but lousy for letters. Other printers may be just the opposite.

Dot-matrix printers are better than laser printers for printing envelopes and address labels. Laser printers are better for just about everything else.

Laser printers may sound dangerous, but their lasers are tiny little things buried deep inside. In fact, laser printers are no more dangerous than copy machines. Nobody makes scary movies about deadly copy machines.

You'll probably have to buy a printer cable; printers rarely come with a printer cable included. Just ask the salesperson for an IBM-compatible printer cable. All printer cables for PCs do the same thing (unless you have a serial printer, which is described at the end of this chapter).

To install a printer, follow these steps:

1. **Turn off your computer.**

   Turning off your computer is a good idea when installing anything but software. Be sure to save your work and exit any programs before turning it off, however.

2. **Remove the new printer from the box.**

   Remove any stray bits of Styrofoam, tape, or plastic baggies. Check inside the box for any stray bits of stuffing. Grab all the manuals and disks; they can get lost amid all the packaging material.

3. **Find the printer cable, your computer's printer port, and the port on the back of your printer.**

   The printer port looks the same on a PC, an XT, an AT, a 386, or any other IBM-compatible computer. Make sure that you're plugging the printer cable into the big port with 25 holes in it, as shown in Figure 8-2. (The big port with 25 pins is a *serial* port.)

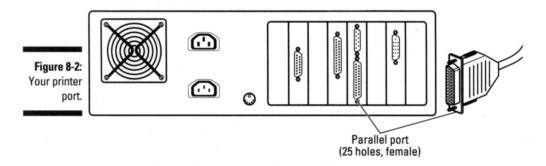

**Figure 8-2:** Your printer port.

Parallel port
(25 holes, female)

Printers usually come with a built-in *self-test* program. You run the self-test program by pushing buttons on the printer's control panel. The program squirts out a piece of paper showing alphabetical rows of letters. The test merely shows that the printer works by itself. The test doesn't prove that the printer is hooked up to the computer right.

## Testing your printer

To test your printer, try this neat trick. Type the following line at the DOS prompt:

```
C:\> DIR > LPT1:
```

That is, type DIR, a space, a greater-than sign, another space, and LPT1:.

If your printer says

```
Write fault error writing device
LPT1
Abort, Retry, Ignore, Fail?
```

then press A. Make sure that your cables are connected and the printer is turned on. Of course, make sure that your printer has paper in it, too. If everything is working, your printer will spit out a list of files on your computer's current directory.

Doesn't work? Maybe your printer is in PostScript mode. Try flicking it to LaserJet mode and try again. If it's not working, something is still wrong with your printer, cable, or printer port.

## Serial printer nonsense

A few old printers want to be plugged into your computer's serial port. If you picked up one of these feisty old printers at a garage sale, here's the procedure:

First, flip the printer's switches until it works at 9600 baud, no parity, 8 data bits, and 1 stop bit.

Then type the following at your C:\> prompt:

```
C:\>MODE9600,n,8,1,p
```

When your computer is ready for more action,

type the following:

```
C:\> MODE LPT1=COM1
```

If your printer is installed on your second serial port, type COM2 rather than COM1.

Last, you'll need to buy a special serial printer cable. The one attached to your modem won't work.

Maybe you should have left it at the garage sale. . . .

# Part III
# The Stuff Hiding Inside Your PC

The 5th Wave        By Rich Tennant

After spending hours trying to get the system up and running, Carl discovers that everything had been plugged into a "Clapper" light socket when he tries to kill a mosquito.

# In this part . . .

**Y**ou're probably pretty familiar with the stuff that lives outside your PC. You've shuffled the pieces around on your desk, pausing occasionally when a cable pops off the back of your PC.

This part of the book, however, describes the stuff you've never touched. Here, you'll find out about the unseen parts of your computer — the pieces that lurk deep inside its case, making ominous humming noises.

This part of the book uncovers what's beneath your PC's cover.

# Chapter 9

# The Motherboard (and Its CPU, Math Coprocessor, BIOS, and Even a Battery)

## In This Chapter

▶ Finding and changing your computer's battery

▶ Deciding on a math coprocessor

▶ Installing a math coprocessor

▶ Replacing your CPU

▶ Understanding overdrive sockets

▶ Upgrading an older computer's motherboard

▶ Replacing your motherboard

▶ Understanding your BIOS

▶ Upgrading your computer's BIOS

*I*f your computer is one big omelet, then your motherboard is the great mass of egg that holds together all the mushrooms, cheese, and occasional bits of sausage.

That's why replacing your computer's motherboard is such a colossal bother. You need to pick *everything* off of your motherboard before you can remove it. You can't overlook a single bit of sausage.

Replacing a motherboard isn't a job for weekend chefs. The task is best left for the technocooks at the computer shop.

If you're *sure* that you want to replace your motherboard, you'll find the recipe at the end of this chapter. A few easier projects are sprinkled in along the way, however. In fact, the first section explains how to replace something nobody expects computers to have — a battery.

# *My Computer Forgot That It Has a Hard Drive, and It Doesn't Know What Day It Is!*

Just like a cheap wristwatch, your computer relies on a battery to keep track of time. That constant flow of electricity lets the computer remember the current time and date, even when it's unplugged from the wall. The computer can also remember what parts have been stuffed inside since it left the shop.

But when the battery starts to peter out (after anywhere from one to ten years), the computer forgets two important things: the date and the type of hard drive it has been using all these years. Frightened, the computer sends out a scary message like the following:

```
Invalid Configuration Information
Hard Disk Failure
```

This is your computer's friendly way of telling you that it needs a new battery.

## A *lot* of effort for a little time

The old PC and XT computers didn't come with batteries, so they couldn't remember the date.

So some time-conscious owners opened 'em up and put special *clock* cards inside. Those cards have a battery that can keep the clock ticking.

However, computers are too dumb to look at a card for the current time and date. Computers need a special *program* to tell them where to look. Without that program, the clock card is useless.

If you buy an old PC or XT at a garage sale, make the people root through their boxes of old floppy

disks until they find that little program. It's usually called SETCLOCK or something equally clock oriented.

Savvy PC and XT users copy the special program to their hard drive and put the program's name on a line in their AUTOEXEC.BAT files. Then each time they turn on their computer, the computer runs that program and fetches the time and date.

That AUTOEXEC.BAT file stuff is wrapped up in Chapter 15. Oh, and clock cards can be installed just like any other card, described in Chapter 14.

# I can't find my computer's battery!

Don't bother looking for a battery in most XTs and old PCs — they don't have one. That's why they beg you to type in the current time and date every time they're turned on.

Some people ignore their computer when it asks them to type in the current time and date. So their computer simply tacks the date January 1, 1980, on every file it creates that day. That makes it rough when you're looking for a file you created yesterday, though, because they'll *all* look 13 years old.

If your computer constantly comes up with the correct date, it's harboring a battery inside somewhere. But where? Computer batteries rarely *look* like batteries.

If you have an XT or old PC, look on its cards for a round, silvery thing. The battery should look like a huge watch battery that is held in place by a little metal flap.

If you have a newer computer, its battery could hail from one of these four tribes:

- ✔ The friendliest computers use AA batteries in a little plastic pack that's taped to the power supply — that big, silver thing in the computer's back corner.

    Wires from the plastic pack connect to little pins on the motherboard. Those AA batteries last about three years.

- ✔ Other computers use a little cube-shaped battery, which is also taped to the power supply.

    Like the AA cells, these guys have wires leading to pins on the motherboard. A cube-shaped battery's life span is about three years.

- ✔ Older computers often use little battery cylinders about the size of a cigar butt.

    Battery cylinders live between little prongs on the motherboard, like the one in Figure 9-1.

- ✔ The most elusive batteries hide inside a chip that looks nothing at all like a battery.

    The chip says *Dallas* and has a little picture of an alarm clock on it. (It's supposed to last about ten years.) When the chip dies, ask your local computer store for a *Dallas Real Time* chip. If the store's clerk stares at you funny, try bugging Dallas Semiconductor at 214/450-0400.

**Figure 9-1:**
Some batteries fit between prongs on the motherboard.

A newer computer's batteries almost always live near where the keyboard plugs into the motherboard.

## How do I install a new battery?

**IQ level:** 80

**Tools you need:** Screwdriver, flashlight, and prying fingers

**Cost:** Anywhere from $5 - $20

**Things to watch out for:**

If your computer's battery looks especially unworldly, try Radio Shack. It can special-order odd-sized batteries from a wide variety of planets.

Some manufacturers were especially vile and *soldered* the computer's battery onto the motherboard. Solder is like molten lead, so just give up. You can melt the solder with a *soldering iron,* but doing so can be both scary and dangerous. Take this one to the repair shop unless you've soldered something before and enjoyed the experience. Melting solder even smells bad.

## Don't forget what your computer is supposed to remember

When you remove the battery, your computer forgets a lot of information about itself. If your battery is dead, it has already forgotten, so this little tip comes too late.

But, if your battery is still grasping at life, head for Chapter 17. In that chapter, you'll learn how to access your computer's CMOS and find out the type number of your hard drive.

After you install the new battery, you need to tell your computer the hard drive type number. If you didn't write down that information beforehand, you'll have to page through dusty manuals and search for the right number to type back in. Yuck.

To install a battery, follow these steps:

1. **Turn off your computer, unplug it, and remove its case.**

   This merry little chore is covered in the cheat sheet at the front of this book.

2. **Find and remove the computer's old battery.**

   Don't know what the battery looks like? Head for the "I can't find my computer's battery!" section earlier in this chapter.

   Be sure to draw a picture of the old battery's position. Each end has a + or – sign. The signs need to face the same way on the new battery as they did on the old battery.

   AA batteries simply snap out of their plastic case, just like in a small radio. The batteries shaped like a cigar butt slip out of their little prong sockets, but this can take some pressure.

   Don't force anything; some batteries may be *soldered* in, which means that you should stop right now and take the computer to the shop.

   If you have a Dallas clock chip, pry it out gently. If you don't have a chip puller tool (and who does, anyway?), grab the chip between your thumb and forefinger and pull straight up with a gentle rocking motion. It's a pretty big chip, so it's easy to grab. Keep track of what direction the chip faces; the new one needs to face the same way.

3. **Take the old battery to the computer store and buy a replacement battery.**

4. **Place the new battery where the old one lived.**

   Make sure that the + and – ends of the new battery face the same direction as they did on the old battery.

   If you've accidentally yanked any wires from their pins on the motherboard, all is not lost. Look for the pin with the number 1 written closest to it. *The red wire always connects to Pin 1:* computer technicians have that on their bumper stickers.

**5. Put the computer's case back on and plug it back in.**

The battery problem should be solved, but the computer won't be grateful. When first turned on, it will probably send out a horrible-sounding error message about your *incorrect CMOS*.

You need to tell your computer's CMOS what type of hard drive you have. (You remembered to write down that information before you started, didn't you?) You'll find that CMOS stuff hashed out in Chapter 17.

## To Ignore This, Press Enter

Even computers with a *working* clock will occasionally query you for the time and date. Your computer will pick up the current time and date from its internal clock, just like normal. But then your computer displays the date and time on-screen and asks you whether it's *really* OK.

Just press Enter to confirm that yes, indeed, the computer already knows the right time and date. This bit of weirdness pops up when a computer can't find an AUTOEXEC.BAT file. With that file missing, the computer gets suspicious and asks you whether it *really* knows the time and date.

Your computer is most likely to question its internal clock when you boot from floppy disks that don't have an AUTOEXEC.BAT file. Are you a little sketchy on what an AUTOEXEC.BAT file is supposed to do? Troop to Chapter 15 for a refresher.

## Can a Math Coprocessor Really Speed Up My Computer?

A *math coprocessor* is a little chip that plugs into your motherboard. With a math coprocessor, your PC is faster at statistics, engineering, and some graphics, which means that your computer is fastest and nerdliest at statistical graphics engineering.

Unless you're doing that kind of work, however, a math coprocessor won't speed up your computer at all.

Note that not any math coprocessor will do. Pick up the math coprocessor that matches your CPU, as listed in Table 9-1.

| Table 9-1 | Math Coprocessors |
| --- | --- |
| *Your CPU* | *The Appropriate Math Coprocessor* |
| 8088, 8086, 80188, V20, V30 | 8087 |
| 286 | 287 |
| 386SX | 387SX |
| 386DX | 387DX |
| 486DX | Doesn't need one; the math coprocessor is already built in |
| 486SX | 487 |

## Utterly trivial math stuff about the 486SX

When Intel made the world's first 486 chip, it tried something new. Intel built all the math coprocessor stuff right inside the 486 chip. Because the math circuits were so close at hand, the CPU could do math faster than ever before.

But then a rival company started selling 486 chips *without* the coprocessor stuff inside. And they were cheaper! So Intel disabled the math coprocessor in some of its chips, called the stripped-down version a 486SX, and sold the 486SX for less money.

So if you buy a 486SX and want faster math stuff, you need to buy a 487 chip. But if you have a 486DX chip, your math coprocessor already lives inside.

Don't confuse that DX stuff, either. A 386DX *doesn't* have a math coprocessor built in, but a 486DX *does.* It's more confusing that way.

## Can I get a math coprocessor for my older computer?

Even an ancient computer can do math a little more quickly with a math coprocessor. But if you're after speed, buy a new computer with a faster CPU. That will speed up *everything,* not just occasional spurts of math.

A 386 with a math coprocessor is still twice as slow at math as a 486DX computer.

## How do I install a math coprocessor?

**IQ level:** 90

**Tools you need:** Chip puller, screwdriver, and strong fingers

**Cost:** Anywhere from $100 - $375

**Things to watch out for:**

This one is basically easy — just push the math coprocessor chip into the empty little socket.

The problem? Well, the chip fits into that socket four different ways, and only one way works. In fact, the other three ways may ruin the chip.

The key is to find the *marked* corner on both the chip and the socket. One corner will have a notch, a dot, an extra hole, or something even harder to spot. Figure 9-2 shows the differences between some chips and sockets.

**Figure 9-2:**
The marked corner of a chip plugs into the marked corner of its socket.

The chip

387          387

Dot in corner          Notch in corner

The socket

Notch inside          Notch outside

Finally, make sure that your math coprocessor is the same speed — measured in megahertz — as your CPU. The math coprocessor can be faster, but it cannot be slower.

To install a math coprocessor, follow these steps:

1. **Turn off the PC, unplug it, and remove its cover.**

   The cheat sheet at the front of this book explains these little chores.

2. **Find the math coprocessor's socket.**

   First, find your CPU. It's almost always the biggest, black, square chip on the motherboard. The numbers 286, 80286, 386, 80386, or 486 are usually printed somewhere along its top.

   The math coprocessor's socket usually lives an inch or two away from the CPU.

3. **Prepare the new math coprocessor chip.**

   Don't touch any chip until you've released any pent-up static electricity. Tap on a doorknob, file cabinet, or bare metal part of your desk. *Then* pick up the chip.

   First, make sure that the new chip is the right size to fit in that little socket. Then make sure that all the chip's little pins are lined up straight. The pins need to fit into all those little holes *exactly,* with no legs hanging off the edge.

4. **Press the chip into its socket.**

   The chip's marked corner rests over the socket's marked corner, like in Figure 9-2.

   Finding the chip's marked corner is easy. The socket is a little rougher. Look at the little lines etched onto the motherboard. Sometimes, the little line surrounding the socket has a notched corner, even if the socket itself doesn't. Some sockets have a little dot or extra hole in one corner.

   Lined up the right corners? Make sure that all the little pins are lined up over all the little holes. Then carefully push the chip down into the socket. It should take some pressure, but don't bend your motherboard. If your motherboard bends more than slightly, stop and let the dealer or repair shop finish the job.

   The letters printed on top of the coprocessor usually face the same way as the letters printed on top of your CPU.

Some sockets have *three* rows of holes, and yet the coprocessor will only have *two* rows of pins. If so, line up the pins in the two rows closest to the center.

Also, the 387SX's socket looks completely different from the 387DX's socket. If something looks wrong, make sure that you've bought the right math coprocessor.

**5. Plug your computer back in and turn it on.**

If the chip came with software, run the software to see whether the chip is working. Didn't come with software? Then run a math-oriented program that knows how to use the chip, and then see whether your computer says *math coprocessor detected* or something just as promising.

If the software can't find the math coprocessor, you'll probably have to dig out your motherboard's manual. You may need to flip a tiny switch somewhere or tell your computer's CMOS about the new chip. Those pressing details are cleared up in Chapter 17.

If the chip is still not working, check to make sure that the chip is firmly seated in its socket and is facing the right way. Also, check for a wandering pin that didn't go into its hole, like the one in Figure 9-3.

**Figure 9-3:**
If a single pin misses its hole, the chip won't work.

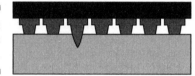

If the math coprocessor is working, put the computer's cover back on and then wipe your hands on your pants. You've earned it.

# Can I Put a 486 Chip in My 386 Computer to Make It Go Faster?

Nope. Motherboards and CPUs work together as a team. Think of the motherboard as a city that has roads connecting the houses and the grocery stores. The roads on the 386 motherboard aren't wide enough to carry all the information the 486 chip wants to start trucking around.

## It's probably too late to worry about this

Normally, you can't just plop a new CPU into an older computer and expect the thing to work. A CPU and a motherboard are pretty much a matched set. However, companies like Dell Computer Corporation broke the rules by selling *upgradable* computers.

The CPU comes on a little card that sits in a special little socket on the motherboard. When a newer, faster CPU hits the stores, the company will sell the CPU mounted on a special card. You pull out your old CPU's card and plop in the new one.

Those particular motherboards have been designed to expect that sort of thing, so it works. But you need to have bought one of these upgradable PCs before you can try this trick.

# Can I Put a 486 Motherboard into My Old IBM PC or XT?

Nope. Motherboards come in two basic sizes: the weird size for the old XT computers and the size everybody has used since.

Therefore, the newer motherboards just don't fit inside your XT's weird-shaped case. But that's not the biggest problem.

See, even if you could jam a 486 motherboard inside an XT, you would have to buy all new memory. An XT's memory chips won't fit on the new motherboard. You'll need a new power supply, too; the old one's not powerful enough. Toss a new keyboard onto the bill, too. Plus, you'll probably want the newer, higher-capacity disk drives.

A completely new computer will cost about the same. Plus, a new computer has a better warranty. And some dealers will toss in a free copy of the latest version of DOS and Windows.

A few companies went off the deep end when it came to the *standard* motherboard size. Some Compaq computers use weird-sized motherboards, which makes replacement difficult. You'll probably have to go to a Compaq dealer for one of those.

# Uh, should I really install the motherboard myself?

Don't replace your motherboard unless you've gotten used to fiddling around inside your computer.

Replacing the motherboard is a tedious, laborious chore. You need to remove every wire that plugs into the old motherboard and then plug the wires into your new motherboard. And they'll probably plug into different places!

You have to pull out every card and every bit of memory off your old motherboard. Then you have to stick it all back onto the new one, in exactly the right spots.

Besides, motherboards are fragile things. When bent too far, motherboards break. Oh, you won't see the break. Just one of those little wires etched along the bottom will break.

And the motherboard won't *always* be broken. The motherboard may work fine when you first turn the computer on. But when it heats up in about an hour, the motherboard will expand slightly, which aggravates the break. That brings on the worst kind of computer problem — a glitch that only happens once in a while, especially when no one's around to believe you.

Don't mess with your motherboard unless you've messed around with all the other parts in your computer first and feel like you've gotten the hang of it.

# I just installed a new 486 motherboard, and it's slower than my old 386!

Installing a new motherboard into a computer is like the Star Trek episode *Return to Tomorrow* where the crew took that alien's *consciousness* out of a can and stuck it into Spock. Although Spock still had pointed ears and everything, he was a completely different person.

The same thing happens to your computer. It looks the same, but that new motherboard gives it a completely different consciousness.

In the computer world, that consciousness is called *CMOS*. Your new motherboard has all sorts of new CMOS settings for you to play with. And if the motherboard is moving slowly, you probably need to fiddle with its *cache settings*. In that case, you'd better head for Chapter 17 where all those little CMOS setting details hang freely in the wind.

## *What's that Overdrive stuff?*

At the race track, the riders often whip their horses to make 'em run a little bit faster.

Intel does the same thing with its *Overdrive* chips. Many motherboards with Intel's 486 chips contain a special Overdrive socket. When you stick the Overdrive chip in that socket, it whips your CPU and makes it work twice as fast.

- ✔ Well, not really twice as fast. Technically, it's twice as fast at *thinking* about stuff and not moving information around. Without getting too bogged down in the difference between *thinking* and *moving,* just figure that the chip can speed up your computer by about 70 percent.

- ✔ Only 486 motherboards can handle those Overdrive chips. When you see a computer billed as a 66 MHz 486DX2, that means it's really a 33 MHz CPU with one of those Overdrive chips that make it run at 66 MHz.

- ✔ Those chips plug in just like math coprocessor chips, so head for that section for the installation scoop.

## *How do I install a new motherboard?*

**IQ level:** 120

**Tools you need:** Big Phillips screwdriver, little screwdriver, tweezers/needle-nose pliers, two hands, and a *lot* of patience

**Cost:** Anywhere from $100 - $1,000

**Things to watch out for:**

Give yourself plenty of time. You need to remove just about everything inside your computer and then put it all back after the new motherboard is inside. Give yourself plenty of room, too. You'll need room to spread out.

If you're dealing with a very old computer, your best bet is to buy a new case along with the new motherboard. That way you can be sure that they match up.

Finally, you'll be dealing with a lot of your computer's parts here. If you're stuck on the memory step, for example, head for Chapter 10 for memory information. All the cards stuff is in Chapter 14. Just check the book's table of contents to see where your confusing part is discussed.

Good luck. (It's not too late to take this one to the shop, you know.)

To install a new motherboard, follow these steps:

1. **Buy the new motherboard.**

   The new motherboard doesn't have to be the same identical size as your old one. In fact, your new motherboard will probably be smaller. However, the motherboard's little screw holes must be in the same place as the old one, or it may not fit into the case.

2. **Write down your computer's CMOS information.**

   Your new motherboard isn't going to know the same things as your old one. So write down the *type* of hard drive your computer uses. (You'll find that information by probing into your computer's CMOS, described in Chapter 17.) Make sure that you know the *density* of your floppy drives, too.

3. **Turn off your PC, unplug it, and remove its case.**

   All this stuff is described in the cheat sheet at the front of this book.

4. **Unplug any wires that connect to the motherboard.**

   Don't touch anything inside your computer until you have released your pent-up static electricity. Tap on a doorknob, file cabinet, or bare metal part of your desk.

   Bunches of little wires plug into little pins or sockets on the motherboard. While unplugging each one, write down any numbers, words, or letters you see next to the spot it was removed from on the motherboard. Those words or letters will help you plug those wires into the right spots on the new motherboard.

   Make sure that you unplug these wires:

   **Power supply:** The power supply is two big multiwired cables that plug into big sockets.

   **Lights:** Unplug the wires leading to the lights along the front of your computer's case. Most computers have a hard drive light and power light; some fancier computers have more.

   **Switches:** The wires from your reset button end up on your motherboard somewhere. Usually, the reset button wire goes next to where the lights plug in.

5. **Remove all the cards and cables.**

   The cables from your printer, mouse, monitor, and other goodies all plug into the ends of cards. You need to remove each cable. Then you need to remove all the cards. They're held in place with a single screw at the back of the case. After you've removed the screws, each card should pull straight up and out.

Keep track of which card lived in which slot. The cards probably don't need to be reinserted in the same order, but, hey, why take chances?

Do you have a card that's not in the same row as all the others? That's probably a 386 computer's special proprietary memory card; it probably won't work in your new motherboard. Sigh.

### 6. Unplug your keyboard.

The keyboard plugs in through a hole in the back of the case. Pull the keyboard plug straight out without turning.

### 7. Remove all the memory chips.

Chapter 10 covers all of this memory stuff. There, you'll learn what type of memory to look for and how to grab it.

You'll also learn whether or not you can stick that memory on your new motherboard. (The answer is rarely good news.)

Either way, save those chips in Ziploc baggies. Some stores let you trade old chips in for a discount on new chips.

### 8. Unpack the new board.

Remove the new board from the wrapper and look for anything grossly wrong: shattered plastic, broken wires, gouges, melted ice cream, or anything loose and dangling.

Don't touch your motherboard until you've released any stray static electricity. Touch a doorknob, file cabinet, or bare metal part of your desk. Even then, handle the board by its edges.

Those innocent-looking silver dots on one side of your motherboard are actually savage metal pokers. If they brush across your hand, they'll leave ugly scratches. People will mistake you for a biker.

Look for any DIP switches; you may need to flick them later. (That DIPPY stuff's all described in Chapter 17.)

### 9. Put memory chips on the new motherboard.

If you could salvage any memory from your old motherboard, stick it onto your new one. Add as many new memory chips as you can afford, as well. Don't know how? Chapter 10 has detailed instructions for putting memory into its rightful place.

### 10. Look at how your old board is mounted.

Usually, two or three screws hold the thing in place. Remember where the screws are so you can screw the new ones in the same place.

### 11. Remove the old motherboard.

Unscrew the screws holding the old motherboard in place. Then gently grasp the board's edge and pull it straight out of the computer. You may need to move the board slightly back and forth until it comes free. Some motherboards need to be slid toward the left before they'll come loose.

### 12. Remove the plastic standoffs.

The screws keep the motherboard from moving around. But little plastic *spacers* keep the motherboard from actually touching the bottom of the case.

You can remove the spacers by pinching their tops and pushing them down into the holes, like in Figure 9-4.

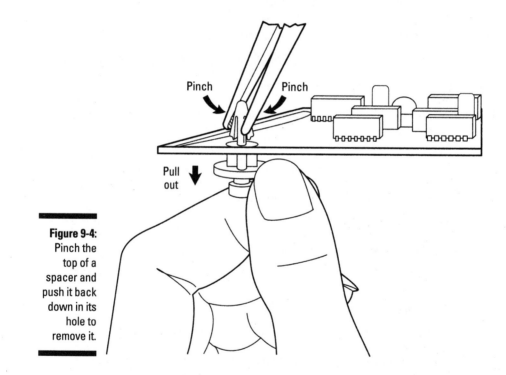

Pinch          Pinch

Pull
out

**Figure 9-4:**
Pinch the
top of a
spacer and
push it back
down in its
hole to
remove it.

### 13. Put the little plastic standoffs on the new board.

Then push those little plastic standoffs into the new motherboard. Push them up into the holes from the bottom.

**14. Slide in the new board and tighten the screws.**

Slide in the new motherboard just like you slid out the old one. Look for the keyboard cable hole because the keyboard plug on the new motherboard needs to go right next to it.

You'll have to fiddle with the motherboard for a while until the little plastic spacers all line up in their little holes. When the board is in firm and all the holes line up, screw it down. Don't screw it in *too* hard because it may crack.

**15. Replace the wires.**

Is it in? Then hook all those little wires from the lights and switches to their spots on the new motherboard. If you're lucky, they'll be marked. If you're not lucky, you'll have to flip through the new motherboard's manual.

The red wire always connects to Pin 1. The two black wires always go next to each other on the power supply's two cables.

**16. Replace cards and cables.**

Put all the cards back in their slots, as described in Chapter 14. Make sure that you don't drop any screws inside the case; if you lose one, curse loudly. Then find the screw before going any further. If a screw lodges itself in the wrong place, it could ruin your motherboard. (Screw extraction tips live in Chapter 2.)

Plug in all your card's cables: the printer, mouse, monitor, and any other odds and ends that need to plug back into the right card.

**17. Plug in the keyboard.**

The keyboard should plug into its hole in the back of the case.

**18. Plug in the PC and turn it on.**

This is the big test. Does it turn on? Do you see words on the monitor?

**19. Put the cover back on.**

If everything works, put the cover back on and breathe a sigh of relief. If the PC is not working, several things could be wrong.

Make sure that all the cards and memory are sitting firmly in their sockets.

You may need to adjust the computer's new CMOS settings, as described in Chapter 17.

Some of your cards may not be compatible with your new motherboard. For example, I had an older VGA graphics card that simply refused to work in a new 486 motherboard.

Through the process of trial and error (and a lot of flipping around from chapter to chapter in this book), you can probably find the culprit. It may be faster to take the whole thing to the computer shop, though. Because you've already installed the motherboard, the shop should charge you a lot less.

# *What's This BIOS Business?*

Sometimes you can stick a new toy in your computer, fire it up, and start playing.

Other times, the computer will balk. If, for example, a computer was built in 1983, it's not going to know how to handle the new technology stuff that came out five years later.

For example, you can install a 3½-inch floppy disk drive into an XT computer. But because that old XT won't recognize the drive, it won't be able to use it. That XT computer's *BIOS* — the built-in instructions for handling computer parts — is stuck in the era of 5¼-inch drives and early Madonna singles.

✔ The decrepit BIOS in some computers can't handle Windows, VGA cards, or other new stuff.

   All is not lost, though. BIOS chips are easy to replace. The old chips can be plucked off the motherboard like ticks from a hound dog. Then the new chips plug right into their place.

✔ The problem comes with *finding* those new BIOS chips.

   Try bugging the dealer who sold you your computer. Show the dealer the receipt listing the specific brand of motherboard that you bought many moons ago. The dealer may have some newer BIOS chips in the back room, which are mixed in with the snack foods.

   If you picked up your PC at a garage sale, check the backs of the thickest computer magazines, where the small ads live. Chances are that you'll find somebody selling ROM BIOS upgrades.

✔ What BIOS chips do you need? Look for a row of up to four chips, usually with little labels stuck to their tops mentioning the word *BIOS*. For example, my 386 computer has four BIOS chips that say "Mylex, 386 BIOS, (c) 1986 AMI, 09/25/88." That doesn't mean much to you or me, but it means a lot to the guy on the phone at the mail-order house.

✔ The new BIOS won't make your computer run any faster. The BIOS is just a Band-Aid that lets an older computer use some newer parts. New motherboards always come with the newest BIOS chips as part of the package deal.

   Some new disk drives come with *device drivers*. After putting the device driver into your CONFIG.SYS file, you'll be able to bypass your BIOS. That driver stuff is driven home in Chapter 15.

✔ Your computer probably has several *types* of BIOS chips. For example, a video BIOS chip probably lives on your video card to make sure that the pictures are showing up on the screen. But, when you hear the word BIOS dropped in casual conversation, the reference is to the BIOS on your motherboard.

Some of the newest computers have a *flash BIOS*. You can upgrade that kind of BIOS by simply running a software program. Upgrading a flash BIOS is so easy that a lot of nerds are up in arms against it.

# How Do I Replace My BIOS?

**IQ level:** 80

**Tools you need:** One hand and a chip puller

**Cost:** Anywhere from $35 - $100

**Stuff to watch out for:**

Like all other chips, BIOS chips don't like static. Be sure to touch something metal — your computer's case or a filing cabinet — before picking up the chip.

Make sure that the little legs on the chip are aligned in a neat little row. Straighten out any bent legs.

Oh, and make sure that you can take your new BIOS chips back if they don't work. BIOS chips can be finicky in different types of computers, and they may refuse to work.

To replace the BIOS, follow these steps:

1. **Turn off your computer, unplug it, and remove its case.**

   If you're new at this game, head for the cheat sheet at the front of this book.

2. **Find your old BIOS chips.**

   They're the chips with the word *BIOS* on a stick-on label. You'll find anywhere from one to five chips. (You may find a keyboard BIOS chip as well.)

   If you have more than one BIOS chip, look for distinguishing numbers on them: BIOS-1, BIOS-2, BIOS-3, or something similar. Write down which chip goes in which socket and the direction each chip faces. The new BIOS chips must go in exactly the same place.

3. **Remove the old BIOS chips.**

   Some of your cards or other computer paraphernalia may be thoughtlessly hovering in the way. You have to remove that stuff before you can reach the chips.

To make it easy to pry out the old chips, some BIOS retailers toss in a chip puller — a weird, tweezers-looking thing. Don't carry a chip puller around? Try this trick: using a small screwdriver, gently pry up one end of the chip, and then pry up the other end. By carefully lifting up each side a little bit at a time, you can gently lift the chip out of its socket, like in Figure 9-5.

**Figure 9-5:**
By gently prying up one side and then the other, you can lift a chip out of its socket.

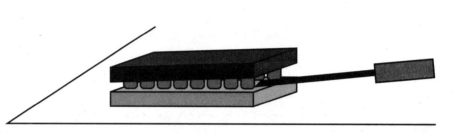

Or look for one of those L-shaped metal things that cover up the slots in the back of your computer. They're called *expansion slot retaining brackets,* and they also work to pry out chips, as shown in Figure 9-6.

**Figure 9-6:**
You can use a slot's bracket cover to pry out a chip.

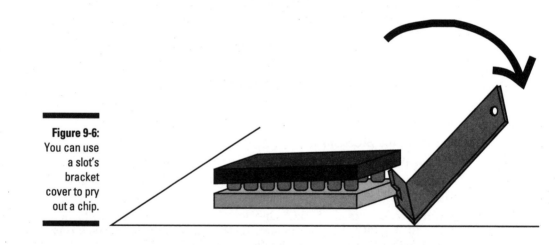

Don't try to pry the chip up from just one side. Doing so can bend or break its tiny little pins. Instead, pry up one side a fraction of an inch and then pry up the other side. By alternating and using gentle pressure, you can remove the chip undamaged.

**4. Insert the new BIOS chips.**

Find your notes and make sure that you know which chip goes into which socket and the direction the chip should face. Can't find your notes? Then make sure that the *notched* end of each chip faces the *notched* or *marked* end of its socket.

Next, make sure that the little pins on the chip are straight. A pair of needle-nose pliers can work here. Or you can push them against a flat desktop to make sure that they're all in a straight line.

Now, follow the steps shown in Figure 9-7.

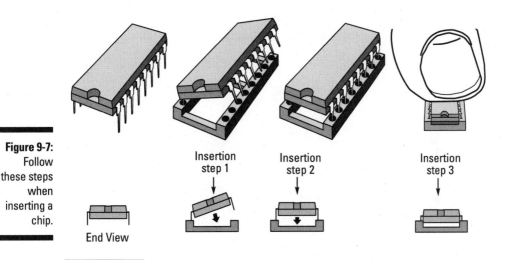

**Figure 9-7:**
Follow these steps when inserting a chip.

End View

Insertion step 1

Insertion step 2

Insertion step 3

Put the first row of little pins into their row of holes and make sure that they're lined up perfectly. Next, line up the other row of pins over their holes and push down until the pins are lined up, too. Finally, give the chip a firm push with your thumb until it rests in the socket.

**5. Replace any cards or other items that had blocked your view.**

**6. Replace the computer's cover, plug the computer back in, and turn it on.**

Your computer should notice its new BIOS chips right away. When you turn on your computer, you'll see the chips' new copyright date on the screen's first or second paragraph.

Doesn't work? Then unplug the computer, take off the case, and make sure that you've pushed those chips all the way into their sockets. Also, make sure that all those little pins are in their sockets. If one hangs out, like in Figure 9-3, things can get pretty goofy.

# Chapter 10
# Memory Stuff You'll Wish You Could Forget

●●●●●●●●●●●●●●●●●●●●●●●●●●●●●●●●●●●●●●●●●●●●●●●●●

## *In This Chapter*

▶ Understanding Windows' memory messages

▶ Dealing with parity errors

▶ Finding your computer's current memory

▶ Telling your computer about its memory

▶ Buying the right memory for your computer

▶ Installing or upgrading memory

●●●●●●●●●●●●●●●●●●●●●●●●●●●●●●●●●●●●●●●●●●●●●●●●●

**S**ome parts of your computer are great fun: joysticks, compact disc players, sound cards, and cool games like Disney's Stunt Island, where you can fly a duck around the tops of New York City skyscrapers.

Unfortunately, one part of your computer sends you screaming in the other direction: your computer's memory. Figuring out your computer's memory is the most devastatingly complicated part of IBM-compatible computing.

And, besides, memory is awfully boring.

In fact, this chapter starts out with awful memory by-products called *parity errors* and closes with migraine-inspired details on pushing memory chips onto your motherboard.

So feel free to ignore this chapter. If you don't want to be bothered with boring memory details, just let the folks at the computer shop handle your memory problems. Buddha would have taken his abacus to the shop if it used single in-line memory modules (SIMMs). Yech!

# *My Computer Keeps Saying* Parity Error *or Something Just as Mind-Numbing*

That parity stuff means that your computer is not getting along well with its memory, and this isn't good.

If you've just installed some new memory, perhaps the computer is just confused. Run your computer's Setup program or adjust the CMOS settings, which are described in Chapter 17. Also, make sure that your computer recognizes your handiwork — its new memory.

If the message persists, though, your best bet is to take your computer to the shop. One of your memory chips is squawking, and the technowizards in the shop can track down the culprit a lot faster than you can.

✔ Try a few tricks before giving up completely, though. Turn off the computer, remove the cover, and look for a little graveyard of memory chips lying flat along the motherboard's bottom left-hand corner. See 'em? Give 'em a little extra push with your thumb. Over the years, those chips tend to rise up from their sockets like ghosts.

Before touching any of your chips, touch a plain metal surface to discharge any static electricity. One stray spark can nuke your chips something fierce.

✔ People with newer computers may not have a chip graveyard. Instead, new computer users should give their memory modules a little push. *Memory modules* are little strips of plastic that have chips hanging off the side. Turn off your computer, take off its case, and give those strips a little push to make sure that they're in there tight.

✔ You'll find more of this thumb-pushing stuff at the end of this chapter.

# *Windows Keeps Saying* Not Enough Memory *or* Insufficient Memory

Windows uses memory the way baked potatoes use butter: the more you have, the better they taste.

If you don't have enough butter, the potato just sits there and tastes dry. But if you don't have enough memory, Windows reminds you of it constantly, as shown in Figure 10-1.

**Figure 10-1:**
When Windows
runs out of memory,
it sends this
uncomfortable-
sounding message.

> **Application Execution Error**
>
> (!) **Insufficient memory to run this application. Quit one or more Windows applications and then try again.**
>
> OK

There are only two ways to stop Windows from complaining. One way is to buy more memory. The other way is to make sure that your computer knows how to use the memory it already has.

✔ Adding memory is usually pretty easy. Just buy more memory chips and stick the chips in the empty sockets inside your computer (after reading the installation instructions at the back of this chapter, that is).

✔ Other computers are maxed out; that is, their motherboards simply can't handle any more memory, even if you won zillions of memory chips from *Reader's Digest.* You'll simply have to buy a newer, flashier computer with bigger memory bowels. Or if you're feeling really ambitious, ogle the directions for installing a new motherboard in Chapter 9.

*TECHNICAL STUFF*

## Playing cards by memory

If your XT computer is maxed out, you can buy a memory card to plug in an expansion slot. The computer can transform the memory card into *expanded memory,* and then the computer can dish the memory out to programs that need more memory. Unfortunately, buying an expanded memory card means that you're sinking more money into a dying investment. Think about spending that money on a newer computer, instead.

Is your 386 or 486 computer stuffed with memory up to its limit? Don't bother with an expanded memory card because it'll be way too slow for those whizbang computers.

Instead, some of those newer computers use special proprietary memory cards, which are available only from the manufacturer. Proprietary memory cards fit in a special 32-bit slot on the motherboard.

Check your motherboard's manual to see whether it has a 32-bit slot before you get too excited about a proprietary memory card. Even if your computer has the slot, those 32-bit proprietary memory cards are expensive.

Confidential to Skip Press in Burbank, California: No, Skip, you can't "hot wire" your 32-bit slot to the $1 slots in Las Vegas. I think your teenage hacker friend has been reading too many adventure novels.

# *How Much Memory Do I Have?*

For the most part, you don't need to know how much memory your computer has. If you don't have enough memory, your computer will tell you through a rude message.

If you're curious, though, watch your computer's screen when you first turn it on for the day.

When you flip the On switch, your computer tallies up its memory faster than a grocer can add up double coupons. The computer is testing all the memory it can find so it knows how much room is available for tallying up numbers.

Keep an eye on the screen for the total. That's how much memory your computer has found to play with. (It is possible, through wrong motherboard DIP settings and wrong CMOS settings, for the wrong amount of memory to be shown during bootup. Read on for more information.)

The second easiest way to discover your computer's memory is to look at the receipt to see how much memory you bought. Of course, it's more reassuring to have the *computer* tell you.

So whether you're using Windows 3.1 or DOS 6, look for the helpful little computer nerd program Microsoft has stashed on your computer. Exit Win-

## My computer can't count RAM right!

My computer has 8MB of random-access memory (RAM), and it counts to 7808K each morning. Why doesn't the computer count to 8000K, which is an even 8MB? Well, a megabyte is *really* 1024K, but people tend to round down to 1000K or 1MB.

So 7MB totals 7168K. That's how much *extended memory* my computer has. Then I add the *conventional memory* DOS can actually use, which is 640K. That brings the total to 7808K, which is the amount my computer displays on-screen.

There's still a 384K chunk of memory leftover, though. That's the *high* memory, which is where some of your computer's hardware goodies hang their hats.

These weird memory terms all get their due in Table 10-1, which is a few pages down the road in this chapter.

dows (or just make sure that you're *really* in DOS) and type **MSD** at the C:\> thing. You'll see the amount of memory your computer thinks that it has next to the word Memory on-screen.

For example, on my computer the MSD program says 640K, 7168 Ext. So if I divide 7168K by 1024K, I get 7 or 7MB of extended memory. And because I have 1MB of regular memory (that's where the 640K comes from), I have 8MB of RAM in my computer.

Yeah, this memory stuff is pretty complicated. And to make matters worse, sometimes your computer has memory but doesn't know that the memory is there. The memory simply doesn't show up on MSD or any other software program! This calamity is covered in the next section.

And the worst part is the way DOS was designed. When DOS programs complain about needing more memory, they're not saying that you need to buy great gobs of memory chips. They're saying that they need more *conventional memory,* which is that small portion of memory all DOS programs fight over.

Some programs refuse to run on a computer. The programs complain, saying that they need 570K of memory. But you only have 550K or something similar. To make these programs run, head for Chapter 2 and make a *System disk.* Then put that disk into drive A and press your Ctrl, Alt, and Delete keys at the same time. When your computer restarts, it will have more memory to share with your hoggy games.

# I Installed a Bunch of Memory, but My Computer Doesn't Know That It's There!

There are two main reasons for your computer not finding new memory.

First, some PCs aren't smart enough to know that you've spent a lot of time and money to stick little memory chip things inside them. To wise 'em up, you probably need to flip a *DIP* switch on the motherboard. (I'm not making this up, as you'll find out in Chapter 17's DIP switch section.) Some computers may make you fiddle with their *jumpers,* which is also covered in Chapter 17.

But the biggest problem is probably this: even when the *computer* knows that the memory's there, the *software* may not know. For example, even after you add 4MB of memory to your computer, most software can still only use 640K of it. Because of the way DOS works, the rest of the memory just sits there unused!

To use any more memory than 640K, you need a special *memory manager* program to dish it around to your programs.

Yep, memory is a horrible, confusing mess. Worse yet, you may need to buy more software.

- ✔ Luckily for thin wallets, Windows, DOS 5, DOS 6, and OS/2 come with a free memory manager that can handle some of these complicated memory-dishing chores. When you install the latest version of DOS, Windows, or OS/2, it automatically starts managing your memory.

- ✔ In fact, the memory management system with Windows is so elaborate that it completely takes over all the memory in your computer. When running Windows programs, you don't need to worry about that 640K memory barrier.

- ✔ If you try to run DOS programs under Windows, however, the problems return. Windows tries to dish out that coveted 640K memory, but sometimes Windows can't scrape up enough memory. That's why some DOS programs don't work right under Windows.

The memory manager in DOS 5 and DOS 6 is called HIMEM.SYS, and it only works if it's mentioned in the first line of your computer's CONFIG.SYS file. When you install Windows, for example, Windows automatically adds the line `DEVICE=C:\WINDOWS\HIMEM.SYS` to your CONFIG.SYS file. DOS puts that line in there, too. And OS/2 uses a much more efficient memory system that I won't bore you with here.

Now, back to our regularly scheduled bulleted items.

- ✔ For real powerhouse memory management, some people buy third-party programs like QEMM or 386MAX. Those programs automatically add up all the memory your computer has, organize it, and dole out the best chunks to your programs. Best yet, you don't have to mess with any of the hard stuff.

- ✔ Memory management is an awesome chore, so don't feel bad if you don't get the hang of it right away. In fact, nobody has ever gotten the hang of it.

# Why Can't I Move Memory off My Old Motherboard and Stick It onto My New Motherboard?

The packaging has changed on memory chips over the years. The memory chips on your old motherboard are probably a different size from the ones you'll need for your new motherboard.

The chips just won't fit — like an 8-track tape won't fit in a CD player.

✔ You can usually tell whether or not your memory chips will work by just looking at them. Most memory today comes on long flat cards called *SIMMs*. Older motherboards used chips called *DIPs* or *SIPPs*. A DIP chip and a SIMM are pictured in Figure 10-2.

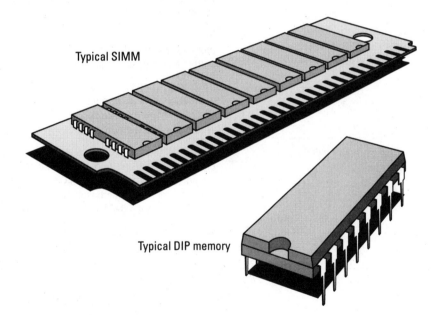

Typical SIMM

Typical DIP memory

**Figure 10-2:** A DIP chip and a SIMM.

✔ If you can't reuse your old chips, save 'em anyway. Some computer stores let you trade 'em in for a discount on the type of chips that *will* work.

✔ Some men use their obsolete chips to make hip costume jewelry for their wives. Their wives, subsequently, serve their husbands 8-track tapes for dinner.

Only nerds know *all* these memory terms. Memory is merely a chalkboard the computer uses to store information while it's divvying up numbers. Unfortunately, DOS divvies up that big chalkboard into bunches of little sections, and each section has its own name and purpose. Table 10-1 explains what all those words mean, just in case you want to be a memory chip for Halloween.

| Table 10-1 | Inane Memory Terms |
|---|---|
| *What It's Called* | *The Point of It All* |
| Memory | Alias: Random-access memory (RAM). Memory comes on chips that live on your motherboard. Almost all new computers have at least 1MB — 1024K — of memory. |
| | Why 1MB? Because the nerd who created your computer figured that was plenty. Who'd need more? |
| Conventional memory | Alias: DOS memory, base memory, or real memory. Your computer takes that 1MB of memory and tosses 640K (about two-thirds of it) to your DOS programs. |
| | In fact, all DOS programs grab for that same 640K memory chunk, no matter how much memory you've stuffed inside your computer. |
| | If a program can't find enough conventional memory, it won't run. Or the program may simply stop working. Often, programs stop working quite abruptly and at the worse possible moments. |
| Upper memory | Alias: High memory, reserved memory, or upper memory blocks. After a program grabs its 640K from the 1MB of memory, the computer has 384K leftover. The computer uses that for mechanical stuff, like making sure that you've *really* put a disk in the floppy drive. |
| | Your computer's BIOS hangs out in that area, as do the brains behind your video card and other bits of computing viscera. |
| Expanded memory | As programs grew huffier and puffier, they soon outgrew their little 640K allotment. |
| | So computer nerds stuck extra memory chips onto a card and stuck that card inside their computers. Then the nerds wrote a complicated memory management program to grab the memory off the card and slip the memory over to the DOS program on the sly. |

| *What It's Called* | *The Point of It All* |
| --- | --- |
| | But only DOS programs written specifically for that expanded memory could grab those extra chunks of memory. All the other DOS programs were still stuck in their 640K closet. |
| Extended memory | As the years rolled on, the new 286, 386, and 486 computers hit the stores. The new computers had gobs of memory stuffed right onto their motherboard. Some motherboards came with 4MB, and other motherboards could hold up to 64MB or more. |
| | The increased memory still didn't liberate DOS programs from their 640K hole, though. But the nerds wrote a special memory manager for that extended memory, just as they'd done for the expanded memory that came on cards. |
| | Windows knows how to use extended memory. In fact, Windows grabs *all* your computer's memory so it can run bunches of programs at the same time. |
| | But most of your DOS programs are stuck with 640K, no matter how much memory's lying around. |
| Virtual memory | Alias: Swap disk. Windows grabs as much extended memory as it can find. |
| | But when Windows wants even *more* memory, it creates its own. Windows grabs part of your hard drive and temporarily stores information there. |
| | When Windows starts using its newly created virtual memory, everything slows down a little: your hard drive is much slower than RAM chips. But, hey, it works. |
| ROM | Alias: Read-only memory. Computers normally use memory for calculating numbers. Computers grab some memory from the pool, work out their problem, and pour the memory back into the pool. |
| | But sometimes a computer needs to store something *forever*. That information is stored on ROM chips. |
| | Standing for read-only memory, ROM chips contain things that never change. Your computer's BIOS is stored on ROM because it contains instructions for things that never change — for example, the way your computer copies information onto a floppy disk. |

*(continued)*

| Table 10-1 | Inane Memory Terms *(continued)* |
|---|---|
| *What It's Called* | *The Point of It All* |
| | In fact, that's why you'll need a new BIOS when a new breed of floppy drives come out. The old BIOS won't know how to deal with those new drives, and the ROM on the old BIOS can't be updated with new information. |
| Cache | Alias: Shadow RAM. After your computer's CPU figures out something, it copies its answer into a slippery memory receptacle called a cache. |
| | Then if the computer needs that information again, it just snatches it from the cache. That's quicker than performing the calculation again or bothering other parts for the answer. |
| | A 486 computer comes with an 8K cache built into the chip. Other computers add CPU caches to the motherboard to speed things up. |
| | Special ultra-fast memory chips are used for caches. These chips are much faster than the ones used for extended memory, and they're also more expensive. |
| RAM disks | Files normally live on a hard disk or floppy disk. Disk drives are slow, though, because they're mechanical: little hamsters run on a treadmill to turn their gears. |
| | To speed things up, some folks bypass the mechanical stuff by telling DOS to take some of their memory and turn it into a virtual disk drive. |
| | Then these folks copy their most often used files to that memory or RAM drive. When the computer needs those files, it sucks them from the RAM. That's a lot quicker than waiting for tired, old hamsters. |

# *Geez, What Memory Should I Buy?*

Everybody knows that they need *more* memory. But what *kind* of memory? Like living rooms, motherboards are all arranged differently. Some motherboards can hold great gobs of memory. Other motherboards can barely squeak by with a sliver.

The only way to know for sure how much memory your motherboard can hold is to dig out the manual and look for the following key words.

## Memory type

Some memory chips plug right into the motherboard, like in Figure 10-3. Called a DIP chip, each chip plugs into its own little socket. DIP chips are the oldest type of memory and the hardest to find and install.

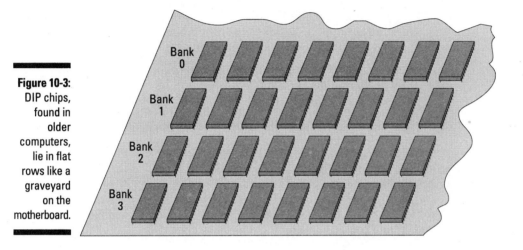

**Figure 10-3:** DIP chips, found in older computers, lie in flat rows like a graveyard on the motherboard.

Other memory chips, called SIMMs, plug into long slots on the motherboard, like in Figure 10-4.

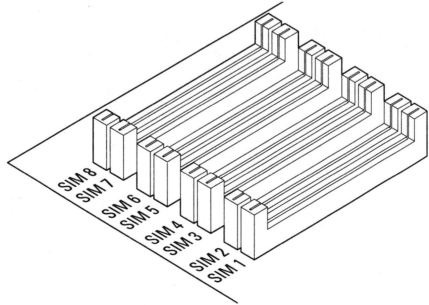

**Figure 10-4:** SIMMs plug into sockets like these.

The last memory type, called a SIPP, plugs into little rows pretty much like the ones in Figure 10-4. The sockets have little holes rather than a slot to accommodate the little feet on the chips.

Most new computers these days use SIMMs because they're the easiest to install. Some computers use DIPs on the motherboard for their first 1MB and SIMMs for the rest.

Have you found the right pages in your motherboard's manual yet?

## Memory speed

Buy chips that are the same speed or faster than your current memory chips. Buying faster chips won't make your computer run faster. Motherboards run at their own, internal limit.

Also, don't buy chips that are slower than your current crop of chips, even though they *are* cheaper.

Chip speed is measured in *nanoseconds.* Smaller numbers mean faster chips: A 70 nanosecond chip is faster than a 100 nanosecond chip.

Dunno how fast your current chips can scoot? Look at the string of numbers written across the roof of the chips. The numbers usually end with a hyphen and are followed by another number or two. Table 10-2 shows what that magic number after the hyphen means.

| Table 10-2 | The Numbers After the Hyphen Display Your Chip's Speed | |
|---|---|---|
| The Number on the Chip | The Speed of the Chip | Computers That Like the Chip |
| -7 or -70 | 70 nanoseconds | Most 386, 486, and newer |
| -8 or -80 | 80 nanoseconds | Most 386, 486, and newer |
| -10 | 100 nanoseconds | Most ATs or 286s |
| -12 | 120 nanoseconds | Most ATs or 286s |
| -15 | 150 nanoseconds | XTs and PCs |
| -20 | 200 nanoseconds | Very old PCs |

## *Memory capacity*

Here's where things get even weirder. For example, suppose that your mother-board says it can handle 8MB of memory. Your computer only has 2MB, and you're rubbing your hands in anticipation of an easy, plug-in-the-chip upgrade.

But when you open your computer, you see that all your SIMM sockets are full of chips, just like in Figure 10-5. How can you fit more memory in there? Where's the crowbar?

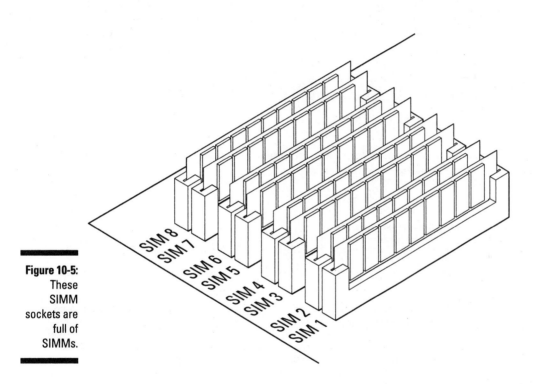

**Figure 10-5:**
These
SIMM
sockets are
full of
SIMMs.

✔ The problem is the capacity of the SIMMs that are sitting in those sockets. Those little strips can hold memory in the amounts of 256K, 1MB, 2MB, 4MB, 8MB, or 16MB.

✔ In this case, those eight SIMMs must be holding 256K of memory. Eight sockets of 256K SIMMs totals up to 2048K of memory, or 2MB.

✔ So to upgrade that computer to 8MB of memory, you need to yank out all those 256K SIMMs and put the higher capacity 1MB (1024K) SIMMs in their place.

✔ Yes, that means those old 256K SIMMs are useless to you. Some dealers let you trade old chips in for a discount on your new chips. Other dealers make you store your old chips in the garage until you forget about them.

# *How Do I Install More Memory?*

**IQ level:** 100

**Tools you need:** Your motherboard's manual, screwdriver, chip puller (optional), and screwdriver

**Cost:** Anywhere from $30 - $80

**Stuff to watch out for:**

Memory has more rules than Mrs. Jackson during her shift on lunch duty:

✔ First, buy memory that fits in your motherboard's sockets. There are several different sizes.

✔ Second, buy memory that's the right speed so your computer can use it without tripping.

✔ Third, buy memory that's the right capacity. Different motherboards have different limits on how much RAM they can handle.

These three details are covered more fully in the preceding section. And be sure that you pull out your motherboard's manual to see what rules to follow.

Actually, installing the memory is the easy part. The hard part is figuring out which chips to buy and where to put them.

If this stuff sounds confusing, feel free to pass this job over to the computer shop, especially if you don't have a manual for your motherboard. The folks in the back room can upgrade memory chips in just a few minutes.

Finally, some companies (IBM included) used some oddball chip sizes. If any of these instructions start sounding weird or something is the wrong size, take the whole thing to the shop.

To install new memory chips, perform the following steps:

1. **Turn off the computer, unplug it, and remove the case.**

   These steps get the full treatment in the cheat sheet at the front of this book.

2. **Figure out what memory your computer uses.**

   Dig out your motherboard's manual to see what sort of memory it's craving. Check for the memory's *type* (motherboards use DIPs, SIMMs, or SIPPs), *speed* (measured in nanoseconds, or ns), and *capacity* (the memory size, listed in kilobytes [K] or megabytes [MB]).

   The most amiable motherboards can handle several different capacities and chip speeds.

3. **Figure out whether there's room for more memory.**

   Ogle your motherboard to see whether it has any empty chip sockets. DIP chips are usually arranged in rows of 9 sockets lying flat on your motherboard, like in Figure 10-3. Are any of them empty?

   Sockets for SIMMs or SIPPs are in little rows near the bottom left-hand corner of your motherboard. Spot any empty ones, like in Figure 10-6? Then you're in luck!

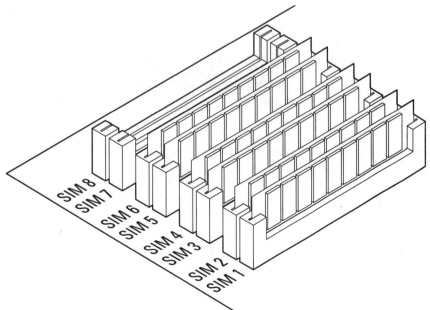

**Figure 10-6:**
Empty
sockets
make
upgrades
easier.

SIM 8
SIM 7
SIM 6
SIM 5
SIM 4
SIM 3
SIM 2
SIM 1

You can add as much memory as you want, under two conditions: First, don't add more memory than your motherboard can handle. (You'll find its limit listed in the manual.) Second, your computer organizes those little sockets into *banks*. Some motherboards say that two sockets make a bank. Other motherboards say that four sockets make a bank.

Regardless, motherboards either make you fill up a bank completely or leave the bank empty. You can't leave a bank half full, or the motherboard will belch.

Also, you can't mix amounts of memory in a bank. For example, you can't put a 1MB SIMM and a 2MB SIMM in a single bank. You either have to use all 1MB SIMMs or all 2MB SIMMs.

If you don't see any empty sockets, your memory upgrade is getting a little more complicated. Check your motherboard's manual to see whether it's maxed out. Your motherboard may already be stuffed to the brim and simply can't handle any more RAM.

If the manual says that the motherboard *can* handle more memory but the sockets are all full, you have to yank out the old chips and replace them with higher capacity chips.

### 4. Buy the right type of new memory chips.

By now, you should know whether you need to buy DIPs, SIMMs, or SIPPs. And your pocketbook (and the motherboard's limit) decides what capacity of chips you buy.

But make sure that you buy the right *speed* of chips, as well. There's really only one rule: don't buy chips that are *slower* than your current ones.

Don't know the speed of your current chips? Head for the "Geez, What Memory Should I Buy?" section for pointers.

### 5. Install the new memory chips.

Make sure that you ground yourself by touching something metallic before picking up any of the chips, or you could destroy them with static electricity.

If you're working in a dry area with lots of static around, take off your shoes. Working barefoot can help prevent static buildup. If you have your own office, feel free to take off all your clothes. Compute naked!

Check your motherboard's manual to make sure that you're filling up the right sockets and rows.

**SIMMs:** Look for the notched end of the SIMM. That notch lets the chip fit into its socket only one way. Position the SIMM over the socket and push it down into place. When the chip is in as far as it goes, tilt it slowly until the little metal tabs snap into place. The whole procedure should look like the three steps in Figure 10-7.

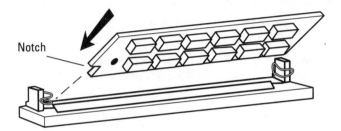

Notch

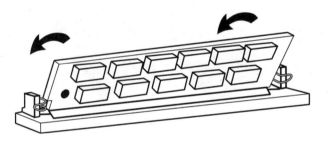

**Figure 10-7:**
SIMMs
snap in like
this.

Some SIMMs, like the ones in Figure 10-5, just push straight down and lock in place. Other SIMMs need to be tilted while they're being inserted. Some SIMMs need to be tilted after being inserted. If you're careful, you'll figure out which way the chips fit.

Be sure that you fill up the bank where you're adding SIMMs.

**DIPs:** Make sure that the little pins on the chips are straight. A pair of needle-nose pliers can help flatten the pins. Or you can push the chips against a flat desktop to make sure that the pins are in a straight line.

Make sure that the chip's notched end is over the notched or marked edge of the socket. Then put the first row of little pins into their row of holes, making sure that the pins line up perfectly.

Next, line up the other row of pins over their holes. Then push down until the pins line up, too.

Finally, give the chip a slow, firm push with your thumb until it rests in the socket. Repeat the process until you've filled up the row.

The process is shown in Figure 10-8.

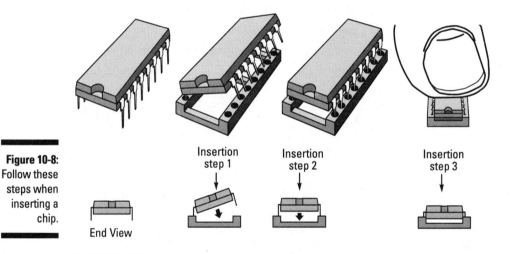

**Figure 10-8:** Follow these steps when inserting a chip.

End View

Insertion step 1

Insertion step 2

Insertion step 3

**SIPPs:** Make sure that the *notched* or *marked* end of the SIPP is aligned with the *marked* side of the socket. Then carefully push the SIPP's little legs into the holes until it's firmly in place.

As with the other SIPPs, make sure that you're filling up the sockets *one bank at a time.*

### 6. Double-check your work.

Make sure that all the DIP chips are facing the right way and make sure that all the legs are in the holes. Also, check the legs to be sure that none are bent underneath or are hanging over the sides.

Check your motherboard's manual to make sure that you've filled up the banks in the right order.

### 7. Flip appropriate DIP switches or jumpers on the motherboard.

Some computers don't automatically recognize the chips you've agonizingly inserted. The computer requires you to flip a DIP switch or move a jumper to tell it how much memory you've added.

Which do you do? Check your motherboard's manual. The manual is the only place you'll find these secrets.

Unsure about how a jumper or DIP switch works? Jump ahead to Chapter 17.

### 8. Replace the case, plug in the computer, and turn it on.

Your computer should greet you with an error message about memory mismatch or something weird. The message sounds scary, but it's good news! Your computer found the memory chips you've stuck inside it.

Your computer is grateful, but it's also a little wary. Your computer wants to show you the amount of memory it found and ask you to confirm that yes, indeed, you did put that much memory inside it.

All this stuff happens in your computer's CMOS area or Setup screen. And all that stuff's tucked away in Chapter 17. (It's not nearly as hard as it sounds, either.)

XTs don't have a Setup program or CMOS area, so XTs just take your word for how much new memory you've installed, based on the DIP switches and jumpers you moved around.

If your computer still doesn't recognize your new memory chips, turn it off and push those chips into their sockets a little more firmly. That may do the trick.

### 9. Put the case back on.

Whew. You've done it. Boot up Windows and see how much faster it runs!

"WE'VE EXPANDED THE MEMORY ON THIS ONE SO MANY TIMES IT'S STARTING TO GET STRETCH MARKS."

# Chapter 11
# Floppy Drives

*In This Chapter*

▶ Tracking down disk errors

▶ Formatting floppy disks

▶ Installing a new floppy drive

*I*nstead of redecorating their living rooms every year, the technical types who work at the world's computer hardware and software factories redesign floppy disks. They either figure out a way to store more information on a disk, or they make the disk smaller. Most likely, they do both.

Then everybody needs to rush out and buy the latest disk drives, or they can't read the new disks. It's a never-ending cycle, like an old dishwasher that's stuck on rinse.

About a year ago, people needed to upgrade to a 3.5-inch disk drive just to be able to install software. Today, you're not in vogue unless you can listen to Garth Brooks on a new CD-ROM drive while formatting your floppy disks.

This chapter explains how to install a new floppy drive so you can keep up with the Joneses and the latest software.

## *My Computer Barfs on My Friend's Disks!*

A floppy disk may work fine in your friend's computer but not in your computer. Instead of reading the disk, your computer barfs a weird error message onto the screen.

For example, my friend Wally could store stuff on disks with no problem. Unfortunately, no other computers in the office could read his disks.

Wally's disk drives were slightly out of alignment with the computers in the rest of the world. A few PC repair shops can tune up a disk drive if its disks don't work in other machines, but the alignment almost always costs more than a brand new drive. Wally didn't buy a new drive, so everybody just avoided his computer. (We still ate lunch with Wally, though.)

Alignment problems aren't the only causes of disk weirdness, however. Some other causes for disk barfs include

- If you have the older, *low-density* drives — the ones that only read 360K or 720K floppies — your computer will barf on a friend's newer, *high-density* floppies — the ones that hold 1.2 or 1.44 megabytes of data. The older drives simply can't decipher that newer, fancier format.

- Also, IBM-compatible computers and Macintosh computers don't like each other. (Neither do their owners, but that's a different story.) Neither computer can read disks used by the other because each sticks stuff on a floppy disk using a different *format.*

- Actually, Macintosh computers have gotten a little friendlier. Some of the newer ones can store files in an IBM-compatible format if their owners tell them to.

# When I Put in a New Disk, it Says Invalid *Something or Other*

A couple of gremlins could be causing this Invalid stuff. The number-one culprit is an *unformatted disk.*

Your computer can't use floppy disks right out of the box. It needs to *format* them first. A new floppy disk is like an empty wall. When a computer formats the disk, it sticks little electronic shelves on the wall so it can store data on them.

To format a disk in drive A, type the following command:

```
C:\> FORMAT A:
```

In other words, type **FORMAT,** a space, and then **A:** (for drive A). The computer responds by telling you to insert a disk in drive A and press the Enter key. Did you put the disk in there? Then press Enter.

After a minute or so, the computer will ask you for a *volume label.* That's a fancy computer word that translates roughly to *name.* So, type in **Tina** or **Lars** or **Ulrich** or whatever name you prefer and then press Enter. (Or just press Enter to forget about the volume label. Write a name on the disk's sticker instead where you can see it.)

When the computer asks whether you want to format another disk, press N. Your newly formatted disk is now ready to roll.

Don't ever format drive C (or D, E, F, or G). Any drive with a letter higher than B is a hard disk, and formatting wipes a hard disk clean. You need to format a hard disk only once, after it's first installed. Then you never format it again.

If your disk is properly formatted, you may get an `Invalid` message for several other reasons:

- ✔ You get an `Invalid` message if you try to use a high-density disk in a low-density drive.

- ✔ Sometimes a floppy disk simply goes bad. If this happens to all your disks, your floppy drive may be acting up. If it just happens on an occasional floppy, just toss the floppy and use another.

- ✔ If you see the `Invalid` message when using your hard drive, you're in for some serious disk trouble. Make a backup copy of your hard drive _immediately._

- ✔ If your computer's having trouble reading its own disks, it may have forgotten what kind of disk drive it owns. To remind it, head for its CMOS area or Setup screen to make sure that it lists the right type of drive. (Better head for Chapter 17 for more information on this one.)

- ✔ Finally, your drive's _controller card_ may be on vacation. Turn off your computer, take off the case, and look for a card with a flat ribbon cable snaking out of it. Push that card down into its socket to make sure that it's snug. Make sure that all those cables are snugly fastened, too. What are controller cards? They're explained near the "How Do I Install a New Floppy Drive?" section later in this chapter.

## Who cares why a 1.2MB disk holds more than a 360K disk?

Computers measure stuff by the metric system, which works out great for everybody except Americans who've been using yardsticks and rulers since kindergarten.

Mainly, computers measure the amount of data they can store either in _kilobytes (K)_ or _megabytes (MB)._ One megabyte is a lot more than one kilobyte. It's _1,000_ times as much. Actually, it's exactly 1,024 times as much, but everybody rounds it down to 1,000 during general everyday breakfast conversation.

So, a 1.44MB disk can hold _twice_ as much as a 720K disk. And a 1.2MB disk can hold _four_ times as much as a 360K disk.

The disks that can hold 1.44MB or 1.2MB of data are called _high-density_ disks. The others, the 360K and 720K disks, are called _low-density_ disks, although some manufacturers call them _double-density_ to confuse the issue.

Finally, the newest disks can hold 2.88MB, and they're called _extended-capacity_ disks. You'll learn more about these in the next section.

# *What's an Extended-Capacity Disk?*

The newest breed of floppy disk, dubbed *extended capacity,* can hold 2.88MB of data. That's twice as much as the former storage champs, the high-density disks. (If you're curious about high-density disks, check out the technical box stuff in the preceding section.)

These new disks are still 3.5 inches wide, just like the older guys, but they have the letters *ED* stamped on a corner.

- Extended-capacity disks are so new that hardly anybody uses them. I've never seen one, but everybody says that they're out there somewhere.

- If you want to use the new disks, you need to buy a special, more expensive disk drive. (I've never seen one of those either.)

- The special, more expensive disk drives can still read the other two varieties of 3.5-inch disks: 720K disks and 1.44MB disks.

- These new disks and drives have been slow to catch on. But, hey, Hollywood snobs booed *Citizen Kane* during the Academy Awards in 1941.

# *My Computer Says That My Sector Isn't Found or My FAT Is Bad!*

This is particularly discouraging news.

If you see a message to this effect while using a floppy disk, try your best to copy the floppy's contents to another floppy or to your hard drive. If you're lucky, you may be able to salvage some of its contents.

If you're not lucky and you *really* need that data back, head to the software store's Utilities aisle and buy a *disk rescue program.* For example, Norton Utilities and PC Tools both can rescue data off a disk that's gone bad. Without one of these special programs, however, there's not much you can do.

If the error message pops up when you're trying to read something off your hard drive, try saving your current work and then push your computer's reset button. Sometimes that fixes it.

If the message keeps popping up, though, you'd better start saving money for a new hard drive. First, though, give one of the rescue programs a shot at it. They're a lot cheaper then a new hard drive, and they can often grab information from a disk you thought was a goner.

✔ Computers toss information onto disks in little areas called *sectors.* When a sector goes bad, it's like a shelf collapsing in the garage: everything spills onto the floor and gets mixed up.

✔ In the old days, almost all hard drives came with a few bad sectors. However, DOS put warning signs next to those sectors so it wouldn't store any information on them. Because the hard drive's hundreds of other sectors still worked, nobody complained.

✔ Your *file allocation table,* dubbed *FAT,* is your computer's index to what stuff it has stuffed in what sectors. When your FAT goes bad, your computer suddenly forgets where it put everything. A bad FAT is even grosser than it sounds.

✔ If you don't have a rescue program and don't feel like buying one, try running CHKDSK, the funny-sounding program described in the next chapter. It comes with DOS, so there's nothing else to buy.

# How Do I Install a New Floppy Drive?

**IQ level:** 80

**Tools you need:** One hand and a screwdriver

**Cost:** Anywhere from $70 - $120

**Stuff to watch out for:**

If you're adding a second floppy drive, better check under your computer's hood to see whether there's room to slide one inside. That magic spot is called a *bay*; see the upcoming Figure 11-3 for a picture of one. Sometimes a second hard disk or tape backup drive can hog all the available bays.

Don't have a drive bay for another drive? Buy a Combo Drive from Teac. It squeezes both a 3.5-inch floppy drive and a 5.25-inch floppy drive into one small unit that fits in a single drive bay. That immediately frees up enough room for more exciting toys like internal CD-ROM drives or tape backup units.

If you're adding one of those high-density 3.5-inch floppy drives, make sure that you're using DOS 3.3 or later. That's the first version of DOS that could handle those drives. If you're using an ancient PC, you may need to update its BIOS chips as well. (That's described in Chapter 9.) Or just swear loudly and buy a new computer.

Don't want to buy new BIOS chips for your ancient computer? Buy a new controller card along with your new high-density floppy drive. Some controller cards come with a Band-Aid BIOS that lets an older computer work with a newer drive.

Your new floppy drive may need rails or mounting brackets before it will fit inside your PC. Some drives come with that stuff right in the box; others don't. If you're *replacing* a drive, you can swipe its old rails. If you're adding a second drive and need rails or brackets, they'll cost a couple bucks at the computer store.

Using a 5.25-inch floppy drive for drive B? Then look for its *terminating resistor* jumper or switch, as shown in Figure 11-1. Sometimes it's marked *TR*. Remove that jumper to use the new drive as drive B; leave it in place if you want the drive to be drive A.

**Figure 11-1:** Terminating resistors often look like this. Pull it out of the socket only if it's on drive B.

See, your computer needs a "plug" on the end of its ribbon cable. Because drive A is at the cable's end, it needs the plug to keep the signals from flowing out the end. If drive B has the terminating resistor, or plug, the signals have to work too hard to reach drive A on the cable's end. If jumpers leave you stumped, check the drive's manual and Chapter 17.

To add or replace a floppy drive, follow these steps:

1. **Turn off the computer, unplug it, and remove the case.**

   These chores are covered in the cheat sheet at the front of this book.

2. **Remove the cables from the old drive.**

   Found the old drive? Floppy drives have two cables plugged into them:

   **Ribbon cable:** The flat ribbon cable connects the drive either to a controller card or to a special socket built right onto your motherboard. Look to see which kind you have so you can replace it if it falls off.

   If you're replacing the drive, grab its ribbon cable by the plug and pull it straight off the drive. It should slide off pretty easily. You can see a picture of the cable and connector in the upcoming Figure 11-6.

   **Power cable:** The other cable is made of four wires that head to the power supply. Like the ribbon cable, the power cable pulls straight off the drive's connector, but it usually takes a *lot* more pulling. Don't pull on the wires themselves; pull on the cable's plastic connector. Sometimes a gentle back-and-forth jiggle will loosen it.

   Drives can use one of two power supply plugs, pictured with their sockets in Figure 11-2.

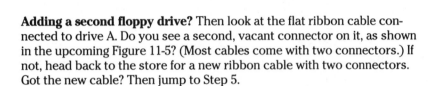

**Figure 11-2:**
Power supply
cables come
in two sizes.
Each size
plugs into its
own socket.

**Adding a second floppy drive?** Then look at the flat ribbon cable connected to drive A. Do you see a second, vacant connector on it, as shown in the upcoming Figure 11-5? (Most cables come with two connectors.) If not, head back to the store for a new ribbon cable with two connectors. Got the new cable? Then jump to Step 5.

3. **Remove the mounting screws holding the drive in place.**

Drives fit inside your computer in two main ways.

**Rails:** Some drives let you screw little rails onto their sides. The rails hold the drive in place as it slides into the computer. Finally, two screws along the front keep the drive from sliding back out. To remove the drive, just unscrew the screws, shown in Figure 11-3.

Choose short screws to attach rails to the drive. If long ones are used, they may damage the drive.

**No rails:** Some drives also slide in but without rails to hold them in place. Instead, they're secured by screws along their sides, as shown in Figure 11-4. The screws along one side may be hidden from view by a particularly long card or even another drive mounted on its side. You'll have to pull out the card to get at the screws, cursing all the while. Note that using long screws may damage the drive.

4. **Slide the drive out of the front of the computer.**

After you remove the drive's screws and cables, grab the drive from the front and slide it straight toward you.

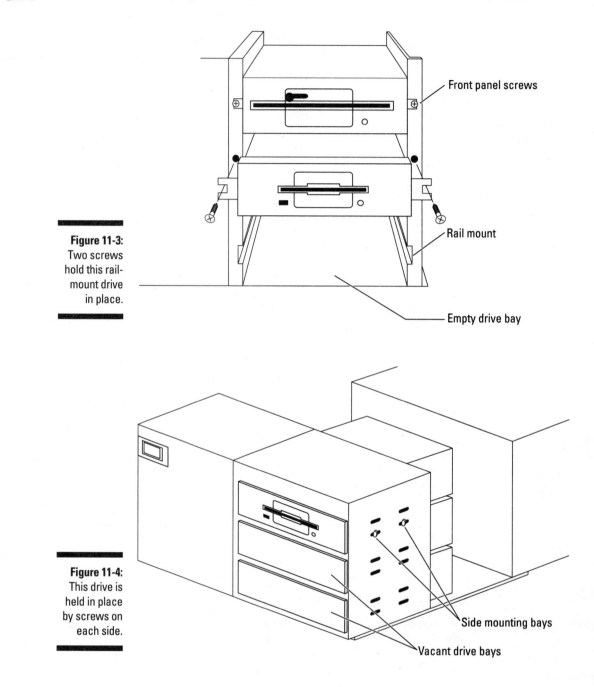

**Figure 11-3:**
Two screws
hold this rail-
mount drive
in place.

Front panel screws

Rail mount

Empty drive bay

**Figure 11-4:**
This drive is
held in place
by screws on
each side.

Side mounting bays

Vacant drive bays

5. **Slide the new drive in where the old one came out.**

   Slide your new drive into the spot where the old drive lived. You may need to remove the rails from the old drive and screw them onto the new drive.

   Adding a second drive? Find an available bay either above or below the other drive and slide the second drive on in.

6. **Attach the two cables to the drive.**

   Sometimes it's easier to attach the cables if you slide the drive back out a little bit first.

   **Ribbon cable:** The plug on the *end* of the ribbon cable attaches to drive A; the plug in the ribbon cable's *middle* goes to drive B, as in Figure 11-5. A little barrier inside the ribbon cable usually makes sure that it can only plug in one way: the right way.

**Figure 11-5:**
The plug on the *end* of the connector goes to drive A; the other plugs into drive B. Note the cable's "twist" leading to drive A.

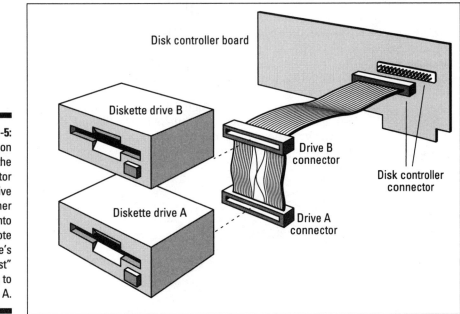

Disk controller board

Diskette drive B

Drive B connector

Disk controller connector

Diskette drive A

Drive A connector

Sometimes the ribbon cable can fit either way. Horrors! Look closely for little numbers printed near the connecting tab on the drive. One edge of the tab has low numbers; the other side has larger numbers in the 30s. The colored edge of the ribbon connector always faces toward the low numbers. It should look like the one shown in Figure 11-6.

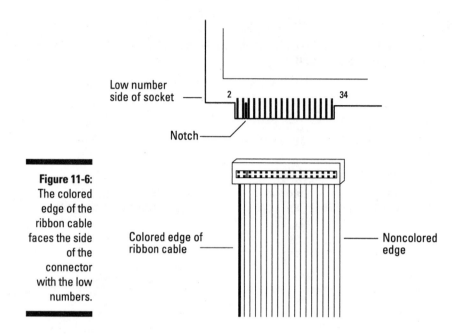

Low number
side of socket

2

34

Notch

**Figure 11-6:**
The colored
edge of the
ribbon cable
faces the side
of the
connector
with the low
numbers.

Colored edge of
ribbon cable

Noncolored
edge

The connector on some 3.5-inch drives doesn't look like the one in Figure 11-6. Instead, it has a bunch of little pins, like the one shown in Figure 11-7. You'll have to head back to the computer store for an adapter if one wasn't included in the drive's box.

**Figure 11-7:**
An adapter
lets you plug a
ribbon cable
into a drive
with pins like
these.

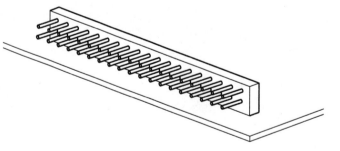

**Power supply:** The power supply cable only fits into the drive's socket one way. Even so, check carefully to make sure that you're not forcing the two together in the wrong way.

If you're adding a second drive, look at all the cables coming out of the power supply and grab one that's not being used. All used up? Then head back to the store and ask for a *Y adapter* for your power supply's drive cable.

### 7. Screw the new drive in place.

If the drive's inserted right, its holes should line up with the holes in the computer's case. Got it? Then put the screws back in the right holes. You may need to slide the drive a little further in or out until the holes line up.

Make sure that you use a screw of the right length to keep from damaging the disk drive.

### 8. Test the drive.

Plug in your computer, turn it on, put a disk in the drive, and see whether the drive works. OK? Then turn if off, unplug it, and replace the cover. You're done!

However, if the drive doesn't work, turn off the computer, unplug it, and try a couple of things before pounding the walls. First, are the cables lined up right? Plugged in firmly?

Check the connection where the ribbon cable plugs into the controller card or the motherboard. Sometimes all that jiggling around can pull it loose.

If you did anything more than simply replacing a dead drive, you probably need to tell your computer about your accomplishment. Computers aren't smart enough to figure out what kind of drive you've installed.

**XT:** If you added a drive to an ancient PC or XT, you'd better pull out your computer's manual. You probably need to flip a switch or change a jumper on the motherboard. (That's covered in Chapter 17.)

**AT, 286, 386, or 486:** For these computers, you probably need to change your computer's CMOS or Setup screen. (That's covered in Chapter 17, too.)

If you're installing one of those new combo drives (the ones with a 5.25-inch drive and a 3.5-inch drive in one little unit), you need to fiddle with the drive's jumpers. That's how the computer knows which one will be drive A and which will be drive B. The drive's manual will explain which way to jump.

## Twisted cable tales

Some floppies don't get along with their ribbon cables. It boils down to whether or not the ribbon cable has a little twist near its end. Some do, some don't. You need to set the drive's *DS switches* accordingly.

Where are those DS switches? They're little switches or jumpers on the side of the floppy drive, as illustrated in the accompanying figure. The drive's manual will say what to start flipping.

```
1 2 3 4
```

✔ If your ribbon cable has a *twist* in its middle, like the one in Figure 11-5, set both your drives' switches to *DS2*. (Most likely, they already came set that way.)

✔ If there's *no* twist in the ribbon cable, set drive A to DS1 and drive B to DS2. (If your switches start at DS0, then set drive A to DS0 and drive B to DS1. Hey, *I* didn't design this stuff . . .)

✔ If your drives already work fine, ignore all this stuff. Finally, for the low-down on jumper flippin', head for Chapter 17.

# Chapter 12
# Hard Drives, CD-ROM Drives, and Tape Backup Drives

● ● ● ● ● ● ● ● ● ● ● ● ● ● ● ● ● ● ● ● ● ● ● ● ● ● ● ● ● ● ● ● ● ● ● ● ● ● ● ● ● ● ● ● ● ●

## In This Chapter

▶ Fixing disk errors with CHKDSK

▶ Understanding types of hard drives

▶ Installing a new hard drive

▶ Installing a CD-ROM drive

▶ Installing a tape backup drive

● ● ● ● ● ● ● ● ● ● ● ● ● ● ● ● ● ● ● ● ● ● ● ● ● ● ● ● ● ● ● ● ● ● ● ● ● ● ● ● ● ● ● ● ● ●

*I*f you've never used a hard drive before, this chapter will change your computing life. If your old hard drive's stuffed, you'll want to stick around, too. You'll find out how to install a hard drive or even two. This chapter also covers CD-ROM drives and even tape backup units.

You may never need to touch a floppy disk again.

## What's This CHKDSK Stuff?

Ever lost your train of thought after somebody snuck up and tapped you on the shoulder? The same thing can happen to your computer.

If the power goes out or a program crashes while a computer's working, the computer loses its train of thought. It forgets to write down where it put stuff on the hard drive.

To patch things up as much as possible, type the following command:

```
C:\> CHKDSK /F
```

That is, type **CHKDSK,** a space, and a forward slash, and then press F. Your computer will respond with some computer words too bizarre to mention here. But if the program asks you, Convert lost chains to files (Y/N)?, press Y.

Your computer then gathers any file scraps and stores them in files like FILE000.CHK, FILE001.CHK, FILE002.CHK — you get the point. Feel free to delete those files. There's nothing worthwhile in them, as you'll quickly discover if you try to open them with your word processor.

- ✔ If there's nothing worthwhile in those files, why bother with CHKDSK at all? Because those little scraps of data are taking up disk space. By rounding them up and deleting them, you can have more room for your own files.

After you've grown confident that those FILE000.CHK files never contain anything of value, don't make them anymore. Press N when CHKDSK asks about converting lost chains to files. CHKDSK simply deletes them, freeing up space on your disk.

- ✔ CHKDSK dredges up a lot of information about your computer. It tells you how big your hard disk is and how much storage space you have left. It also lets you know how much memory your computer has, too.

- ✔ Computers work well with numbers, but they're terrible with commas. While looking at those big numbers on the screen, mentally add your own commas between every third number, working from right to left, and everything will look clearer. For example, when CHKDSK says 78409728 bytes available on disk, it really means 78,409,728 bytes. That translates to about 78MB, which is quite a bit of space. (Let the kids add their new missions for Wing Commander.)

# My Hard Disk Sure Isn't as Fast as It Used to Be

When your computer first copies a bunch of files onto the hard drive, it pours them onto the disk in one long strip. When you delete some of those files, the computer runs over and clears off the spots where those files lived.

That leaves holes in what used to be a long strip. When you start adding new files, the computer starts filling up the holes. If a file's too big to fit in one hole, the computer breaks the file up, sticking bits and pieces wherever it can find room.

A single file can have its parts spread out all over your hard drive. Your computer still can find everything, but it takes more time because the hard drive has to move around a lot more to grab all the parts.

To stop this *fragmentation,* a concerned computer nerd released a defragmentation program. The program picks up all the information on your hard drive and pours it all back down in one long strip, putting all the file's parts next to each other.

- ✔ If you notice your hard drive slowing down, it may need to be defragmentized. Some people defragment their drives once a week to keep things running smoothly.

- ✔ DOS 6 comes with a built-in defragmentation program. Type **DEFRAG** at the command line, and the program recommends how your disk should be *optimized.* Press Enter, and the program starts raking your fragmented data back into one big pile again.

- ✔ Defragmenting a hard drive can take several minutes, especially if you haven't done it for a while. In fact, on some slow drives, the process may take up to an hour. The more often you defragment a drive, however, the less time it takes.

While you're browsing defragmentation programs, check out the *hard drive cache* programs as well. These programs can speed things up, too. (If a computer guru is around, have him or her install SmartDrive. It's a program that comes with DOS 5, DOS 6, and Windows that can make your hard drive spit up information more quickly and with less work.)

# What's a Controller Card?

A controller card plugs into one of the slots inside your computer. Long flat ribbons run from the controller card over to your disk drives, as illustrated in Figure 12-1.

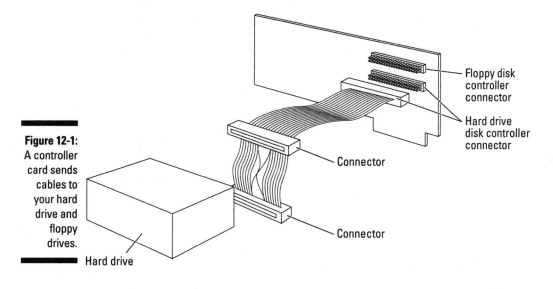

**Figure 12-1:**
A controller card sends cables to your hard drive and floppy drives.

Floppy disk controller connector

Hard drive disk controller connector

Connector

Connector

Hard drive

When your computer wants some information, it tells the controller card. The controller card grabs the right information from the drive through the cable and shoots it back to the computer.

- In the big, bulky, olden days of yesteryear computing, controller cards were big, bulky things with lots of circuitry and expensive little chip things.

- Today, though, the controller card's pretty much been bypassed. Most of its circuitry has been hot-wired right into the disk drives themselves.

- In fact, more than 90 percent of the hard drives sold today are called *IDE drives,* which is short for *Integrated Drive Electronics.* IDE drives don't need controller cards; the old chores once handled by the large controller cards are now integrated into the drive. The cables for these drives just plug straight into sockets on new motherboards.

- If your hard drive plugs straight into your motherboard, your floppy drives probably do the same thing. They usually plug in near the power supply — in the back right corner of your computer. (That's the same location where the tuba players sit in an orchestra pit.)

- If your older motherboard doesn't have those special IDE sockets, buy an IDE controller card. It's just a cheap little thing that plugs into a slot and gives you a place to plug in the drive's cables.

# Should I Buy an ST506, a SCSI, an ESDI, or an IDE Drive?

Today, everybody wants to upgrade from their old-technology drives. Not only are the drives dying fast, but they have ugly, old-technology names like *ST506* and *ESDI.* In an attempt to spice things up, the nerds sometimes referred to the ST506 drives as *MFM* and *RLL* drives.

Rich folks prefer SCSI drives because those drives are quick and can hold gobs of data. But if you're installing a new drive today, the choice is pretty clear: about 90 percent of the drives on the shelves today are the new IDE drives.

These drives don't need fancy controller cards, described in the preceding section. They're the easiest drives to install, too. Good news!

If you're replacing your older hard drive with a new IDE drive, you need to replace your old controller card also. Luckily, a controller card for an IDE drive is the cheapest controller card on the market.

IDE drives turn up their noses at older-technology drives. If you want to add an IDE drive as your second hard drive, your *first* hard drive must be an IDE drive, too. If you've been using an older-style ST506 drive, you'll have to ditch it.

- ✔ If you're using an older-style drive, don't feel too bad about ditching it for an IDE drive. IDE drives are faster and more reliable than the older ones. Plus, most newer computers come with special sockets designed specifically for IDE drives.

- ✔ IDE drives are designed to work in XTs, 286/386/486-style computers, and IBM's MCA-style computers. But you need a different IDE depending on which style of computer you own. You can't take one built for an XT and stick it in your 386 or vice versa. When buying an IDE drive, make sure that you're getting the right one for your kind of computer.

- ✔ Some folks are excited about SCSI-style hard drives. Theoretically, you can plug a SCSI card into your computer and "chain" up to seven other computer toys, including hard drives, CD-ROM drives, scanners, and tape backup drives. Unfortunately, SCSI drives are harder to set up, expensive, and prone to conflicting standards. That's why this book sticks to the less frustrating, more friendly, and far more popular IDE drives.

- ✔ Dunno what all those other hard drive words mean? Check out Table 12-1.

**Table 12-1    What Do All Those Hard Drive Words Mean?**

| *This Word* | *Means This* | *So Look for This* |
|---|---|---|
| Capacity | The amount of data it can store | The more megabytes, the better. If you use Windows, you want at least 60MB. Buy the biggest drive you can afford. |
| Access time | How long it takes your drive to locate stored files, measured in milliseconds (ms) | The smaller the number, the better. You want speed, and 15 ms is considered pretty speedy. CD-ROM drives are considerably slower. The fastest ones are about 200 ms, with most averaging about 350 ms. |
| Data transfer rate | How fast your computer can grab information from files after it finds them | The higher the number, the better. Don't place *too* much stock in it, though; it has become a meaningless statistic bandied about by vendors. |

*(continued)*

| Table 12-1 | What Do All Those Hard Drive Words Mean? | *(continued )* |
|---|---|---|
| *This Word* | *Means This* | *So Look for This* |
| MTBF | Mean Time Between Failures | The higher, the better. This is the number of hours the drive should last. For example, an MTBF of 30,000 means the drive will last through about 3½ years of continuous spinning. (That's about 10 years of 8-hour days.) |

# How Do I Get the Drive Lights to Turn On and Off?

If your floppy drive's light comes on when you use the drive but never turns off, check out Step 6 of the installation section, coming up next. Somebody may have fastened the flat ribbon cable connector upside down when pushing it onto the disk drive.

If the hard drive light on the front of your computer never comes on, you need to push the light's little wires onto a *jumper* that lives on your hard drive or controller card. (Jumper pushing is discussed in Chapter 17.)

Some hard drives even have a little jumper that lets you choose one of two options: you can keep the little light on all the time, or you can have it turn on when the hard drive's actually fetching data. (Traditionalists stick with the fetching data option.)

# How Do I Install or Replace an IDE Hard Drive?

**IQ level:** 100

**Tools you need:** One hand, a screwdriver, and a system disk

**Cost:** Roughly $200 - $400; huge ones can cost $1,000

**Stuff to watch out for:**

Make sure that you have a System disk on hand, as described in Chapter 2. Don't have one nearby? Race back to Chapter 2 for instructions. You need some of the programs on that disk.

IDE drives don't work with the older-style ST506 (MFM or RLL) drives. If you have one of those, pull it out and try to sell it. It was probably going to die soon, anyway.

If you had an older-style ST506 (MFM or RLL) drive, you also need to buy a new IDE controller card to go with your new IDE drive. The older controllers don't work with IDE drives.

If you're adding a _second_ IDE drive, you have to tell your computer which drive you want to be drive C. (Drive C is the one the computer looks at first and boots from.) That drive's the _master,_ and the second is the _slave._ You need to move a little jumper on the second drive to make that drive work as the slave (see Figure 12-2).

Some hard drives also ask you to move a jumper depending on whether you're using one hard drive or two. Others automatically set themselves up for one hard drive if they're set up as the master. You may have to check the drive's manual on this one.

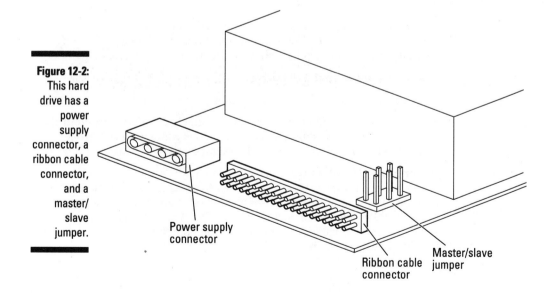

**Figure 12-2:**
This hard drive has a power supply connector, a ribbon cable connector, and a master/ slave jumper.

Power supply connector

Ribbon cable connector

Master/slave jumper

XT computers can't handle two IDE drives. The other AT class or 386 class computers can't handle more than two IDE drives, or things start getting *really* complicated; you'll find yourself in a mess involving Scotch tape and *IRQ14 monitoring.*

You may need rails to fit your hard drive in your computer. Some drives come with rails; others don't. If you're replacing an old drive, you can swipe its old rails. Otherwise, you may need to head back to the store to buy some.

If you're adding a hard drive to a PC that's never had one, you may need a new power supply. Your PC's going to be drawing a little more power now. Chapter 13 puts power supplies into perspective.

Don't have room for a second hard drive or don't want to get rid of your old, incompatible one? Buy an *external* hard drive. It's a box that plugs into your printer port. You pay a little more money for the convenience.

You do have one other choice: a *hard card.* Hard cards are hard drives stuck on little cards that plug inside your computer. Unlike IDE drives, hard cards still work alongside older-technology drives. They cost a little more, unfortunately.

The following steps show you how to install an IDE hard drive.

1. **Back up your hard drive, turn off the computer, unplug it, and remove the case.**

   Be sure to back up your hard drive before playing with it. You don't want to lose any of your data. You'll find instructions for removing the computer's cover in the cheat sheet at the front of this book.

2. **Remove cables from the old drive.**

   Hard drives have two or three cables plugged into them.

   **Ribbon cable:** The ribbon cable leads from the hard drive to its controller card. Older-style drives have *two* ribbon cables going to the controller card. Either way, ribbon cables pull straight off the drive pretty easily.

   **Power cable:** The other cable is made of four wires that head for the power supply. Power cables come in two sizes, as shown in Figure 12-3. Like the ribbon cable, the power cable pulls straight off the drive's socket; it usually takes a *lot* more pulling, though. Don't pull on the wires themselves; pull on the cable's plastic connector. Sometimes a gentle back-and-forth jiggle will loosen it.

**Figure 12-3:**
Your hard
drive uses
one of these
two sizes for
the power
cable.

**Adding a second IDE drive:** If you're adding a second IDE drive, check out the flat ribbon cable connected to the first drive. Do you see a second, vacant plug on it, like the one shown in Figure 12-1? If not, head back to the store for a new ribbon cable. It needs to have *two* connectors. (Most already do, luckily.) You second-drive installers can jump ahead to Step 5.

**3. Remove the mounting screws holding the drive in place.**

Some drives are held in place by two screws in front. Other drives are held in place by screws in their sides. The screws on one side may be hidden from view by a particularly long card, or even another drive, mounted on its side. That means you have to pull out the card or remove the obstructing drive just to get at the screws!

**4. Slide the old drive out the computer's front.**

After you remove the old drive's cables and screws, you should be able to slide it out of the front of the computer. Give it a gentle tug.

Drives that mount on their sides slide out toward the computer's center; be sure not to gouge your motherboard while pulling out the drive.

**Replacing a controller card:** Are you pulling out your old-style drive to replace it with an IDE drive? Then pull out your old controller card as well. You can see a picture of one in Figure 12-1. Look for the card where all the ribbon cables end up. Found it? Pull all the ribbon cables off, including the ones heading for your floppy drives.

See that tiny screw holding the controller card in place? Remove the screw and pull the card straight up out of its slot. (For more card details, head for Chapter 14.)

**5. Slide the new drive in where the old one came out.**

Your new IDE drive should slide in place right where the old one came out. Doesn't fit? If the new drive's smaller than the old one, you need to add rails or mounting brackets to make it fit.

Adding a second IDE drive? Slide it into a vacant bay, which usually is next to the first drive. Check your computer's manual; you may be able to mount the drive on its side.

**6. Add the new controller card if necessary.**

Are you replacing your older-style drives with IDE drives? Then you need a new controller card to go with it.

Handling the card by its edges, push it down into the slot where the old controller card sat. Then fasten it down with the screw. (You'll find more card installation tips in Chapter 14.) Check the controller's manual; you need to push ribbon cables onto the controller's connectors for your floppy disks and hard disk.

**7. Attach two cables to the hard drive.**

Try sliding the drive out a little bit to connect the two cables more easily.

**Ribbon cable:** The plug on the ribbon cable should push onto little pins on the end of the drive. The other end of the cable goes either to the controller card or to a socket on the motherboard.

If you're installing a second hard drive, the ribbon cable should have a spare connector on it. (If not, head back to the store.) It doesn't matter which connector goes onto which drive; the computer looks at the drives' master/slave jumpers to figure out which one's drive C.

**Power supply:** The power supply cable only fits into the drive's socket one way. Even so, check the ends to make sure that you're not forcing it in the wrong way. Check out Figure 12-3 to make sure that you've found the right power cable socket.

Power supply cables come with both large and small connectors. The connectors are supposed to fit only one way, but the small ones often fit either way. The trick? Look for the number 1 somewhere near the drive's little socket. The power supply connector's red wire fastens onto the number 1 prong.

**Adding a second IDE drive:** If this is your second drive, look for its master/slave jumper. Make this second drive the slave drive. You can see the jumpers in Figure 12-2. The drive's manual will tell you which jumpers need the "bridge." Chapter 17 tells you how to set those jumpers.

Note that some hard drives also ask you to move a jumper depending on whether you're using one hard drive or two. Others automatically set themselves up for one hard drive if they're set up as the master. You may have to check the drive's manual on this one.

IDE drives usually come configured as master drives. If you're installing just a single IDE drive in your computer, you usually don't need to mess with any of the jumpers.

8. **Replace the screws.**

Cables attached? Master/slave jumper set? Then fasten the drive in place with those little screws. Make sure that they are short screws to prevent damage to the inside of the hard drive.

9. **Replace the cover, plug in the computer, and turn it on.**

Chances are, your hard drive won't work right off the bat. Hard drives must be prepared before they start to work, unfortunately. Take a deep breath before heading for the next step. Exhale. Now move on.

10. **Configure CMOS for the new drive.**

Here's where things get the most complicated. Your computer needs to know some arcane details about the drive you've just installed.

Your absolute best bet is to buy a hard drive setup program like EZ-Drive from MicroHouse (to order, call 303/443-3388). This program introduces your new hard drive to your computer and has the drive shaking hands with DOS in less than 60 seconds.

If you bought a used hard drive from a friend, it may boot right up, in which case you won't have to fiddle with this stuff. If you have a new hard drive, though, holler for a computer guru friend, hand your guru the following section, and tell him or her to break in your new hard drive. No guru around? Then you may have to brave it yourself. There's nothing to break; the drive just won't work until it's set up right.

# Breaking in a New Hard Drive

Here are the last few hoops you need to jump through before your computer starts speaking to its new hard drive:

**1. Set the CMOS.**

Your CMOS, described in Chapter 17, is where your computer keeps track of the equipment connected to it. It needs to know what kind of hard drive you installed before you can use it. IDE drives deal with the CMOS in three possible ways:

Some drives check the CMOS to see what hard drive your computer expects to find and then automatically mimic that drive. Blissfully simple! Move on to Step 2.

Other IDE drives let you pick *any* hard drive that's listed in your computer's CMOS table. So just choose any drive that's the same capacity (in megabytes) as your IDE drive, and all will be fine. A bit bothersome, but still workable. Head for Step 2.

The pickiest IDE drives make you look for information buried in their manual. Specifically, you need to look for the IDE drive's recommended *cylinders, heads,* and *sectors.* Then you need to plug those numbers into your CMOS' *user-defined* area. Yeah, it's a little complicated. But if you're lucky, the first two options will work. If you're not lucky, head for Chapter 17.

**2. Partition the drive.**

Partitioning a drive completely wipes out any information stored on it.

When you're through setting the CMOS, you need to *partition* your drive. The simplest method is to make one big DOS partition. Type **FDISK** at the DOS prompt; that brings the partition program to the screen.

If you replaced your old drive, tell FDISK to make a *Primary DOS Partition.* To do that, press Enter twice and then press Y.

If you added a second drive to be a slave to your first, you see a new option, `Change Current Fixed Disk Drive.` Pick that option to switch to your second drive; then create a *Logical DOS Partition* to make that drive your drive D.

When you exit FDISK, it reboots your computer. If you just installed a single hard drive, better put a System disk in drive A so your computer will start up.

**3. Format the drive.**

Formatting a disk completely wipes out any information stored on it.

Never try to "low-level format" an IDE drive, no matter what anyone tells you.

Here's the last step: You need to *format* the new drive after it is partitioned. If your computer only has one hard disk, type the following at the A:\> prompt of your System disk:

```
A:\> FORMAT C: /S
```

If you installed a second drive and partitioned it to be drive D, format it by entering this command:

```
A:\> FORMAT D:
```

Done? Then remove the System disk from drive A and reboot your computer, and everything should work fine.

If it doesn't work, start by double-checking all your cables. On tight? Upside down? In the right place? Is the drive partitioned right? Formatted correctly? If you installed a second disk drive, twice as many things could have gone wrong.

If your two IDE drives just won't work right, try switching the master/slave relationship. Sometimes IDE drives from different manufacturers just don't like to work with each other, no matter who's in charge. You may have to exchange one IDE drive for one that's the same brand as the other.

If you have to turn your computer on several times in the morning before the hard drive starts working, you may need a new power supply. The power supply may not provide enough power to bring the drive up to speed quickly enough. You'll find power supplies dissected in Chapter 13.

# *How Do I Install a CD-ROM Drive?*

**IQ level:** 90

**Tools you need:** One hand and a screwdriver

**Cost:** Anywhere from $250 - $600

**Stuff to watch out for:**

Compact disc players (CD-ROM drives) come in two types, *Internal* and *External*. The external ones are little boxes that take up room on your desk. The internal ones slide into the front of your computer like a floppy disk.

Both kinds come with a card that plugs into one of your computer's slots. Better pop the cover and make sure that you have an empty slot before doing anything else.

## *Installing an external CD-ROM drive*

1. **Turn off your computer, unplug it, and remove its case.**

   You'll find complete instructions in the cheat sheet at the front of this book.

2. **Plug the CD-ROM drive's card into one of your available slots and screw it down.**

   Chapter 14 describes cards and how to stick them in the right place.

3. **Replace your computer's cover and plug in your PC.**

4. **Plug the CD-ROM drive's cable into the card.**

   You'll find a thick cord in the box with the CD-ROM drive. One side of the cord plugs into the connector now peeking from the back of your PC; the other end fits into the back of the CD-ROM drive.

5. **Plug in the CD-ROM drive and turn it on.**

   External CD-ROM drives have a power cord that needs to be plugged into the wall.

   Don't have enough power outlets? Head back to the computer store and buy a power strip. These gadgets let you plug in six or more accessories into one outlet.

**6. Turn on your computer.**

**7. When it boots up, install the CD-ROM's software.**

You have to put the disk in drive A and type **INSTALL** or **SETUP,** depending on what your manual says.

Chances are, the program will stick a *device driver* into your computer's CONFIG.SYS file and reboot your computer. That driver stuff's hammered down in Chapter 15.

For a few extra tips and tricks, head to the end of the "Installing an internal CD-ROM drive" section.

# Installing an internal CD-ROM drive

**1. Turn off your computer, unplug it, and remove its case.**

You'll find complete instructions in the cheat sheet at the front of this book.

**2. Plug the CD-ROM drive's card into one of your available slots and screw it down.**

Cards — and how to install them — are described in Chapter 14.

**3. Slide the CD-ROM drive into the front of your computer.**

You need a vacant drive bay, which is an opening where your disk drives normally live. The drive should slide in the front. For tips, check out Chapter 11. The CD-ROM drive slides in the same way as a floppy drive.

Don't have an empty drive bay for your CD-ROM drive? Buy a Combo Drive from Teac. It squeezes both a 3.5-inch floppy drive and a 5.25-inch floppy drive into one small unit that fits in a single drive bay. That immediately frees up enough room for an internal CD-ROM drive.

**4. Connect the cables.**

First, connect the cable between the CD-ROM drive and the card you installed in Step 2. It should only fit one way.

Next, rummage around the tentacles of wires leading from your power supply until you find a spare power connector. That plugs into your CD-ROM drive. Those drives usually use the small-sized connector shown back in Figure 12-3.

**5. Screw the drive in place.**

Although some drives screw in from the sides, most fasten with two screws along the front.

6. **Replace your computer's cover, plug the computer in, and turn it on.**

7. **Run the CD-ROM drive software.**

The software should take over the rest of the installation chores. If it tosses bits of weirdness, like `interrupts` or `drivers`, page on ahead to Chapters 15 and 17.

CD-ROM drives almost always use SCSI ports and cards. If you already have a SCSI card in your computer, things can get either better or worse. Here's the scoop:

**The Good News:** SCSI ports can chain a handful of other SCSI devices. That means that you should be able to hook your CD-ROM drive into your chain. For example, if your sound card comes with a SCSI port, you won't need the CD-ROM drive's card. Just plug the CD-ROM drive's cable into the sound card's SCSI port, saving time and, more importantly, a slot.

**The Bad News:** Different brands of SCSI ports aren't always compatible with each other. Sometimes they work; sometimes they don't. Before investing in SCSI devices, call the manufacturers to be sure the devices will all get along.

# How Do I Install a Tape Backup Unit?

**IQ level:** 90

**Tools you need:** One hand and a screwdriver

**Cost:** Anywhere from $200 - $800

**Stuff to watch out for:**

The easiest tape backup units live in little boxes. You just plug a cable between the box and your parallel port. That's it! Just pop its installation floppy in your disk drive and you're through.

An internal backup unit is a little rougher to install, but not much. Just follow these steps:

1. **Turn off your computer, unplug it, and remove its cover.**

This step is covered in the cheat sheet at the front of this book.

**2. Push the unit into a drive bay.**

You need a free drive bay — one of those spots into which you can slide floppy disk drives. If you don't have one, you can remove drive B to make room. Be sure to tell your computer's CMOS you don't have a drive B anymore, however; that cautious task is explained in Chapter 17.

**3. Fasten the unit down.**

If the unit has rails on the sides, fasten it in place with two screws along the front. If it doesn't use rails, put two screws in each of its sides.

**4. Attach the cables.**

**Power cable:** Find a spare power cable hanging out of your power supply. Don't have one? Head to the store for a Y adapter.

**Ribbon cable:** The drive comes with its own ribbon cable. Unplug your floppy drive's old ribbon cable from your controller card and plug in the new backup unit's cable.

See the extra connector on the backup unit's ribbon cable, about an inch away from where it's plugged into the card? Plug your floppy drive's cable into that new little connector. Then plug the end of the backup unit's new ribbon cable into the backup drive.

The cables should fit only one way, but look at the ribbon's colored edge: that's the side that plugs into Pin 1.

**5. Replace the computer's cover, plug in the computer, and turn it on.**

That should do the trick. Now you have to run the tape backup unit's installation software.

Whew. No more feeding 40 backup disks to the computer every week. Don't you wish you bought this a year ago when you first bought your computer?

If any of these steps leave you scratching your head, flip back to Chapter 11. Tape backup drives are installed almost exactly like floppy drives.

# Chapter 13
# Power Supplies

● ● ● ● ● ● ● ● ● ● ● ● ● ● ● ● ● ● ● ● ● ● ● ● ● ● ● ● ● ● ● ● ● ● ● ● ● ● ● ● ● ● ● ● ● ● ●

*In This Chapter*

▶ Listening to your computer's sounds

▶ Diagnosing your power supply

▶ Understanding an uninterrupted power supply

▶ Buying the right power supply

▶ Replacing your power supply

● ● ● ● ● ● ● ● ● ● ● ● ● ● ● ● ● ● ● ● ● ● ● ● ● ● ● ● ● ● ● ● ● ● ● ● ● ● ● ● ● ● ● ● ● ● ●

*Y*ou can't see it, but you can sure hear it: your computer's power supply sits inside one corner of your computer and whirs away.

This chapter covers that restless little beast that sucks up electricity all day long. When the power supply stops grabbing power, this chapter tells you how to grab the power supply and replace it with a new one.

## My Computer Makes a Constant Whining Noise

Some power supplies wail like a Volkswagen from the early '60s. Other power supplies purr quietly like a BMW.

The noise comes from the fan inside the power supply that blows air across the power supply's innards. The fan cools off the inside of your computer at the same time.

As for the racket? Well, many power supplies are just noisy little beasts. There's just no getting around the racket.

✔ If your power supply is *too* noisy, consider replacing it. Today's power supplies are often a little quieter than the rumblers released five or more years ago.

✔ If your power supply doesn't make any noise at all, you're in even *worse* trouble. Hold your hand against the fan hole in the back. If you don't feel any air blowing out, the fan has died. Buy a new power supply — right away. Your computer can overheat like a car in the desert, but you won't see any dramatic radiator leaks. Some of your computer's parts will just stop working.

Don't try taking apart your power supply and quieting down the fan. Power supplies soak up electricity and can zap you, even when they're unplugged. Don't mess around inside a power supply.

# Nothing Happens When I Turn On My Computer

Nothing? No little lights go on along the front? No purr from the fan whirring merrily?

If you're sure that your computer is plugged in, then your power supply probably died during the night.

## Is it your hard drive, or is it your power supply?

Sometimes it's hard to differentiate between a noisy power supply fan and a noisy hard drive. Both have a constantly running motor, so both are susceptible to the burned-out bearing syndrome.

To tell whether the noise is from your power supply or your hard drive, turn off your computer, unplug it, and open the case. Then pull the power supply's cable out from the back of your hard

drive. Plug your computer back in and turn it on. Because the hard drive won't be getting power, it won't turn on with the rest of your computer. If you hear a noise, it's your power supply.

If you don't hear a noise, it's your hard drive. Unfortunately, hard drives cost a lot more to replace, as discussed in Chapter 12.

✔ First, plug a lamp in your power outlet to make sure that the outlet *really* works. Or you may have a blown circuit breaker. That's a lot cheaper.

✔ A lightening bolt that barrels down your electric line can kill your power supply. The power supply has been designed to sacrifice itself for the good of the whole computer. Chances are that you can replace the power supply, and then everything will return to the prelightening state.

✔ Power supplies are pretty easy to replace, though. Just grab a screwdriver and page through to the section "Installing a New Power Supply."

# *My Computer Forgets the Date, Even After I Changed the Batteries!*

Drinking fountains never work the same way. Some fountains make you bend down really low and press your cheek against the gross, crusty metal part to get any driblets of water. Other fountains squirt up and hit you in the forehead.

Power supplies, however, are specifically designed to provide a steady stream of electricity at just the right voltage. If the power level strays from the norm, even by just a few volts, it can interfere with your computer's lifestyle.

If your power supply is not dependable, replace it.

✔ Uh, how can you tell whether your power supply is dependable? Well, if your computer constantly forgets the date and the hard drive type, even after you've changed the battery, the power supply is a likely suspect. Sometimes, the power supply won't deliver enough power to keep your computer's CMOS settings in place.

✔ After you've changed the power supply (or battery), head for Chapter 17 to restore your computer's CMOS settings to the right place. Luckily, XT computers don't have these setting problems. Unfortunately, XTs have enough other problems to keep their owners busy.

Your computer's power supply and its battery are two different things. The power supply gives your computer electricity when it's turned *on* so it can accomplish computer-like things. The computer's battery provides electricity when your computer is turned *off* so it can remember what computer-like things have been installed.

✔ Have you been replacing a lot of your computer's disk drives lately? The power supply may be producing too much power. Being off just a few volts can burn up your computer's disk drives or make them work erratically.

✔ If you've recently added a second hard drive or extra cards to a computer with an older power supply, consider upgrading your power supply. The old one may not be putting out enough watts to support all the extra gadgets. See the "What Kind of Power Supply Should I Buy?" section later in this chapter.

# What's a UPS or Backup Power Supply?

When your computer loses its power, *you* lose your work. Everything that you haven't actually saved to a disk just sort of dribbles away.

If the power suddenly fails and the lights go out, your computer will go out, too. To protect against such scariness, some people buy an *uninterrupted power supply,* which is often called a *UPS.*

The UPS is a big box that connects your computer and its power outlet. The big box constantly sucks up power and stores it, like a huge car battery. Then, if the power dies, the big box instantly turns itself on and provides uninterrupted power to your computer.

Then the big box provides you with a rewarding feeling of accomplishment for having bought and installed a UPS before the power died.

✔ The more money you spend on your UPS, the more time you'll be able to work in the dark. Common times range from ten minutes to a half hour.

✔ For the most part, the UPS isn't designed to keep your computer running all day in the dark. The UPS just keeps your computer going when the power dies, which gives you a few extra minutes to save your work, turn off your computer, and drink a Pepsi until the lights go back on.

✔ Some uninterrupted power supplies also work as a *line conditioner,* which filters out any nasty voltage spikes or surges that may come through the power lines. A line conditioner can make your computer last longer.

✔ A UPS isn't cheap; one costs anywhere from $120 to $400. Still, a UPS can be an important investment if you live in an area prone to power outage problems.

# What Kind of Power Supply Should I Buy?

If you expand your living room by knocking down a wall, you'll need more than a single 100-watt bulb to light everything up. Computers work in a similar way.

Like a light bulb, a computer's power supply is rated in watts. The more gizmos you've plugged into your computer, the more watts you'll need to feed them.

An XT can survive with a 135-watt power supply, but the more powerful AT computer is more reliable with a 200-watt power supply.

If you're using a 386 or 486 computer with great gobs of memory, more than one hard drive, or lots of cards, make sure that your power supply is rated at 250 watts or more.

✔ Don't think that more is *always* better, though. For example, there's no reason to stick a 235-watt power supply in an XT. Your electricity bill will rise, but your computer's performance won't.

If you've been upgrading a lot of computer parts lately — a new motherboard, a second hard drive, extra cards, or a tape backup drive — your next purchase should be a more powerful power supply.

# Installing a New Power Supply

**IQ level:** 90

**Tools you need:** One hand and a screwdriver

**Cost:** Anywhere from $70 - $120

**Stuff to watch out for:**

Power supplies can't be repaired; they're simply replaced. Throw the old power supply away.

Don't ever open your power supply or try to fix it yourself. The power supply stores powerful jolts of electricity, even when the computer is turned off and unplugged. Power supplies are safe but only when they are not open.

Also, the shelves in the back room of the computer store are filled with different kinds of power supplies. To find the right replacement, bring in your old power supply and say, "I need another one of these."

To install a new power supply, perform the following steps:

1. **Turn off your PC, unplug it, and remove its cover.**

   If you've never gone fishing inside your computer before, the cheat sheet at the front of this book covers how to remove your computer's cover.

2. **Unplug the power supply's cables from the motherboard, the drives, and the power switch.**

   Your power supply is that big, boxy, silver thing in your computer's top right-hand corner. Bunches of cables run out of a hole in the power supply's side.

   Each cable has one of several types of plugs on its end. The plugs are all shaped differently to keep them from plugging into the wrong place.

   Even so, put a strip of masking tape on the end of each plug and write down its destination. You and your computer will feel better that way.

   Here's a rundown of the plugs, their shape, and their destination:

   **Motherboard:** The two biggest plugs attach to connectors on the motherboard, like in Figure 13-1.

**Figure 13-1:**
These rectangular-shaped plugs pull straight up and off of sockets on your motherboard.

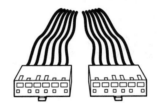

**Drives:** Disk drives, tape backup units, and other internal goodies get their power from two different sizes of plugs, as shown in Figure 13-2.

**Figure 13-2:**
Newer disk drives favor the smaller plugs; older disk drives tend to prefer the larger plugs.

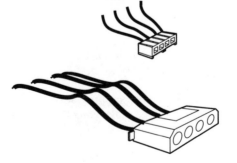

**Switch:** Some older power supplies have an on/off switch built right into their chest. Other power supplies have a wire that connects to an on/off switch along the computer's front or side. Those power supplies have little connectors like the one in Figure 13-3.

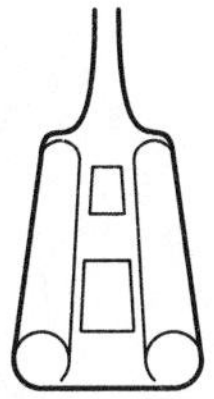

**Figure 13-3:**
This connector fits onto your computer's power switch.

The plugs only fit into their sockets one way. The power switch tabs can be rough, though, so draw a picture of which colored wire connects to which tab.

Unless your computer is packed to the brim with goodies, you'll probably have a few stray cables leftover. Those cables are thoughtfully supplied to power any future additions.

3. **Remove the screws holding the power supply to the back of the computer's case.**

   Look on the back of your computer near the fan hole and you'll see several screws. Some of these screws hold your power supply in place. But other screws hold your fan inside your power supply.

   With the case off, you can usually tell which screws hold the power supply in place. Try loosening the screws slightly; that sometimes makes it easier to tell which screws are which.

   The screws that hold the power supply in place are generally closer to the outside edge of the computer's rear. The screws that hold the fan are generally closer to the fan's edge. Don't loosen the screws if you can help it.

4. **Lift out the power supply.**

   Does the power supply come out easily? If the power supply is cramped, you may need to loosen the floppy drives and pull them forward a bit. (Loosening floppy drives is described in Chapter 11, if you're not sure how the floppy drives are mounted.)

If the power supply still won't come out, make sure that you've removed all the screws. Some power supplies have extra screws around their base to hold them down.

Some XT power supplies are held in place by little metal tabs; if so, slide the power supply toward the front of the case, and then it should come loose.

Power supplies are pretty hardy beasts, so don't be afraid to pull hard.

**5. Take the power supply to the store and get a new one, just like it.**

That's the best way to make sure that you get the right-sized replacement. If you're planning on adding some other computer toys — such as compact disc players or sound cards — or filling up your slots with more gadgets, consider buying a power supply with a higher wattage, as discussed earlier in this chapter.

**6. Put the new power supply where the old one sat.**

Sometimes it's easier to reconnect the cables before sliding the power supply in place.

**7. Reconnect all the cables to the motherboard, the drives, and the power switch.**

Grab any little pictures you drew and look at any masking tape labels you put on the old power supply's cables.

Forgot to label them? Well, it doesn't really matter which disk drive gets which plug.

On the motherboard, the *black* wires on the two plugs almost always face each other. But make sure that you hook up the power switch connectors according to your notes. There aren't any hard and fast rules.

**8. Replace the screws holding the power supply to the back of the computer's case.**

Do you have the cables back on? Then screw the power supply back into place. Be sure that you tighten down any disk drives you may have loosened.

Also, check to make sure that you haven't knocked any other cables loose while moving around inside your computer.

**9. Make sure that the voltage is set correctly.**

Look on the back of the power supply, which is near the fan. A switch usually lets you toggle the power to either 120 volts or 220 volts. If you're in America, make sure that the switch is set to 120 volts. If you're overseas, flip the switch to the 220-volt setting.

If you take your computer overseas and expect it to work, be sure that you toggle the voltage setting switch.

10. **Reconnect the power cord.**

    Plug your computer back in; its power cord should push into the socket near the fan.

11. **Turn on the power and see whether it works.**

    Do you hear the fan whirring? Does the computer leap to life? If so, then all is well. If the fan is not spinning, though, something is wrong with the new power supply or your power outlet.

    Try plugging a lamp into the outlet to make *sure* that it works. If the outlet works, take the power supply back. The computer store sold you a bad power supply.

12. **Turn off the computer and put the case back on.**

    Is everything working right? Then turn off the computer, put its case back on, and put a cool glass of iced tea in your hands. Congratulations!

# Chapter 14
# Stuff on Cards

● ● ● ● ● ● ● ● ● ● ● ● ● ● ● ● ● ● ● ● ● ● ● ● ● ● ● ● ● ● ● ● ● ● ● ● ● ● ● ● ● ● ● ●

## In This Chapter

▶ Making cards fit in slots

▶ Repairing cards that aren't working

▶ Understanding card varieties

▶ Installing new cards

● ● ● ● ● ● ● ● ● ● ● ● ● ● ● ● ● ● ● ● ● ● ● ● ● ● ● ● ● ● ● ● ● ● ● ● ● ● ● ● ● ● ● ●

*M*ost computer upgrades are a shoehorn process: trying to force an old computer to do something it wasn't really designed to do.

Adding expansion cards, however, is a different story. Cards provide the 100 percent approved way of upgrading your system. That means that this is going to be easy. So, relax. Smile! You're playing with cards, remember?

## My Card Doesn't Fit!

Unlike other computer organs, expansion cards have remained remarkably uncomplicated over the years. In fact, most people need to worry about only one thing: card size.

Cards come in two sizes — big and small. The small ones are called *8-bit cards* and look like the one shown in Figure 14-1.

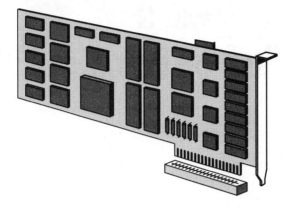

**Figure 14-1:**
The 8-bit
cards have
a single tab
on the
bottom that
plugs into a
single slot.

The bigger versions are called *16-bit cards*. They're a newer breed, so the gray-haired XT computers don't have any of them. Figure 14-2 shows a 16-bit card.

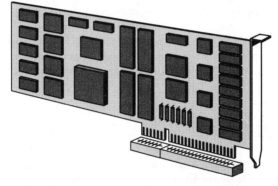

**Figure 14-2:**
The 16-bit
cards have
two tabs
that plug
into a longer
slot inside
your PC.

You can plug an 8-bit card into a slot of any size. No problem there. But you can't plug a 16-bit card into an 8-bit slot. Well, you can, but the card usually won't work.

✔ Because the old XT computers don't have 16-bit slots, they can't handle the latest, fanciest sound cards, video cards, and other goodies.

✔ Also, some really picky old XT computers don't like just *any* card in the slot closest to the power supply. Save that slot for last.

✔ Sometimes a card is too long. If you push the card into the slot, the end bumps into some memory chips or something near the front of your computer. These troublesome long cards are called *full-length cards.*

✔ Some cards are too fat. They fit into the slot but bump up against the cards in the slots next to them. This problem pops up most often on really old cards.

✔ How do you handle cards that are too fat or too long? Well, you can break off the troublesome parts that don't fit. But then the card doesn't work. Your best bet is to move the cards around, trying different positions until they all fit. It's kind of like packing bags in the car trunk on the way home from the grocery store. You have to try different combinations before the trunk lid will close.

✔ A few 16-bit video cards will still work in an 8-bit slot. Most of the other types of 16-bit cards won't work in an 8-bit slot, though.

## Which bus are you on?

Computer nerds call a computer's row of expansion slots a *bus.* Although there are three types of buses, you probably have an *ISA bus.* The majority of cards on the store shelves are ISA cards, so they'll work in your computer without any problems.

If your computer has an *EISA bus,* you spent a lot more money for it. An EISA bus can still use the same old ISA cards filling the shelves. It also can use the more expensive EISA cards, if you can find one.

The people who need to watch out are those who have an *MCA bus.* Short for *Micro Channel Architecture,* MCA was designed by IBM for its PS/2 series of computers. If you have an MCA bus, you can't use the ISA or EISA cards everybody else is buying. You must ask for MCA cards *specifically,* or the cards won't work on your computer.

# My Card Doesn't Work!

Not much can go wrong when you install a card. The biggest problem is remembering to turn off the power to your computer first.

Always turn off the power to your computer and unplug it before inserting or removing a card. If you forget, you may see sparks and a dead card.

Chances are, your nonfunctioning card *does* work; the computer just doesn't know it's attached. The card lies unnoticed, like a dribble of spaghetti sauce on the corner of a mouth.

✔ Most cards come with an installation program. The program tells the computer to make contact with the card and report its progress. It usually takes three steps.

✔ First, the installation program may put a *driver* program onto your computer's hard disk.

✔ Second, the program may tell you to change a *jumper* on the card.

✔ Finally, the program may ask you to flip a *DIP switch* on the card.

✔ All this stuff's covered in Chapter 17.

If one of your older cards stops working, turn off your computer, unplug it, remove the cover, and remove the card. Then take a plain old pencil eraser and rub it over the contacts on the part of the card that fits into the slot. This can remove any corrosion or buildup of crud.

Another reason older cards stop working is because their driver was disturbed. You need to check your AUTOEXEC.BAT or CONFIG.SYS file, described in Chapter 15.

Also try pushing the card more firmly into its slot. Sometimes the cards creep up and out with age.

# What Kinds of Cards Can I Buy?

Hundreds of cards fill the store shelves. But here's a look at the most popular. You probably have at least two of these cards inside your computer right now.

**Video cards:** These give your monitor a place to plug into. Every computer has a video card, except for the ones with the video circuitry built right into the motherboard. (In fact, you need to disable that motherboard circuitry if you ever put a video card in a slot. Better check the motherboard's manual.)

Computers expect only one video card. Don't confuse your computer by leaving your old video card in place after adding a new one.

An *accelerated* video card can display images faster than the boring old cards. They cost more, but they can really speed up Windows and other graphics-hungry programs.

**I/O cards:** You know where your printer plugs into the back of your computer? It's plugging into the back of your I/O card. Chances are, there's a serial port above your printer port, too. A mouse or modem usually plugs into that port.

**Controller cards:** All sorts of flat ribbon cables sprout from these cards. The cables connect to your floppy drives and hard drives. Some newer computers recently fired the controller card. The ribbon cables just plug straight into the motherboard on these machines.

Put your controller card in a slot close to the power supply; that way, the ribbon cables don't have to reach so far to connect to your drives.

**Sound cards:** Bought a sound card? Fun! The hard part is configuring them to a special *IRQ address*. That technical stuff's covered in Chapter 17.

You won't hear anything from a sound card unless you also bought speakers. Another alternative is to buy a *long* phono cord and run it from the sound card to your stereo's tape or auxiliary jack. The hard part then becomes trying not to trip over the cord.

**Modems:** Modem cards cause two main problems. First, they need to be configured for a COM port so your computer has an electronic doorway to yell in and out of. (COM ports are covered in Chapter 17.)

Second, modem cards come with *two* phone jacks on them. Your phone line plugs into one, and you can plug your telephone into the other. But those phone jacks are rarely marked. Which one goes where? Grab that manual or just try connecting the wires one way; if it doesn't work, try the opposite plug.

**Memory cards:** Some people, hungry for more memory, stick memory chips on a card and then stick the card into their computer. It's a last-resort operation, though, reserved for when your computer's motherboard is already filled up with memory chips. Memory on a card always works more slowly.

Some 386 computers come with a *proprietary* memory slot. You can buy a memory card for that slot from the computer's maker, but no other card will work. The card looks different from the other cards, so you don't have to worry about getting your memory cards mixed up. It's just as fast as any other memory, but it costs a lot more.

**Interface cards:** You plug in one of these guys to put a new connector on the back of your computer. For example, you can plug in a CD-ROM drive, a mouse, or a PCMCIA card reader for those little credit-card-sized laptop disks. Some Roland music synthesizers use an interface card, as do the latest robotic arm controllers.

✓ All types of cards plug in the same way. No special tricks.

✓ Not all cards work right away, though. You may have to flip some switches on them or move some jumpers around. That's covered in Chapter 17.

✓ The biggest problem you'll probably have with cards is finding room for them. Most computers come with eight slots. After you plug in your video card, controller card, and I/O card, you'll realize how quickly those slots get used up.

When fastening a cable to the back of a card, look for little screws on the cord's end. Some have big thumbscrews designed especially for clumsy people. (Thank goodness.) Others have tiny screws that frustrate the myopic. Either way, screw the cord tightly onto the back of your computer. That keeps it from falling off whenever you adjust your computer's position on your desk.

# How Do I Install a New Card?

**IQ level:** 90

**Tools you need:** One hand and a screwdriver

**Cost:** Anywhere from $70 - $120

**Stuff to watch out for:**

Cards are particularly susceptible to static electricity. Tap your computer's case to ground yourself before touching the card.

Be careful not to bend the cards while installing them. That can damage their circuitry.

Cards are pretty easy to install. They're self-contained little units. For example, they suck electricity right out of that little slot they plug into. You don't need to plug special power cables into them.

Cards are delicate, however. Handle them only by their edges. The oil from your fingers can damage their circuitry.

Also, those little silver dots on one side of the card are actually sharp metal pokers that can leave scratches across the back of your hand. In fact, the scratches on one computer nerd's hand resembled a tattoo so closely that chummy hoodlums dragged him into a biker bar. (He ended up recalibrating the Quiz Whiz arcade unit.)

Different-sized cards need different-sized slots. You may need to rearrange some of your cards to accommodate different lengths and thicknesses.

To install a card, follow these steps:

1. **Turn off your computer, unplug it, and remove the cover.**

   Don't know how that cover comes off? Flip to the cheat sheet at the font of this book for the answers.

2. **Find the right size slot for your card.**

   See the row of slots along the back wall of your computer, as shown in Figure 14-3? Your new card will plug into one of those slots. Don't confuse your computer's expansion slots — the ones where the cards plug in — with its memory slots, where the memory-chip-laden SIMMs plug in.

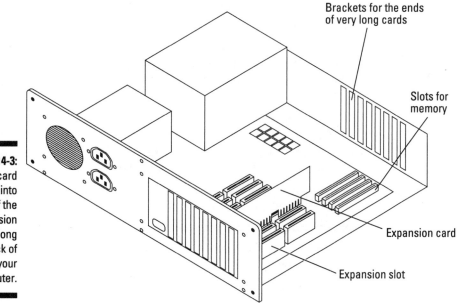

Brackets for the ends
of very long cards

Slots for
memory

**Figure 14-3:**
A card
pushes into
one of the
expansion
slots along
the back of
your
computer.

Expansion card

Expansion slot

Check out the pictures in Figure 14-1 and 14-2 so you know whether you have an 8-bit or 16-bit card. Or just look at its bottom: two tabs make it a 16-bit card; just one tab makes it an 8-bit card.

You can stick an 8-bit card in a 16-bit slot, but rarely vice versa.

You may have to shuffle your cards around until there's room for the new card.

If you have a lot of room, keep your cards spaced as far apart as possible. That keeps them cooler.

**3. Remove the slot's cover.**

Unused slots have a little cover next to them to keep dust from flying in through the back of your computer. With a small screwdriver, remove the screw that holds the cover in place. Don't lose the screw! You need it to secure the card in place.

Dropped the screw in there "somewhere?" Head for Chapter 2 for tips on getting it back out. (You can't just leave it in there, or your computer will choke on it and possibly electrocute itself.)

Got the screw out? Keep it handy, and keep the little bracket, too. You can use it as a makeshift chip puller, as seen in Figure 9-6 in Chapter 9.

**4. Push the card into its slot.**

To spare yourself some possible aggravation, first check your card's manual to see if you need to flip any of the card's switches or move any of its jumpers. Then you won't have to take the card back out if it's not working right.

Holding the card by its edges, position it over the slot. The edge with the shiny metal bracket should face toward the *back* of your computer. Got it?

Push the card slowly into the slot. You may need to rock it back and forth gently. When it pops in, you'll feel it come to rest. Don't force it!

Don't let any card come into contact with any other card. That can cause electrical problems, and neither the card nor the computer will work.

**5. Secure the card in the slot with the screw.**

Yep, all those expensive cards are held in place by a single screw. Make sure that you *use* a screw, however; don't just leave the card sitting there. Cards need to be grounded to the computer's case. Without a secure connection, they may not work.

6. **Plug the computer back in, turn it on, and run the card's installation software.**

   Here's where you find out whether or not all those little switches and jumpers were set correctly. If it works, carefully put the cover back on. You're done!

If it doesn't work, try the following:

✔ Check the manual to make sure that the card's switches and jumpers are set right.

✔ Sometimes you have to run the card's software and then reboot your computer before it will work. That's because the card puts a driver in one of your computer's special files. Your computer only reads that file when it's first turned on or when it's rebooted.

✔ Make sure that the card is seated securely in its slot and screwed in reasonably tight.

✔ Make sure that the card's in the right slot: 8-bit or 16-bit.

✔ It can take some fiddling to get a card working right.

✔ Nine times out of ten, however, the problem lies with the software. The card's sitting in the slot just right; the software is conflicting with some other software or not talking with the card correctly.

✔ If the card still doesn't work, root around in its box for the manual. Most manuals list a technical support phone number you can call for help. Be sure to read the tail end of Chapter 4 before calling; it'll save you a lot of time.

# Part IV
# Telling Your Computer What You've Done

"HEY, I NEVER SAW A SLOW RESPONSE TIME FIXED WITH A PAPER WEIGHT BEFORE."

# In this part . . .

Upgrading a computer is kind of like recording something on a VCR. The easy part is stuffing the videotape inside. The hard part is making the VCR automatically record the late show while you're snoozing so you can watch the show the next day and fast-forward through all the commercials.

Computers present a similar situation. The easy part of upgrading your computer often turns out to be sticking in the new part. The hard part is making the computer recognize that new part and start putting it to work.

That's where this part of the book comes in. It helps avert that sinking sensation — that feeling you get when you've finally tightened the last screw, but the ungrateful computer *still* doesn't recognize your handiwork.

Hold on; you're almost there.

# Chapter 15
## That AUTOEXEC.BAT and CONFIG.SYS File Stuff

- - - - - - - - - - - - - - - - - - - - - - - - - - - - - - - - - - - - - - - - -

### In This Chapter

▶ Understanding your CONFIG.SYS file

▶ Understanding your AUTOEXEC.BAT file

▶ Taking a look at paths

▶ Creating a PATH statement

▶ Adding a driver to a CONFIG.SYS file

▶ Changing your AUTOEXEC.BAT file

▶ Understanding what really happens when you turn on your computer

- - - - - - - - - - - - - - - - - - - - - - - - - - - - - - - - - - - - - - - - -

*W*hen your computer wakes up in the morning, it reaches for its cup of coffee. However, a computer thinks *everything* is either a file or piece of electronic circuitry, so its cup of coffee certainly isn't made by Folgers.

No, the coffee for a newly wakened computer consists of two small files: AUTOEXEC.BAT and CONFIG.SYS.

You've probably seen those weird names either in a directory on your hard drive or in a manual somewhere. Normally, you don't have to mess with these files, thank goodness. But when a program or manual tells you to *modify your AUTOEXEC.BAT/CONFIG.SYS files,* follow the numbered steps in this chapter.

## What's a CONFIG.SYS File?

A CONFIG.SYS file is simply a file filled with text. However, it's designed for your *computer* to look at, not you. That's why its contents look like the fine print on a bottle of multivitamins. For example, look at the nerdy verbiage in the CONFIG.SYS file shown in Figure 15-1.

```
DEVICE=C:\WINDOWS\HIMEM.SYS
DEVICE=C:\WINDOWS\EMM386.EXE NOEMS
DOS=HIGH,UMB

DEVICEHIGH=C:\UTIL\DEV\MDSCD_FD.SYS /D:MSCD000 /N:1
DEVICEHIGH=D:\COMM\FAX\SATISFAX.SYS IOADDR=0310
DEVICEHIGH=D:\SOUND\PROAUDIO\MVSOUND.SYS D:3 Q:7

STACKS=9,256
FILES=80
BUFFERS=40
LASTDRIVE=Z
```

What is all that stuff? Well, a CONFIG.SYS file contains mostly the names of *drivers* — pieces of software that help your computer talk to mice, sound cards, extra chunks of memory, and other gadgets. The CONFIG.SYS file lists where all those drivers live on your hard drive; it's sort of like a phone book for computer parts.

Whenever you turn on or reboot your computer, it flips open its CONFIG.SYS file to see all the drivers listed in there. As it reads each driver's name, it finds that driver's software on the hard drive. It then reads the driver to learn how to carry on a conversation with whatever component the driver represents.

The computer immediately forgets about the drivers as soon as you turn it off. But when you turn it back on again, it heads straight back to the CONFIG.SYS file and calls those drivers back into action. Sure, it's repetitious. But computers never get bored.

- ✔ If your computer can't find a part's *driver,* it probably won't be able to find the part, either. In fact, it won't even know it's supposed to *look* for the part. And if it stumbles across the part accidentally, it won't know how to talk to the part, leading to arguments and general discomfort.

- ✔ When everything's working correctly, your computer reads its CONFIG.SYS file so quickly and automatically that you don't have to mess with the file at all — except when you need to toss a new driver in there.

- ✔ Some computer parts come with installation programs that automatically place their drivers in the CONFIG.SYS file. Others computer parts are lazy and make you put the driver in yourself.

- ✔ Your computer looks at the CONFIG.SYS file only when it's rebooted or turned on. That's why so many installation programs want to reboot your computer when they're through — it's how they force your computer to notice their changes.

- ✔ Not *all* computer parts force you to fiddle with a CONFIG.SYS file or a driver. Some make you fiddle with an AUTOEXEC.BAT file instead. (That file is described next.) Others don't make you fiddle with *anything*: the computer handles all the fiddling chores itself. The boxes that the parts come in rarely give much of a clue as to what you should expect, unfortunately.

The lines listed in a CONFIG.SYS file aren't commands you can type at the DOS prompt. Your computer will probably spit out an error message if you try. Your computer can only understand those lines when they're packaged in the CONFIG.SYS file.

✔ Your computer's picky about the location of its CONFIG.SYS file. It only looks for CONFIG.SYS in your *root* directory — that C:\> directory. If you move the file to a directory like C:\DOS> or C:\WINDOWS> or any other directory with words in the name, your computer won't be able to find it.

# *What's an AUTOEXEC.BAT File?*

Imagine that it's your first day on the job. You walk into a new, unfamiliar office and don't know where to start. Then you see a "to-do" list the boss tacked to the desk.

An AUTOEXEC.BAT file is a "to-do" list for your computer. It's simply a text file filled with commands you'd normally type at the C:\> prompt. You can see a sample of an AUTOEXEC.BAT file in Figure 15-2.

Whenever you turn on or reboot your computer, it looks for a file called AUTOEXEC.BAT. If it finds one, it reads the file line by line and carries out all the instructions in the file. It AUTOmatically EXECutes all those commands when you first turn it on. (Get it?)

An AUTOEXEC.BAT file is a sneaky way to make computers do some of their start-up work automatically so you don't have to boss them around for every little thing.

✔ An AUTOEXEC.BAT file contains a list of commands for the computer to run whenever it's turned on or rebooted. In fact, those are the only times the computer ever bothers reading the AUTOEXEC.BAT file.

✔ If the AUTOEXEC.BAT file ever changes, the computer won't notice until the next time it's rebooted. That's why the installation programs for most new computer parts insist on rebooting your computer. Rebooting forces your computer to notice their changes.

**Figure 15-2:**
A typical AUTOEXEC.BAT file. Yours probably differs from this one.

```
PATH C:\DOS;C:\WINDOWS
SET TEMP=C:\DOS
C:\WINDOWS\SMARTDRV.EXE
C:\WINDOWS\MOUSE.COM
PROMPT $p$g
```

✔ Like the CONFIG.SYS file, the AUTOEXEC.BAT file lives in your root directory, the one you see when you type **DIR** at the C:\> prompt. Sure, you can put those two files anywhere on your hard drive you want. However, your computer won't be able to find them unless they're in the root directory.

✔ Some computer parts want to stick some lines into your CONFIG.SYS file. Others prefer adding to the AUTOEXEC.BAT file. Some want to put a line in *both* files. Other, more easy-going parts don't use *any* drivers or programs, sparing you from bothering with this entire chapter.

✔ There's no surefire way to tell whether a certain computer part prefers to stake its mark in the CONFIG.SYS file or the AUTOEXEC.BAT file. It depends on the manufacturer and whoever invented the part. Only the manual knows for sure.

Keep a backup copy of your AUTOEXEC.BAT and CONFIG.SYS files on a floppy disk. If something goes wrong, you can copy them back over to your root directory. Feel free to keep a printout of them on hand, too. Just be sure to update your printout or floppy disk whenever the files change.

# *What's a Path?*

Computers aren't terribly clever beasts. When you copy a file or program to your computer's hard drive, your computer doesn't always pay attention. It won't automatically be able to find the file or program later.

That's why a *path* comes in so handy. A path is a computer's road map — it shows where a particular file is located.

For example, perhaps your file COUGH.EXE is in your C:\SYMPTOMS>sub-directory. After the C:\> prompt, you type COUGH and press Enter, like this:

```
C:\> COUGH
```

But your computer doesn't run COUGH. Instead, it gives off the following confused shout: Bad command or file name.

That's because the computer couldn't find COUGH. It looked in the directory it was in at the time — the C:\> directory — and couldn't find COUGH, so it gave up.

However, if you add COUGH's *path,* the computer knows where to look for the file. So to make the computer run COUGH, you type the subdirectory as well as the filename, like this:

```
C:\> C:\SYMPTOMS\COUGH
```

The point? If all the programs and drivers in your CONFIG.SYS and AUTOEXEC.BAT files include paths, your computer will always be able to find them.

✔ If you see the words Bad command or file name while your computer is booting up, it's a sure sign that the computer couldn't find a file listed in your AUTOEXEC.BAT file.

✔ The problem probably occurred because the file's name or path is spelled wrong, no matter how subtly. Or it may be that you moved the file to a different place on your hard drive. If you did, your computer won't be able to find it anymore — you'll have to update the file's path in your AUTOEXEC.BAT file to reflect its new location.

✔ When your computer can't find something in your CONFIG.SYS file, it's a little more specific about the problem: it not only lists the name of the driver it can't find, but also the line number in your CONFIG.SYS file that's causing the problem.

## PATH=C:\WHO\CARES>

This path stuff is a bother. Why can't the computer just look *everywhere* on the hard drive and find files automatically? Well, because that can take a long time. If you have an old computer and an older hard drive, it can take a *very* long time.

DOS offers a compromise. It lets you put your most popular directories on a special list. When you type the name of a program at the C:\> prompt, the computer searches for the file in the current directory, just as it normally does. But if it doesn't find the program there, it *also* searches the directories you placed on the special list.

This special list is called the PATH statement, and it lives in the AUTOEXEC.BAT file. In the AUTOEXEC.BAT file in Figure 15-2, for example, the PATH looks like this:

    PATH C:\DOS;C:\WINDOWS

See those subdirectories listed after the word PATH? Those are the directories your computer staggers through when searching for files. In Figure 15-2, for example, the computer automatically searches through the C:\DOS and C:\WINDOWS directories for your programs.

Listing a program's directory on the PATH can make things easier. You can type a program's name from anywhere on your hard drive, and if its directory is on the path, your computer finds and runs the program.

In fact, that's part of the problem. Because it's so easy to find and run a program that's on the PATH, almost *every* installation program wants to put its directory on the PATH.

DOS bylaws decree that a PATH statement can be no longer than 127 characters. If it's 128 characters or longer, DOS simply ignores the PATH statement, leaving you with no PATH at all. Nothing.

The solution? When your PATH gets too long, open up your AUTOEXEC.BAT file and give it a trim. You need to keep Windows and DOS in there, that's for sure. But you may be able to cut out some other, less-frequently used directories. The PATH may list some directories you deleted years ago in a fit of hard-drive housekeeping.

# *How to Edit a CONFIG.SYS or AUTOEXEC.BAT File*

Sooner or later, some new program or gadget will send you a blast of rudeness. From out of the blue, its manual will tell you to modify your CONFIG.SYS file or edit your AUTOEXEC.BAT file. If you spot a floppy disk in the box with your new computer part, chances are that the program on that disk wants to fiddle with your CONFIG.SYS or AUTOEXEC.BAT file.

Some installation programs make all the changes automatically; others make *you* wear the file-changing hat. When you're forced to change your CONFIG.SYS or AUTOEXEC.BAT file, carefully follow these steps.

Before starting, make sure that you're at the *real* DOS prompt and not at the counterfeit DOS prompt that Windows sometimes hands you. Not sure which is which? Then type **EXIT** at the C:\> prompt and press Enter. If Windows doesn't pop back up on your screen, you're safe: Windows wasn't lurking in the background after all.

### 1. Find the file.

Your CONFIG.SYS and AUTOEXEC.BAT files live in a place called the root directory. That's the place that gives you a simple looking C:\> prompt. To get there, type the following command.

```
C:\> C:
```

In other words, press C, a colon, and the Enter key. That takes you to drive C even if you're currently visiting drive D, a CD-ROM drive, or something even more expensive.

Next, type this command:

```
C:\> CD \
```

That is, type **CD,** a space, and the backslash character, (*not* the slash that shares the ? key), and then press Enter.

These two steps always bring you to your root directory, home of your CONFIG.SYS and AUTOEXEC.BAT files.

### 2. Make a backup copy.

Before fiddling with these important files, make a backup copy so you have a place to turn if the weather starts getting rough. Type the following two commands at the C:\> prompt, pressing Enter after each line:

```
C:\> COPY CONFIG.SYS CONFIG.GOD
C:\> COPY AUTOEXEC.BAT AUTOEXEC.GOD
```

By entering these commands, you make a backup copy of each file. The names of the backup files end in GOD — that stands for "Good" file. (Of course, a little divine intervention wouldn't hurt either.)

Feel free to put a copy of the files on a floppy disk, too. Type the following at the C:\> prompt, pressing Enter at the end of each line:

```
C:\> COPY CONFIG.SYS A:
C:\> COPY AUTOEXEC.BAT A:
```

Make sure that you have a floppy disk in drive A. You can never have too many backup copies.

3. **Open the file.**

Now you're ready to start changing the file. If the manual says to add a line to your CONFIG.SYS file, type the command below:

```
C:\> EDIT CONFIG.SYS
```

That is, type **EDIT,** a space, and **CONFIG.SYS.** Then press Enter.

Or if you're supposed to add a line to your AUTOEXEC.BAT file, type **EDIT,** a space, and **AUTOEXEC.BAT,** and press Enter:

```
C:\> EDIT AUTOEXEC.BAT
```

The Edit program pops up on the screen, letting you see your weird-looking CONFIG.SYS file.

Not using DOS 5 or greater? Then you don't have the convenient Edit program, and you just see an error message. You have to use a word processor to do your editing. And there's another catch: You need to save the file in a special format called *ASCII* or *Plain Text* or *DOS text.* Windows' Notepad will do the trick. If something goes horribly wrong, however, you can head back to steady seas with your backup files; that's described at the end of this section.

4. **Add the new line.**

Do you see the contents of your file inside the Edit program? If you're editing your CONFIG.SYS file, for example, your screen should look something like the one shown in Figure 15-3.

Whether you're adding the new line to the CONFIG.SYS or AUTOEXEC.BAT file, put it at the very bottom of the file. Unless the manual says otherwise, that's probably the safest spot.

Hold down the Ctrl key, press the End key, and release them both. That moves you to the last line of the file. Press Enter.

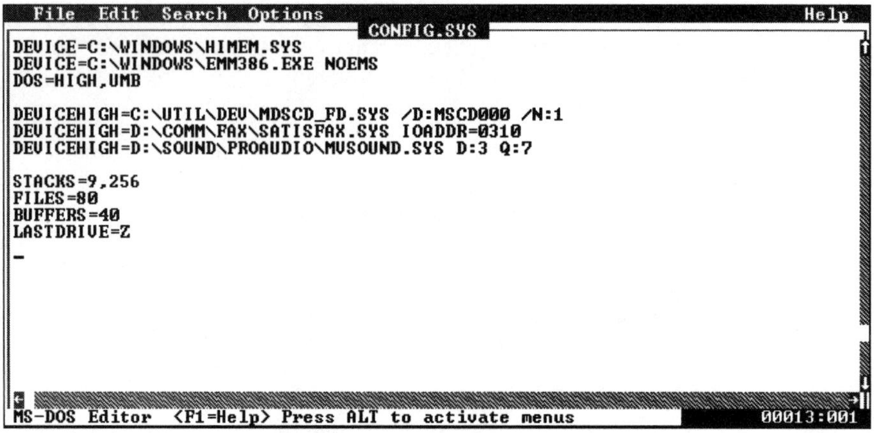

```
 File  Edit  Search  Options                              Help
                          CONFIG.SYS
DEVICE=C:\WINDOWS\HIMEM.SYS
DEVICE=C:\WINDOWS\EMM386.EXE NOEMS
DOS=HIGH,UMB

DEVICEHIGH=C:\UTIL\DEV\MDSCD_FD.SYS /D:MSCD000 /N:1
DEVICEHIGH=D:\COMM\FAX\SATISFAX.SYS IOADDR=0310
DEVICEHIGH=D:\SOUND\PROAUDIO\MVSOUND.SYS D:3 Q:7

STACKS=9,256
FILES=80
BUFFERS=40
LASTDRIVE=Z
_




MS-DOS Editor  <F1=Help> Press ALT to activate menus        00013:001
```

**Figure 15-3:**
This
CONFIG.SYS
file is
loaded into
the Edit pro-
gram and is
ready to be
changed.

Now type in the line you're supposed to add. It'll be listed in the new part's manual or whatever else is forcing you do all this nonsensical stuff.

Be sure to include the file's path so the computer can find the file. (Paths had their own section earlier in this chapter.) Check for typos, too. If you don't spell everything 100 percent correctly, your computer will grow a hair bun and give you cross looks.

Done typing in the line? Then press Enter.

5. **Save the file.**

Did you double-check your work? Then it's time to save the file. Press and release Alt and then press F. A little menu drops down from the top of the screen.

Press S to Save the file.

6. **Exit the program.**

The computer saved your work, so press and release the Alt key and press F. Again, the little menu appears. This time, however, press X for Exit. The Edit program disappears into nothingness, leaving you at your C:\> prompt.

7. **Reset the computer.**

Your computer only reads its AUTOEXEC.BAT and CONFIG.SYS files when it's rebooted. So push your computer's reset button. The screen clears, your computer gathers itself together, and you're ready for the big moment: it reads those AUTOEXEC.BAT and CONFIG.SYS files.

✔ Watch your computer closely when it reboots after you change these files. If the screen says something like `Bad or missing file name` or `Error in CONFIG.SYS line 13`, something's wrong. Jump back to Step 3 and check to see that you spelled everything right and the program's path is correct.

✔ If you did everything correctly, your computer won't toss anything strange onto the screen, not even a thank-you message. Try using your new part or program; chances are, your computer will finally recognize it.

✔ If you mess something up terribly and your computer freaks out, here's how to restore sanity. Simply copy your backup copies over the messed up ones. Type the following commands at the `C:\>` prompt:

```
C:\> COPY CONFIG.GOD CONFIG.SYS
C:\> COPY AUTOEXEC.GOD AUTOEXEC.BAT
```

Then reboot your computer, and it will come back to normal. You still need to find a computer guru to make those changes for you, however. Tell 'em you made an honest effort at doing it yourself. That and a fresh box of Count Chocula cereal often gets a guru's attention.

Sometimes you need to *change* a line, not add a new one. To be safe, find the line you need to change and type the word **REM** in front of it. For example, a program may want to change an AUTOEXEC.BAT file line that looks like this:

```
PROMPT $p$g
```

To change the line, put the word REM in front of it and type the new, changed line directly beneath it, like this:

```
REM PROMPT $p$g
PROMPT $D$_$T$_$P$G
```

The REM stands for *remark*. Because remarks are designed for humans, DOS ignores any line starting with REM.

If something goes wrong with your change, delete the line that messed things up and remove the REM from the original line — the one that worked. Doing that brings things back to normal. Well, as normal as computers can be, anyway.

One last note: If you try this tactic in a version of DOS earlier than 3.3, DOS says `Unrecognized command in CONFIG.SYS` when the computer boots up. Just tell the computer to hush up; everything's fine.

Do you want your computer to start Windows automatically when you turn it on? Then add this word to its own line at the very end of your AUTOEXEC.BAT file:

```
WIN
```

Your computer reads that line when it reboots and loads Windows automatically.

# What Are Those Weird Sounds and Words When I Turn On My Computer?

A computer jumps through the same hoops whenever you press its Reset button or flip its On switch. Here's a rundown of its same ol' run-around:

1. **The switch turns on, and electricity starts flowing.**

   When you first turn on your computer, you hear the power supply's fan start to spin and your hard drive begin to whir. All the circuits inside your PC get a waking burst of electricity.

2. **The BIOS begins.**

   After the computer's CPU wakes up, it heads straight for its *BIOS* — basic, gut-level instructions stored inside special *BIOS* chips on the motherboard. (More BIOS babble bubbles in Chapter 9.) By reading its BIOS, the computer knows how to talk to its floppy drives and other basic parts.

3. **The computer tests itself (POST).**

   After the computer figures out how to talk to its parts, it begins testing them with the *POST,* or *Power On Self Test.* The POST is described more fully in Chapter 4.

   **XT:** On these oldsters, the POST looks at the DIP switches on the motherboard. The switches tell the POST what parts are inside your computer, and then the POST goes looking to make sure that the parts are *really* there.

   **Other:** If you're using a 286, 386, or newer computer, the POST looks for the equipment list stored in your computer's CMOS. The CMOS, covered in Chapter 17, contains a battery-backed up list of the parts inside your computer. The POST grabs the list and starts looking for everything that's listed.

As the POST goes around kicking tires, it lets you know what's going on. For example, you see an on-screen tally as the POST counts your memory chips. You hear your floppy drives gnash their teeth as the POST gives 'em a quick spin. Your hard drive's little red light flashes as the POST peeks inside.

If the POST finds something askew, it flings out a coded series of beeps (which are decoded in Chapter 23) or flashes a cryptic error message (decryptified in Chapter 22). Or both.

If everything's fine and dandy (most of the time), the computer gives one affirmative, head-nodding beep and moves to Step 4.

4. **The computer looks for DOS.**

The computer first looks for DOS on drive A. That's because *everybody* used to keep their DOS system disk in drive A. (Hard drives weren't invented yet.)

The computer is searching for the DOS *boot sector.* If the computer finds a disk in drive A but there's no boot sector to be found, it stops dead, leaving this epitaph:

```
Non-system disk or disk error
Replace and strike any key when ready
```

Odds are, you accidentally left a normal, everyday disk in drive A. DOS couldn't find its life-giving boot sector, so it gave up. Remove the disk, tap the spacebar, and the computer will continue.

When it can't find a disk in drive A, the computer moves on to the hard drive, looking there for the DOS boot sector.

## Boring boot sector balderdash

What's the computer looking for in the boot sector? Two files with important DOS information. Normally, the two files are invisible, so you don't have to bother with them, thank goodness.

One file, called IBMBIO.COM or IO.SYS depending on your version of DOS, helps DOS communicate with your computer's hardware. The other file, called either IBMDOS.COM or MSDOS.SYS,

holds computer-language answers to barebones DOS questions: what are files, what is memory, and other questions answered in *DOS For Dummies.*

While you work in some programs, you may see these two files sitting on your hard drive. Don't delete them, or your computer won't be able to get out of bed.

### 5. The computer looks for the CONFIG.SYS file.

Next, the computer looks for a CONFIG.SYS file. Described earlier in this chapter, this file contains mostly drivers: bits of software that help a computer deal with things like compact disc players, memory managers, mice, video cards, and other gadgets attached to it.

### 6. The computer runs the COMMAND.COM program.

You may have noticed this file sitting on your hard drive or a floppy disk. It contains more basic DOS stuff — form-letter reactions to commands you type at a C:\> prompt, for example.

### 7. The computer runs AUTOEXEC.BAT.

The computer's had its fun; now it gives the user a chance to jump in. It reads each line in the AUTOEXEC.BAT file, covered earlier in this chapter. The computer treats each line as if the user typed in the command at the DOS prompt.

For example, if you end your AUTOEXEC.BAT file with the line WIN, your computer ends its reboot flurries by loading Windows. Quick and convenient. Unless, of course, you were just turning on your computer to grab a quick phone number, and you now have to wait for Windows to finish loading before you can call out for the pizza.

# Chapter 16
# Telling Windows about a New Part

• • • • • • • • • • • • • • • • • • • • • • • • • • • • • • • • • • • • • • • • •

## In This Chapter

▶ Adding a different keyboard

▶ Adding a new monitor or video card

▶ Adding a new mouse

▶ Changing video modes

▶ Adding a new sound card, CD-ROM drive, or other gadget

▶ Finding new drivers

▶ Adding a new printer

• • • • • • • • • • • • • • • • • • • • • • • • • • • • • • • • • • • • • • • • •

*F*or such a flashy program, Windows can act shy in front of newcomers. It won't walk across the room to meet the new parts you install in your computer.

Introducing your new part to DOS usually isn't enough. You'll probably have to doff your hat and *personally* introduce Windows to your new part, or the two will never get along.

The secret is to install the Windows *driver* for the new gadget. A driver is a little piece of software that lets Windows know how to talk to the new part without embarrassing itself.

Chances are, the Windows driver came packed inside the gadget's box. No disk in there? Well, Windows comes with bunches of drivers on its own disks. (Hopefully, you remember where you stashed your Windows box.)

Wherever you find the driver, this chapter tells you how to install it and make Windows greet your latest addition with open arms.

# *Introducing Windows to a New Mouse, Keyboard, Video Card, or Monitor*

Sometimes Windows works like the easy-to-use wunderkind that's advertised on TV: it recognizes your new part automatically, and everything works, with no button-pushing or mouse-sliding on your part.

For example, if you merely replace your mouse, keyboard, video card, or monitor with another one of the same kind, you needn't do anything special. Just plug it in, and Windows will treat it just like the old part.

If you buy a part that uses a different *mode* however, you have to make some changes. Here's a rundown of the modes used by various computer gadgets:

**Mouse:** Most mice operate in two modes: *Microsoft mode* and some other funky, third-party mode, like *Logitech* or *Genius.* If your new mouse runs in the same mode as your old one, you don't need to fiddle with Windows. If it runs in a different mode, however, you need to follow the steps later in this section. (More mouse information lives in Chapter 6.)

Your best bet is to set your new mouse to Microsoft mode and choose that mode when installing the mouse. Microsoft mode seems to cause the fewest problems.

**Keyboard:** Most new keyboards today are Enhanced Keyboards, which have 101 keys. If you're replacing your old Enhanced Keyboard, you don't have to mess with Windows. If you're upgrading from an 84-key keyboard or adding some offbeat third-party brand of keyboard, however, follow the steps later in this section. (Chapter 5 is packed with keyboard stuff.)

**Video card:** Video cards can work in many different modes. The different modes let you choose the number of colors your monitor can display and the monitor *resolution* — the amount of information that can fit on the screen.

If you upgrade to a fancier video card, Windows still boots up on your screen, but it looks like it did with your old video card. To make Windows take advantage of your new card, follow this section's instructions on installing your new card's Windows drivers. Then head for the section on switching between video modes, also in this chapter. You can try your new card's different video modes until you find one you like.

**Monitor:** Bought a new monitor? You need to tweak Windows under only one condition: if you finally bought a monitor that can take advantage of your video card's fancier video modes. To try out those new modes, you need to change the Windows <u>D</u>isplay options, described later in this chapter.

To introduce Windows to your new brand of mouse, keyboard, or video card, follow these steps:

1. **Double-click on the Windows Setup icon in the Program Manager's Main window.**

   The Windows Setup icon lets you tweak the major Windows hardware settings:

2. **Click on Options in the Windows Setup window's menu bar.**

   The Options menu tumbles down, as shown in Figure 16-1.

3. **Click on Change System Settings.**

   Yet another window pops up, as seen in Figure 16-2. Here's where you can change your display, keyboard, mouse, or network. If you're at the office, though, you'll probably get yelled at for fiddling around with the network. Don't click on that one.

4. **Click on the box next to the kind of toy you want to add.**

   For example, to change to a different brand of mouse, click inside the box next to the word Mouse. A menu drops down, as shown in Figure 16-3.

   Press your up-arrow or down-arrow key to see all the listed brands. If you're lucky, Windows lists your particular brand of toy by name.

   If you're *not* lucky, click on Other mouse (Requires disk from OEM)... and jump to Step 6. That "Other" business means Windows doesn't have a driver for your mouse; you need to use the driver on the disk that came with the mouse.

5. **Click on the name of the gadget you installed.**

   When you click on one of the listed gadgets, the menu snaps back into position and looks just like it does in Figure 16-2. This time, however, the box lists the gadget you just selected from the list.

6. **Click on the OK button.**

**Figure 16-1:**
Click on Options, and the menu tumbles down.

Windows Setup

Options  Help
Change System Settings...          mall Fonts)
Set Up Applications...             and Non US
Add/Remove Windows Components...
Exit

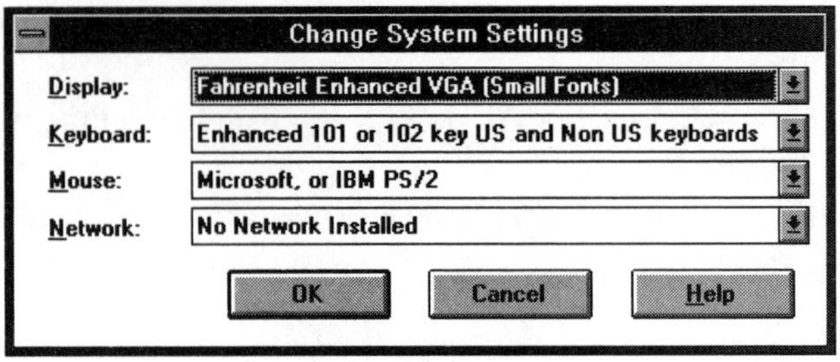

**Figure 16-2:**
This window lets you change your display, key-board, mouse, or, heaven forbid, your network.

Yet another box pops up, as seen in Figure 16-4. If Windows asks you to put one of your Windows disks in drive A, rummage around in your Windows box until you find the correctly numbered disk. Then stick it in drive A and press Enter.

Or, if you clicked on the Other mouse (Requires disk from OEM)... option in Step 4, rummage around in the new gadget's box for a floppy disk. Then stick *that* disk in drive A and press Enter.

If your disk only fits in drive B, feel free to stick it in there. Then change the A:\ in the Windows Setup window to B:\ and press Enter.

Either way, Windows copies the files it needs onto your hard drive so it can use your new toy. Next, Windows almost always asks permission to reboot your computer. Click on Restart Windows when you see the permission box, shown in Figure 16-5. Windows disappears and then reappears. This time, however, it's ready to use your new part.

About time, eh?

✔ Sometimes Windows doesn't ask you to insert a floppy disk. Instead, itautomatically knows how to talk to your new gadget, saving you the bother of rummaging around for the right disk.

✔ Other times, Windows says it *already* has a driver for the new gadget on board. Go ahead and install the driver that came in the gadget's box any-way, though. Those drivers that came with Windows are getting pretty old by now. The one that came with your gadget probably is more up-to-date.

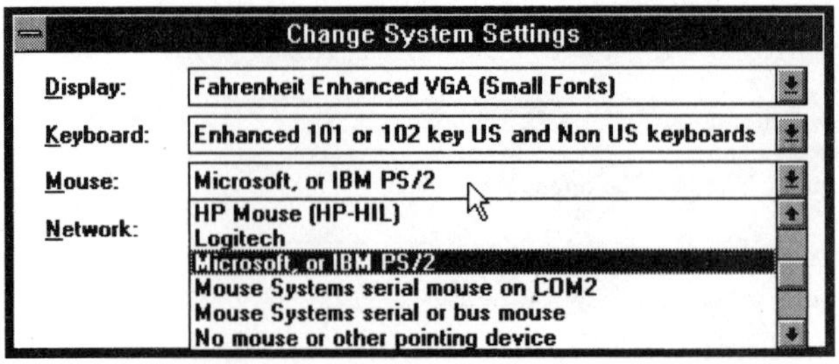

**Figure 16-3:**
Choose your new brand of mouse from the list that drops down.

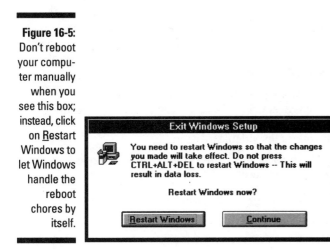

**Figure 16-4:**
Insert the
right disk
into drive A
and press
Enter.

**Windows Setup**

Please insert the Microsoft Windows 3.1 Disk #2.

If the files on this disk can be found at a different
location, for example, on another drive, type a new
path to the file below.

`A:\`

[ OK ]     [ Cancel ]     [ Exit Setup ]

✔ The driver doesn't work? Head for the "My Driver's Too Old and Cruddy to Work Right" section later in this chapter.

✔ If you installed a new video card, Windows may be so disturbed it won't even show up on the screen. If you can't get Windows off the ground, head for the "I Changed Video Modes, and Now Windows Is Broken!" section later in this chapter.

✔ If your new mouse doesn't work in Windows, making it impossible for you to switch to the mouse's new driver, head for the "I Changed Video Modes, and Now Windows Is Broken!" section. It shows you how to use the DOS version of Setup so you can avoid the Windows Setup program.

✔ The Windows Setup program works well for switching to a new mouse, keyboard, video card, or monitor. But that's *all* it can set up. If you added a sound card, compact disc drive, satellite dish controller, or something even more fun, head for the "Introducing Windows to a Sound Card" section later in this chapter.

**Figure 16-5:**
Don't reboot
your compu-
ter manually
when you
see this box;
instead, click
on Restart
Windows to
let Windows
handle the
reboot
chores by
itself.

**Exit Windows Setup**

You need to restart Windows so that the changes
you made will take effect. Do not press
CTRL+ALT+DEL to restart Windows -- This will
result in data loss.

**Restart Windows now?**

[ Restart Windows ]     [ Continue ]

# I Want More Colors and Higher Resolution!

Most video cards can display more then one video *mode*. For example, some let you choose between seeing 16 or 256 colors on the screen. Others let you change *resolutions* and pack more information onto the screen.

Just as some people prefer different brands of toothpaste, some people prefer different video modes. To figure out which mode's right for you, try all the modes your card has to offer and stick with the one you think looks best.

Here's how to change video modes:

1. **Double-click on the Windows Setup icon in the Program Manager's Main window.**

2. **Press and release these three keys in this order: Alt, O, C.**

3. **Click on the Display option.**

   Now choose between VGA, SuperVGA, or any other modes your video card can dish out. In fact, if your video card came with a drivers disk, click on the Other display (Requires disk from OEM)... box.

4. **Follow the directions on the screen, pressing Enter when asked.**

5. **Finally, click on the Restart Windows button.**

   Windows reboots and returns in its new video glory!

✔ Sometimes Windows *doesn't* return in its new video glory. In fact, it doesn't return at all. If so, tiptoe to the next section for the cure: use the DOS version of the Windows Setup program.

✔ When Windows reappears on the screen after you switch between video modes, part of it sometimes hangs off the edge of your screen. If this happens, feel around the edge of your monitor for its vertical and horizontal control knobs. When you find them, turn them back and forth until Windows is centered on your screen.

If you switch the video mode from 16 colors to 256 colors, be sure to try the Windows wallpaper called 256COLOR.BMP. Almost all Windows programs use only 16 colors, so that wallpaper lets you see why you spent the extra money on your fancy video card.

✔ Switching to higher resolutions and more colors makes Windows look prettier, but don't get carried away. Windows works a lot slower when it has to push all those graphics around.

# I Changed Video Modes, and Now Windows Is Broken!

Windows is a very accommodating program. In fact, it's so accommodating, it cheerfully lets you choose a new video mode that your video card can't even display.

You'll know right away if you choose a video mode that's past your computer's limits: When you reboot Windows, it won't reappear. Instead, it'll flash an error message that will move too fast for you to read. Then it will leave you sitting at the DOS prompt.

To bring Windows back to life, use the DOS version of the Windows Setup program. Follow these steps:

1. **Exit Windows, or any other program, until you're at the DOS prompt.**

   To exit Windows, press Alt+F4 from within the Program Manager. If that action leaves you at a menu, press the key that lets you exit to the DOS prompt. Can't find that key? Try pressing Esc or holler for the person who set up your menu.

2. **Move to your Windows directory.**

   From the DOS prompt, change to your Windows directory. If your Windows directory is on drive C, type these two commands, pressing Enter after each one:

   ```
   C:\> C:
   C:\> CD \WINDOWS
   ```

   These commands bring you to drive C and leave you in the Windows directory. If your copy of Windows lives on drive D, however, substitute **D:** for **C:** in the first command.

3. **Type SETUP and press Enter:**

   ```
   C:\> SETUP
   ```

   The DOS version of the Windows Setup program will appear on the screen.

4. **Change your Windows settings.**

The DOS version of Setup, shown in Figure 16-6, works almost identically to the Windows version, described in this chapter's first section. Change the video mode back to VGA or a mode you're *sure* your card and monitor can handle.

```
Windows Setup

     If your computer or network appears on the Hardware Compatibility List
     with an asterisk next to it, press F1 before continuing.

     System Information
        Computer:              MS-DOS System
        Display:               Fahrenheit Enhanced VGA (Small Fonts)
        Mouse:                 Microsoft, or IBM PS/2
        Keyboard:              Enhanced 101 or 102 key US and Non US keyboards
        Keyboard Layout:       US
        Language:              English (American)
        Codepage:              English (437)
        Network:               No Network Installed

     Complete Changes: Accept the configuration shown above.

     To change a system setting, press the UP or DOWN ARROW key to
     move the highlight to the setting you want to change. Then press
     ENTER to see alternatives for that item. When you have finished
     changing your settings, select the "Complete Changes" option
     to quit Setup.

     ENTER=Continue   F1=Help   F3=Exit
```

**Figure 16-6:**
The DOS
version of
Setup
comes in
handy when
Windows
refuses to
load.

Feed your computer any disks the Setup program asks for. When it's done, the program will close, saving your changes. When Windows boots back up, you should be able to see it this time.

The DOS version of Windows Setup comes in handy whenever Windows refuses to load. Feel free to use it if Windows doesn't like your choice of mouse or keyboard, too.

Windows' DOS Setup program can get confused if you're not working in the Windows directory when you call it up. If the Setup program starts talking about *installing* Windows — not merely *changing* its settings — press F3 twice to exit. Then make *sure* that you're in the Windows directory before trying again.

# Introducing Windows to a Sound Card (or CD-ROM Drive or Other Gadget)

Windows tends to segregate its toys. For example, the keyboard, mouse, and video card are all installed through the Setup program, described earlier in this chapter.

Everything else (including the *really* fun stuff) gets introduced through a second program: the Windows Control Panel. The following steps explain how to tell Windows about your new sound cards, CD-ROM drive, or anything else that's not a keyboard, mouse, or video card:

1. **Double-click on the Control Panel icon in the Program Manager's Main window.**

   The Control Panel icon lets you add drivers for new computer gadgets:

2. **Double-click on the Drivers icon.**

   When the Control Panel window pops up (see Figure 16-7), double-click on the Drivers icon. It looks like a little recording studio.

   A box like the one in Figure 16-8 appears, listing the drivers that Windows is currently using.

3. **Click on the Add... button.**

   When you click on the Add... button, a dialog box like the one shown in Figure 16-9 pops up. The box contains a list of brand names.

4. **If you see your gadget's brand name, click on it.**

   Do you see the name of your particular gadget? Press PgUp or PgDn to scroll through the list. If you see your gadget, double-click on its name. If your gadget's *not* listed, double-click on the Unlisted or Updated Driver option.

   A box like the one in Figure 16-10 appears. It asks you to insert one of your Windows disks or, if you chose the Unlisted or Updated Driver option, to insert the disk that came with your new gadget. Either way, insert the disk in drive A and press Enter. (If you're inserting your disk in drive B, change the A:\ to B:\ first. Otherwise, you hear that terrible gnashing sound as your disk drive tries to read a floppy that's not there.)

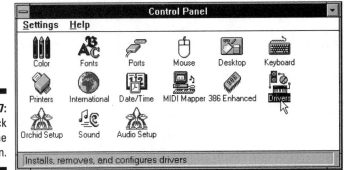

**Figure 16-7:** Double-click on the Drivers icon.

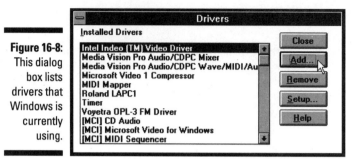

**Figure 16-8:**
This dialog box lists drivers that Windows is currently using.

5. **Let Windows restart your computer.**

After Windows copies the drivers off the disk, it asks politely whether it may restart your computer, as seen in Figure 16-11. Click on the Restart Now button. The screen clears, and Windows reappears. This time, however, Windows recognizes your new gadget.

✔ If Windows doesn't recognize your new gadget when it reboots, try turning your new gadget back on. If Windows still doesn't recognize it, head for Chapter 17; you may need to change some of its settings.

✔ Before Windows can recognize some gadgets, like compact disc drives, you need to install drivers in DOS. Make sure that you run any installation programs that come with your new toy. *Then* try to install it in Windows.

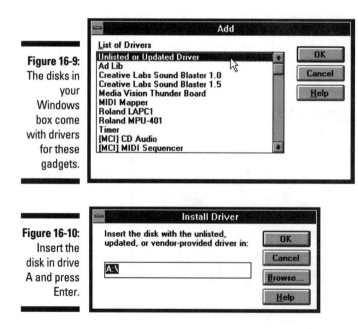

**Figure 16-9:**
The disks in your Windows box come with drivers for these gadgets.

**Figure 16-10:**
Insert the disk in drive A and press Enter.

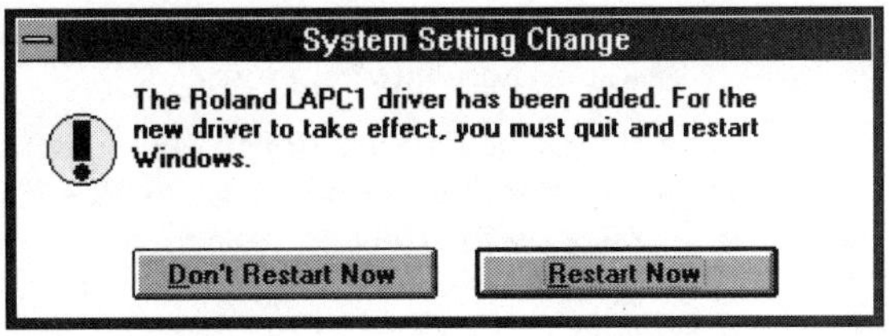

**Figure 16-11:**
Don't reboot your computer manually when you see this box; instead, click on Restart Now to let Windows handle the reboot chores by itself.

> **System Setting Change**
>
> ⊘ The Roland LAPC1 driver has been added. For the new driver to take effect, you must quit and restart Windows.
>
> [ **Don't Restart Now** ]  [ **Restart Now** ]

- ✔ Windows is getting old. Some of the drivers that came with it — the ones for the SoundBlaster sound card, for example — don't work well anymore. You should use the driver that comes in the box with your new gadget.

- ✔ If the driver that came with your new gadget won't work, it may be old, too. Head for the next section for tips on finding the most up-to-date driver available.

# My Driver's Too Old and Cruddy to Work Right!

After you buy a new gadget — a sound card, for example — it's not going to change.

But its *driver* will change. Drivers, like any other piece of software, are subject to perpetual tinkering. The programmer will add bits of code here and there, making the driver faster and less likely to start arguments with other pieces of software.

In fact, some companies release a new driver every two months. When a gadget doesn't work right or conflicts with some other part, your first step should be updating the gadget's driver.

In fact, that's usually the *second* thing you hear if you call the company's tech support line: "Are you using the latest driver?" (The first thing you hear usually is, "All lines are busy right now.")

- ✔ Windows works best when you're using the latest driver for all your gadgets.

- ✔ Your best bet is to call up the gadget's manufacturer. Sometimes they'll mail you a new driver for free. Other times, they'll give you the number of a company BBS. If you know how to use a modem, you can dial the BBS and download the latest driver.

- ✔ If you subscribe to CompuServe, GEnie, or other on-line services, join one of the Windows forums. They usually have the latest drivers within a few days of their release.

✔ Some new drivers come with an installation program that automatically loads them into Windows.

✔ If your new driver doesn't come with an installation program, install it as explained in the "Introducing Windows to a Sound Card" section. Then click on the New button when Windows asks whether you want to use the New driver or the Current driver.

# Adding a New Printer

Congratulations! Don't you love that "new printer" smell?

You need to introduce your new printer through the Windows Control Panel, as described next:

**1. Double-click on the Control Panel icon.**

The Control Panel icon lives in the Program Manager's Main window:

Control Panel

**2. Double-click on the Printers icon.**

When the Control Panel window pops up, double-click on the Printers icon, seen in Figure 6-12.

**3. Click on the Add >> button.**

A double-click on the Add >>button makes the bottom half of the menu appear, as seen in Figure 16-13. Déjà vu! It's the same list of printers you saw when you first installed Windows.

**4. Choose your new printer from the list.**

Press PgUp or PgDn until you see the name of your new printer. Press Enter or double-click on the printer's name. Windows then asks you to stick one of its setup disks into a drive. Insert the disk, press Enter, and listen to the grinding noises as Windows grabs its appropriate printer driver files.

**5. Click on the Set As Default Printer button and click on the Close button.**

That's it!

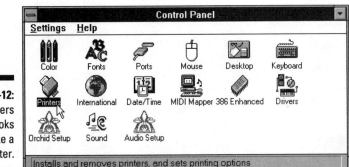

**Figure 16-12:**
The Printers icon looks like a printer.

- ✔ Printer not listed? Then look for the printer it *emulates.* Chapter 8 talks about this emulate stuff.

If you don't want to wade through all those printer names, just press the first letter of your printer: *W* for *WangLDP8,* for example. Windows automatically jumps down to the printers starting with the letter W. This slick trick works in just about any list Windows tosses at you.

- ✔ If Windows still doesn't recognize your new printer, make sure that the printer is plugged into the same spot that your old one held on the back of your computer. Then check the old printer's settings, listed under the Connect... button. Make sure that your new printer matches the same settings listed there.

- ✔ After your new printer's working fine, remove your old printer from your Windows menus. Follow Steps 1 and 2 from the preceding steps. Then click on your old printer's name and click on the Remove button. Done!

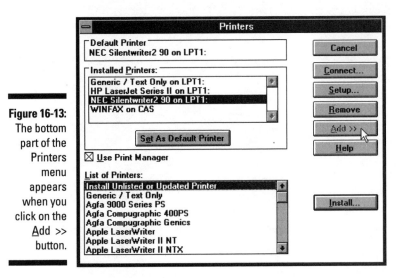

**Figure 16-13:**
The bottom part of the Printers menu appears when you click on the Add >> button.

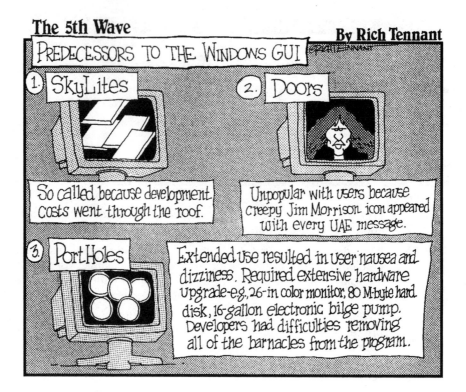

# Chapter 17
# Fiddling with Settings

● ● ● ● ● ● ● ● ● ● ● ● ● ● ● ● ● ● ● ● ● ● ● ● ● ● ● ● ● ● ● ● ● ● ● ● ● ● ● ● ● ● ● ●

## In This Chapter

▶ Figuring out COM ports

▶ Resolving irritating IRQ conflicts

▶ Avoiding DMA and address conflicts

▶ Yanking jumpers

▶ Flipping DIP switches

▶ Understanding the CMOS scene

● ● ● ● ● ● ● ● ● ● ● ● ● ● ● ● ● ● ● ● ● ● ● ● ● ● ● ● ● ● ● ● ● ● ● ● ● ● ● ● ● ● ● ●

*T*his is by far the book's scariest chapter. It's full of disturbing, psychoanalytical words like *conflicts* and *interrupts*. If your computer's acting normally, you don't need to bother with this chapter at all.

But if things start to go haywire after you install a new part — or if the part simply refuses to work — you need to muddle through this conflict and interrupt stuff.

See, some new parts will work as-is, right out of the box. Your computer embraces them like old friends and invites them to dinner, and nobody spills wine on the tablecloth.

Other new parts, however, can start arguing over territory with the older parts, and the resulting brawl can get ugly, fast. The solution? You need to change some of your computer's settings so each part can get its own space.

This chapter tells you how to change the settings on your computer, as well as on some of your newest gadgets. Tweak a few settings here and there, and nobody gets snubbed, especially you.

## My COM Ports Are Arguing!

Chapter 6 covers all you need to know about plugging a mouse or modem into a serial port. But you probably wound up in this section because of a DOS eccentricity: computer gadgets don't like to share serial ports.

If a gadget like a modem needs a serial port, it needs its *own* serial port. A mouse wants its own serial port, too. If you inadvertently set up two gadgets to use the same port, fisticuffs break out and neither gadget works.

Gadgets that plug into the back of your computer usually don't cause much of a problem. You can plug a mouse into one port, for example, and a modem into the other. As long as your mouse and modem software know which part's plugged into which port, everybody's happy. (Chapter 6 tells how to figure out which one's plugged into which port.)

But things get trickier when you plug cards inside your computer. For example, sometimes you plug an internal modem card inside your computer, but it doesn't work. Not only that, it knocks your once-healthy mouse out of commission, too.

That usually happens because the modem and mouse are fighting over the *same* serial port. They've both been told to use the same port, but when they try, they see the other part blocking the way.

The answer is to cajole the internal modem into using a different serial port. You usually do that by a moving a *jumper* or *DIP switch* on the modem's card — a relatively simple, anesthesia-free operation described later in this chapter.

Don't know what COM port to assign to your latest internal gadget? Let Table 17-1 be your guide.

### Table 17-1   What COM Port Should I Give My Internal Gadget?

| If Your Computer's Like This COM Port | Let Your Internal Gadget Use This |
|---|---|
| No COM ports at all | COM2 |
| Only COM1 is installed, but something's plugged into it | COM2 |
| Only COM2 is installed, but something's plugged into it | COM1 |
| Both COM1 and COM2 are installed, but something's plugged into COM1 | COM4 |
| Both COM1 and COM2 are installed, but something's plugged into COM2 | COM3 |
| Both COM1 and COM2 are installed, and something's plugged into both of them | Buy an A/B switch, described in the following section |
| Golly, I don't know what a COM port looks like or who's using it | Turn to Chapter 3 |

✔ A serial port and a COM port are the same thing: a "doorway" through which your computer passes information. If two gadgets try to pass information through the same doorway at the same time, everything gets stuck.

✔ Computers can access *four* serial ports, but there's a catch: only *two* of those ports can be used at the same time. You'll find two serial ports on the back of many computers. The bigger one is usually COM2; the smaller one is usually COM1. (You'll find sexy COM port pictures in Chapter 6.)

✔ If you assigned one gadget to COM1 and a second to COM2 but they're still fighting, try reversing them. Assign the second gadget to COM1 and the first to COM2.

✔ How do you assign a serial port — a COM port — to a gadget? Usually by checking its manual and moving the right jumpers or DIP switches, as described later in this chapter.

After you assign a COM port to your modem, you usually need to tell your modem software what COM port your modem's hogging. Some modem software is getting a little smarter, however; a few programs can find the right port all by themselves. It's about time, too.

✔ You can assign gadgets that plug inside your computer to COM3 and COM4. However, COM1 and COM3 can't be used at the same time, and COM2 and COM4 can't be used at the same time. Short attention span, those computers.

If you want a gadget to use either COM3 or COM4, you need DOS 3.3 or later. Otherwise, your computer's stuck with two serial ports, COM1 and COM2.

✔ Some older internal modems only like serial ports COM1 and COM2. If COM1 and COM2 are already being used, free up a port with an A/B switch, described in the following tip.

Don't have enough COM ports? Buy an *A/B serial port switch*. It's a little box with a switch on the front. You plug a cable from the box into one of your computer's COM ports. Then you plug two gadgets into the two ports on the box. For example, you can plug a serial printer into the box's A port and plug an external modem into the B port. To use the printer, you flip the box's switch to A. To use the modem, you flip the switch to B. Don't be surprised if you forget to flip the switch back to the printer when you want to print; everybody does.

✔ As you figure out which gadget's using which COM port, fill out Table 17-2. You'll save yourself the trouble of figuring everything out again the next time this hassle comes up.

| Table 17-2 | Who's Using My COM Ports? |
|---|---|
| *The Port* | *The Owner (Mouse, Modem, Scanner, or Other Gadget)* |
| COM1 | |
| COM2 | |
| COM3 | |
| COM4 | |

# How to Resolve Irritating IRQ Conflicts

Like squabbling siblings, computer gadgets often argue over *interrupt* rights.

Computers, like harried parents, concentrate on one thing at a time. When a parent's cooking dinner and a kid wants some attention, the kid pulls on the parent's pant leg. Computer gadgets work the same way. Computers have pant legs known as *interrupts*.

An interrupt, often dubbed an *IRQ,* is sort of a virtual pant leg that gadgets can tug on to get your computer's attention. When you move your mouse, for example, it tugs on one of your computer's pant legs — an interrupt — and tells the computer that it moved. The computer takes note and updates the mouse arrow's position on screen.

Just as a pair of pants has only two legs, a computer has a limited number of interrupts. And if two gadgets — a sound card and a scanner, for example — try to use the same interrupt, the harried computer doesn't know which one to listen to. So it usually ignores both of them and keeps on cooking dinner.

The solution is to assign a different interrupt — a different IRQ — to each gadget. Sounds simple enough, eh? But here's the problem: when you try to assign an interrupt to a new part, you find that gadgets like disk drives and keyboards have already grabbed most of the available interrupts for themselves, as you can see in the horribly technical Table 17-4.

✔ For such a laborious subject, interrupts have amazingly simple names. They're merely numbers, like 3 or 12.

✔ When a gadget wants an interrupt on an AT, 386, or faster computer, try assigning it to IRQ 5 or IRQ 7. If you're installing a gadget on a tired old PC or XT model, try IRQ 2 or IRQ 7.

✔ How do you assign an interrupt to a computer part? For the most part, by moving a jumper or flipping a DIP switch, a hobby described later in this chapter. Other gadgets let you choose interrupts from their installation software.

✔ If you inadvertently choose an interrupt that another part's already holding onto, nothing explodes. Your new gadget just doesn't work. Keep trying different interrupts until one finally works. It's like driving around in front of the grocery store until you find a place to park. The parking process can be bothersome, but it's quickly forgotten once you're inside, looking at the fresh strawberries.

✔ If you don't feel like using trial and error to find an unused interrupt, write down which interrupts your computer's gadgets are using. When a new IRQ-hungry part comes along, you'll know which interrupts are unavailable. Table 17-3 provides a handy spot to write down your IRQ assignments. Put the name of the part (such as *sound card* or *internal fax/modem*) in the first column and write down which IRQ the part snapped up in the second column.

**Table 17-3      My Computer Parts Use These IRQs**

| *This Gadget* | *Currently Uses This IRQ* |
| --- | --- |
| My internal modem | |
| My scanner | |
| My sound card | |
| | |
| | |
| | |

If you don't want to use the chart, at least write down the IRQ on the front of the gadget's manual. Chances are, you'll need to dish out that information to any software that wants to play with the gadget.

**Table 17-4    Interrupts and Who Usually Gets Them**

| Interrupt | Owner | Comments |
| --- | --- | --- |
| IRQ 0 | Timer | Your computer already grabbed this one. |
| IRQ 1 | Keyboard | Your computer already grabbed this one. (Your keyboard interrupts your computer each time you press a key.) |
| IRQ 2 | Some video cards on AT and faster computers | This one's usually up for grabs if you have an XT computer instead of an AT, 386, or faster computer. |
| IRQ 3 | COM 2, COM 4 | These two serial ports share this interrupt. (That's why you can't use both these COM ports at the same time.) |
| IRQ 4 | COM 1, COM 3 | These two serial ports share this interrupt. (That's why you can't use both these COM ports at the same time.) |
| IRQ 5 | Second printer port | Try this one on AT, 386, and faster computers. |
| IRQ 6 | Floppy disk controller | Your computer already grabbed this one. |
| IRQ 7 | First printer port | Try this one. |
| IRQ 8 | Your computer's clock | Your computer already grabbed this one. |
| IRQ 9 | Network stuff | This one *may* be free. |
| IRQ 10 | Nothing | This IRQ may be free, but gadgets rarely let you choose it. |
| IRQ 11 | Nothing | This one may be free, but gadgets rarely let you choose it. |
| IRQ 12 | Nothing | This one may be free, but gadgets rarely let you choose it. |
| IRQ 13 | Coprocessor | Your computer already grabbed this one. |
| IRQ 14 | Hard drive | Your computer already grabbed this one. |
| IRQ 15 | Nothing | This interrupt may be free, but gadgets rarely let you choose it. |

# *Address and DMA Stuff*

Some gadgets get greedy. They not only ask for things like an IRQ, described in the preceding section, but also for more arcane bits of weirdness such as an *address* or *DMA*.

Your computer assigns an address to some of its parts so it can find them later. Not all gadgets want or need their own addresses. But some newly installed gadgets ask for their own address and expect you to act as a knowledgeable Realtor.

Because your computer usually has plenty of addresses to spare, most gadgets simply choose an address at random, hoping nobody else is using it. But if some other gadget's already living at the address, the two parts start bickering and neither one works.

The same thing happens when a newly installed gadget grabs a DMA channel that another gadget already snagged. The new gadget simply won't work.

DMA stands for *Direct Memory Address channel.* But who cares?

A DMA channel lets a part squirt information directly into your computer's memory. That's why havoc breaks out if two parts try to squirt in the same place.

The solution is to change your new gadget's address or DMA. You usually need to fiddle with jumpers or DIP switches on a card in order to do this. But sometimes you can change the DMA and address through the gadget's installation software — you don't even need to pop off your computer's case.

Which address or DMA should you choose? Unfortunately, your best bet is the trial-and-error approach. Just keep trying different addresses or DMAs; it shouldn't take long to stumble upon a home that nobody's claimed.

You won't damage anything by inadvertently choosing the wrong address or DMA. Your gadget just won't work until you choose an address or DMA that's vacant.

After you choose a DMA or address, write it down on the front of the gadget's manual. You'll probably need to give that information to any software that wants to play with the gadget.

I/O addresses for *memory* and I/O addresses for *hardware* are different. Software (spreadsheet programs, word processors, and so on) looks for addresses in memory; hardware (sound cards, scanners, and the like) looks for hardware addresses. The two kinds of addresses — memory and hardware — are on completely different streets.

# Jumper Bumping and DIP Switch Flipping

Most people talk to their computer by typing on the keyboard. But sometimes you need to probe *deeper* into your computer's psyche. To talk to your computer on a "low grunt" level, you need to move around its little *jumpers* and *DIP switches.* By wiggling these little doodads around, you tell your computer parts to behave in different ways.

It's easy to change a gadget's jumpers or switches. All you need is the gadget's manual and a magnifying glass. These little switches are *tiny*.

## Moving jumpers around

A *jumper* is a little box that slides on or off little pins. By moving the little box around to different sets of pins, you instruct the computer part to act in different ways.

The part's manual will tell you what pins to fiddle with. The pins themselves have little labels next to them, giving you a fighting chance at finding the right ones.

For example, see the little numbers and letters next to the little pins in Figure 17-1? The jumper box is set across the two pins marked *J1.* That means the jumper is set for J1.

If the manual says to *set jumper J2,* slide the little box up and off the J1 pins and slide it down onto the pins marked *J2.* The pins then look like the ones shown in Figure 17-2.

Quick and easy. In fact, the concept was *too* easy for computer designers, so they complicated matters. Some jumpers don't use *pairs* of pins; instead, they use a single row of pins in a straight line, as shown in Figure 17-3.

In Figure 17-3, the jumper is set between pins 1 and 2. If the manual says to move the jumper to pins 2 and 3, slide the jumper up and off. Then slide it back down over pins 2 and 3, as shown in Figure 17-4.

By moving the little box from pin to pin, you can make the gadget use different settings. It's sort of a gearshift knob for computer circuitry.

**Figure 17-1:**
This jumper
is set for J1.

**Figure 17-2:**
This jumper
is set for J2.

**Figure 17-3:**
This jumper is set between pins 1 and 2.

1 2 3

**Figure 17-4:**
This jumper is set between pins 2 and 3.
1 2 3

- ✔ The hard part of moving jumpers is grabbing that tiny box thing so you can slide it on or off. A pair of tweezers or needle-nose pliers can help.

- ✔ Dropped the little box inside your computer? The last section of Chapter 2 offers tips on fishing out dropped obstacles.

If the manual says to remove a jumper, *don't* remove it! If you slide the little box off the pins, it will camouflage itself amid the paper clips in your desk drawer and you'll never find it again. Instead, leave the little box thing hanging on *one* prong, as shown in Figure 17-5. The computer will think you removed the jumper. But because the jumper's still attached to a pin, it's handy if you ever need to slide it back on.

- ✔ When the little box is over a pair of pins, that jumper circuit is considered *closed.* If the box is removed, that jumper is called *open.*

- ✔ Sometimes a jumper's little box comes with wires attached. For example, the wires leading from your computer's reset button probably push onto pins sticking up from your motherboard, as illustrated in Figure 17-6. That little wire thing can be pulled on or off, just like any other jumper. The wires stay connected to the little box; the little box just slides on and off.

  Don't know which wire should connect to which pin? Look for little numbers printed near base of the pins. The red wire always connects to pin #1.

- ✔ If you don't have a manual, how do you know which jumpers relate to which setting? You don't. You have three options: call the gadget's manufacturer and ask for a new manual; see if the store has a manual lying around; or keep moving the jumpers around until you stumble across the combination that works.

**Figure 17-5:**
If you're told to remove a jumper, just leave it dangling off one pin. That way it won't get lost and will be handy if you ever need it again.

J3
J2
J1

1 2 3

**Figure 17-6:**
Little wires connect to this jumper.

RESET
1 2

## *Flipping a DIP switch*

The first personal computer didn't have a keyboard. Its owners bossed it around by flipping dozens of tiny switches across the front of the computer's case. It took them a *long* time to balance the checkbook, but hey, they were pioneers.

Today's computer owners still have to flip little switches, but not nearly as often. And thank goodness! The few remaining switches have shrunken to microscopic level. In fact, they're too small to flip with your finger. You need a little paper clip or ballpoint pen to switch them back and forth.

These little switches are called *DIP switches.* Figure 17-7 shows a few different switch varieties.

See the little numbers next to each switch? And see how one side of the switch says *On*? When you push or flip a switch toward the On side, you turn on that numbered switch.

In Figure 17-7, for example, both DIP switches show switch numbers 4 and 6 turned on. All other switches are turned off.

✔ DIP switches and jumpers are pretty much on their way out. Some of the latest cards and motherboards let you control all the settings using software. The process is just as aggravating, but at least you don't need a magnifying glass.

Before flipping any DIP switches, draw a little picture of the way they're currently set. If something dreadful happens, you'll be able to flip them back to the way they were.

✔ The first DIP switch pictured in Figure 17-7 has *sliding* controls. You slide the little box toward *On* to turn on that numbered switch. Slide it away from *On* to turn it off.

✔ The second DIP switch in Figure 17-7 has *rocker* controls. You depress the switch toward *On* to turn on that numbered switch. Depress the switch *away* from *On* to turn it off.

**Figure 17-7:**
The first DIP
switch has
sliding controls;
the second has
rocker switches.

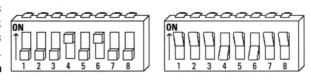

Feel free to flip a DIP switch with the tip of a ballpoint pen, but don't use a pencil. The tip of a pencil can break off and jam the switch, leading to much embarrassment.

✔ You need to flip DIP switches on almost *all* XT motherboards when you add memory.

✔ Although some 386 and 486 motherboards make you push around DIP switches, the switches show up mostly on cards. (Chapter 14 has all the card-playing instructions.)

✔ Some manufacturers felt that labeled switches were too easy for consumers to figure out. So they left out the words *On* and *Off* and put a little arrow on one edge of the switch. Just remember that the arrow points in the *On* direction.

✔ To further confuse things, some manufacturers use the word *Open* instead of *Off* and *Closed* instead of *On*.

✔ Some really offbeat manufacturers label their DIP switches with a *1* for *On* and *0* for *Off*.

Nobody needs to know that DIP stands for *Dual In-line Package*.

# *Sailing the CMOS Sea*

A CMOS, found in AT, 386, and faster computers, is like the sticker in the window of a new car. It lists the machine's most important accessories.

Instead of listing accessories like air conditioning and driver's side air bag, however, the CMOS (pronounced *see-moss*) keeps track of more computer-nerdish details: the size of your disk drives, the size of your hard drive, how much memory you could afford to buy, and other geekoid facts.

Old PC and XT computers don't have a CMOS. Instead, they keep track of what's inside themselves by looking at the way the DIP switches and jumpers are set on the motherboard. (DIP switches and jumpers got their due in the preceding section.)

A CMOS provides a much more convenient system. You can update it by typing stuff in from the keyboard. That's a lot faster than trying to figure out what DIP switches to flip after you've installed some extra memory.

✔ Your computer's CMOS remembers all this stuff even when the computer's turned off or unplugged. A little battery inside your computer keeps the information backed up on a tiny chip.

✔ If that little battery ever dies, however, the information in your CMOS disappears, giving your computer a bad case of amnesia. When you turn the computer on, it won't remember the time, or the date, or the fact that it has a hard drive. (You can find out how to replace a dead battery in Chapter 9.)

✔ You need to update your CMOS if you change your computer's battery, type of disk drives (floppy or hard), memory, motherboard, video card, math coprocessor, or a plethora of other parts. The next section provides more specific details.

✔ If you have an AT (286) computer, you probably need a CMOS disk or Setup disk to change your CMOS. The disk should have been packaged with your computer. Most IBM PS/2s come with a Setup disk as well.

Keep track of what's in your CMOS in case the battery ever dies. Table 17-5 provides a handy spot. Dunno what words like *Cyls, LZ,* and *RAM* mean? Those nerdy details are covered in the next section.

| Table 17-5 | My CMOS Says This Stuff |
|---|---|
| *This* | *Is Set Up Like This* |
| Drive A | (circle one line) |
| | Uses 1.44MB and 3½-inch disks |
| | Uses 1.2MB and 5¼-inch disks |
| | Uses 720K and 3½-inch disks |
| | Uses 360K and 5¼-inch disks |
| Drive B | (circle one line) |
| | Uses 1.44MB and 3½-inch disks |
| | Uses 1.2MB and 5¼-inch disks |
| | Uses 720K and 3½-inch disks |
| | Uses 360K and 5¼-inch disks |
| Drive C | Type ____ |
| | Cylinders ___ Heads ___ WPcomp ___ LZone ___ |
| | Sec __ Capacity ___ |

| This | Is Set Up Like This |
| --- | --- |
| Drive D | Type ____ |
| | Cylinders ___ Heads ___ WPcomp ___ LZone ___ |
| | Sec ___ Capacity ___ |
| Amount of RAM | Base memory _____ |
| | Extended memory _____ |
| Notes | |
| | |
| | |
| | |
| | |
| | |

# *How Do I Change My CMOS?*

Of course, it would be too simple if you could use the same method to update the CMOS in all computers. So here's a rundown of the most common ways to update your computer's master inventory list.

**Old PC or XT:** These oldsters don't have a CMOS. You have to pull off the case and move jumpers or DIP switches, as per the manual's instructions. Your computer looks at those jumpers and switches to figure out what's packed inside it.

**AT/286:** These computers usually come with a Setup program. It calls the CMOS information to the screen, where you can update it.

**386/486/586/Pentium:** These computers keep their CMOS information locked up inside a chip on your motherboard. You don't have to pry out the chip to change your CMOS, though. In fact, you don't have to pop the computer's cover, either.

Instead, you need to figure out what *secret access code* your CMOS uses. Different brands of computers use different codes, but the following paragraphs provide some of the more common ones. Give 'em all a shot before rooting through the file cabinet for your motherboard's manual. (The code is usually listed in the manual under *BIOS.*)

When you reboot your computer, look for words like these:

```
Press <DEL> If you want to run SETUP or DIAGS
```

If you see that message, press Delete quickly, before the message disappears. If you press Delete before the message clears, you're in: your computer brings its master list of parts and settings to the screen. It may look something like the CMOS shown in Figure 17-8.

Other computers take different approaches. On my Dell 450DE, I press Ctrl, Alt, and Enter simultaneously at the C:\> prompt. The screen clears, and the CMOS appears, as shown in Figure 17-9.

On my wife's 486 clone, I press Ctrl, Alt, and Esc simultaneously to access the CMOS screen.

If none of these tricks works for you, it's time to grab the manual for your computer or its motherboard.

Got the CMOS up on the screen? The following list covers things you need to change:

**Battery:** When you change your computer's battery, your CMOS turns off like a flashlight. It won't remember anything when you turn it on, so you have to re-enter all the information. Hopefully you entered the most important stuff in Table 17-5 before the battery died. If not, then make sure that you tackle every item in this list.

```
              C M O S     S E T U P
==============================================
Current date is ................... 09-09-93
Enter new date (MM-DD-YYYY)? ..... 09-09-93
Current time is ................... 14:59:24
Enter new time (HH:MM:SS)? ....... 14:59:30
Primary display is ............... Color display
Current screen width is .......... 80 columns


Fixed disk drive C type .......... 14
Fixed disk drive D type .......... Not installed
Diskette drive A is .............. 1.2 MB, 5¼" drive
Diskette drive B is .............. 1.44 MB, 3½" drive
Base memory size is .............. 640 KB
Expansion memory size is ......... 7168 KB
OS/2,RAMDISK support option (1/2)? 1
Numeric processor ................ Present
80287 or 80387 (1/2)? ............ 1

Are these options correct (Y/N)? _
```

**Figure 17-8:** This CMOS screen appeared on a computer when the user pressed Delete immediately after rebooting.

```
                         Dell Computer Corporation
      Screen 1 of 2              System 450DE Setup

      Time:  15:12:25   Date: Sun  Jun  6, 1993   │ This category sets the time in
                                                   │ 24-hour format (hours:minutes:
        Diskette Drive A:    3.5 inch, 1.44 MB     │ seconds) for the built-in system
        Diskette Drive B:    5.25 inch, 1.2 MB     │ clock.

      Hard Drives  Type  Cyls  Hds  Pre  LZ   Sec  │ To change the value in a field,
        Drive 0:    46    683   16   -1  683   38   │ enter digits or use the left- or
        Drive 1:    39    919   16   -1  919   17   │ right-arrow key to decrease or
                                                    │ increase the value.
            Base Memory:        640 KB             │
            Board Memory:       640 KB             │ Changes take effect immediately.
         Fast Video BIOS:       On                 │
         Extended Memory:       11264 KB           │
             CPU Cache:         On                 │

            CPU Speed:          50 MHz            ├─────────────────────────────────
             Num Lock:          On                │        System BIOS: A09
         Speaker Volume:        High              │         Video BIOS: Disabled
                                                  │    Math Coprocessor: Internal
                                                  │       Total Memory: 12288 KB

      TAB,SHIFT-TAB change fields|←,→ change values|Alt-P page|Esc exit|Alt-B reboot
```

**Figure 17-9:** This CMOS screen appears on my Dell 450DE when I press Ctrl-Alt-Enter at the C:\> prompt.

**Time/Date:** Because your CMOS has a constant battery backup, it's a convenient place to keep track of the current time and date. You can change the time and date here. Or you can change the time and date simply by typing **TIME** or **DATE** at any C:\> prompt.

**Floppy drives:** The CMOS usually lets you choose between four different types of floppy drives, all listed in Table 17-5. If you swapped the cables between your drive A and drive B, be sure to swap the drive's settings in your CMOS, too. You won't be able to choose the higher-density disk drives in some of those old XTs, though. You may have to upgrade your computer's BIOS (Chapter 9) or get a new *controller card* (Chapter 11).

**Hard drives:** If you're lucky, you'll find a Type number for your hard drive somewhere in your hard drive's manual. Put that number — which is usually between 1 and 47 — into the hard drive's Type column.

Can't find a Type number? Well, if you're using an IDE drive, try choosing the Type number of any drive that comes closest to, but not over, the capacity of your hard drive.

Not using an IDE drive? Then you're stuck with the agonizing technical details in the following sidebar, "Cylinders, Heads, and Other Hard Drive Hazards."

If you don't like agonizing details, head to the store and buy a hard disk installation program such as SpeedStor or EZ-Drive. These programs can prevent a lot of aggravation by handling the most onerous installation chores.

## Cylinders, heads, and other hard drive hazards

If you can't find a Type number listed either in the hard drive's manual or your CMOS, you have to dig through the manual for numbers assigned to these words: Number of cylinders (Cyls), Number of heads (Hds), Write PreCompensation (W-PComp), Landing Zone (LZone), Sectors (Sec), and Capacity (Size).

Then you have to enter those numbers in the user-defined area of the CMOS hard drive chart. You can usually get there by entering Type number 47 or 48 and filling in the blanks.

Can't find these numbers? Check with the store where you bought the drive or call the drive's technical support line. You also can try calling a local BBS via your modem and asking if somebody has the same kind of disk drive. You'll be able to track the numbers down eventually. If you can't, consider buying a hard drive installation program, described earlier.

**Memory:** Your CMOS needs to know when you pop in some more memory chips, but the job's pretty easy.

See, your computer *automatically* counts all the available memory whenever you turn it on or reset it. If your computer's quick little tally doesn't match the tally currently stored in your CMOS, your computer gets cautious: it sends out an error message and says to update your CMOS through the setup.

You merely have to call up your CMOS setup and confirm that yes, the computer *did* count up the memory total correctly — the numbers didn't match because you added some more memory! Sometimes, the CMOS already reflects the computer's new count; you just have to save the new total and exit the CMOS screen.

Some older motherboards make you flip a DIP switch to show how much memory you added. If you don't flip the switch, these motherboards won't be able to find the memory. (They won't even bother looking for it, either.) Check your motherboard's manual to figure out which DIP switches to flip. You'll probably still have to update the CMOS setting for those lazy little beggars.

The CMOS of a 286, 386, or faster computer usually calls your first 640K of memory *base* memory; it calls the rest of it *extended* or *expansion* memory.

**Motherboard:** When you buy a new motherboard, you're going to be dealing with a different CMOS, too. Before removing the old motherboard, call up its CMOS settings and write them down. Then enter the same settings into the new motherboard's CMOS.

Some of the latest motherboards have several pages of advanced settings that are far too authoritarian for this easy-going book.

However, make sure that you turn on any memory caches. Your computer will run much faster. If you're searching for speed, try turning on some of the *ROM shadows;* if you run into trouble, change the setting back. It's important to make your changes *one at a time* so you can identify the culprit if your computer freaks out after a change. Just turn that ROM shadow back off, and all will be well.

**Math coprocessor:** Some computers automatically recognize a newly installed math coprocessor. Others can't figure it out for themselves. Some can't even tell if you installed a 287 or a 387 coprocessor. Fill out the appropriate line in the CMOS, and the computer should recognize your new chip. If it doesn't, you may need to flip some switches or move some jumpers on your motherboard. That means it's time to dig out the manual.

**Display:** Sometimes, you have to update the CMOS when you install a new video card. Usually, you only have to choose between *monochrome* or *color.* Some picky systems make you choose between *CGA* or *EGA/VGA.* And some picky motherboards make you flip one of their switches or move a jumper.

After you change a CMOS setting, look for a menu item that *saves* your changes. If you don't specifically tell the CMOS to save your changes, all your work will be for naught.

✔ Most computers don't let you access your CMOS while you're working in Windows. You usually need to be at the C:\> prompt before any of those weird access-code key combinations take effect.

✔ After you update your CMOS and tell it to change the information, your computer either resets itself or tells you to punch the reset button. When the computer comes back to life, it should recognize your new part.

# Part V
# The Part of Tens

## In this part . . .

Those of you with sharp eyes will realize something scandalous right away: Some of the lists in this section don't contain ten items. Actually, very few of them do. Most have a wee bit more information or a wee bit less.

But by the time most people get to this part of the book, they're tired of counting numbers anyway. In fact, these lists *aren't* numbered. They're just a bunch of facts tossed into the basket.

So when you read these lists, remember that it's quality, not quantity, that matters. Besides, would you want to read a fake tip about 8255 PPI (U20) just because one of the lists needed a tenth tip?

# Chapter 18
# Ten Cheap Fixes to Try First

## In This Chapter

▶ Making sure that the computer's plugged in

▶ Turning the computer on and off again

▶ Removing disks before booting up your computer

▶ Checking for overheating

▶ Booting from a system disk

▶ Reseating chips, cards, and connectors

▶ Cleaning card connectors with a pencil eraser

▶ Installing a new power supply

▶ Running CHKDSK

*B*efore spending any money at the shop, try these cheap fixes on your computer. You might get lucky. If you're not lucky, give yourself a good stretch and flip back to Chapter 4 for some more system-sleuthing tips.

## Plug It In

Sure, it sounds silly. But industry experts get paid big bucks to say it's the leading cause of "electrical component malfunction." Check your PC's power cord in *two* places: it not only can creep out of the wall outlet, but also out of the back of your computer.

Sometimes a yawning leg stretch can inadvertently loosen the cord from the wall. Rearranging a computer on the desk almost always loosens cables that aren't screwed tightly into the back of the computer.

And, uh, the machine's turned on, isn't it? (That's the leading cause of printer malfunction, by the way.)

# Turn the Computer Off, Wait 30 Seconds, and Turn It Back On

Sometimes the computer just gets confused for no apparent reason. If your computer's drifted off into oblivion, with no return in sight, try tapping the spacebar a few times. Try pressing Esc.

Sill no return? Then it's time to get ugly. The next few steps mean you'll lose any work that hasn't been saved to either your hard disk or a floppy disk.

- Try rebooting the computer: press the Ctrl, Alt, and Delete keys simultaneously.
- If the computer's still acting like an ice cube, head for the next level of attention grabbing: press the reset button.
- If the computer's *still* counting marbles on some virtual playground, turn it off. Then wait 30 seconds. (That 30-second part is important.) Finally, turn the computer back on and see if it returns in a better mood.

You'd be surprised how much good a little 30-second vacation can accomplish.

# Remove Your WordPerfect Floppy and Then Turn On Your Computer

Ever turn on the computer only to be greeted by a message like this?

```
Non-System disk or disk error
Replace and press any key when ready
```

Chances are, you got that message because a floppy disk is sitting in drive A, where it's confusing the computer's start up process.

Remove the floppy and, as the saying goes, "press any key when ready." A tap of the spacebar does the trick. Your computer returns to life.

# Check for Overheating

Nobody likes to work when it's too hot, and your computer's no exception. Your computer normally works naked, but after a few months it wears a thick coat of dust.

Your first step is to look at the fan's round grill on the back of the computer. See all the dust flecks clinging to the grill, swapping barbecue stories? Wipe them off with a rag, being careful to keep the worst grunge from falling inside.

Don't just *blow* on them, either. The microscopic flecks of spittle in your breath can cause problems with the computer's moisture-sensitive internal components.

Don't tape cards or "cheat sheets" across the front of your PC's case. That can block your PC's air vents, which are disguised as avant-garde ridges across the front of the case. When air can't circulate inside your PC, your computer heats up in a hurry.

Don't keep your computer pushed up against the wall. It needs some breathing room so its fan can blow out all the hot air from inside the case.

# Boot from a System Floppy Disk

If a program says it needs more memory to run, try booting it from a system disk. That makes your computer bypass its AUTOEXEC.BAT and CONFIG.SYS files and run as cleanly as possible.

System disks, described in Chapter 2, contain nothing but the bare-bones basics required to make your computer run. Sometimes they're all a program needs.

After making the disk as described in Chapter 2, put it in drive A and reboot your computer. Then try running your recalcitrant program. When you're done running the program, remove any disk from drive A and reboot your computer to bring things back to normal.

# Reseat Cards, Chips, and Connectors

When your computer's been running for a while, it heats up and expands. When you turn your computer off, it cools off and contracts. This constant expanding and contracting can play subtle tricks on your computer's internal components. Specifically, it can make those internal parts slide out of their little compartments.

If your computer acts up, turn it off, remove the case, and give all the cards a little extra push into their slots. Give the chips a little extra push into their sockets as well. That can cure memory errors. While you're in there, make sure that all those internal cables are plugged snugly into their connectors.

Sometimes taking this step clears up some intermittent problems, especially the ones that appear after the computer's been turned on for a while.

# Clean Card Connectors with a Pencil Eraser

Is your computer still acting up, even after you pushed the cards a little more deeply into their sockets? Then try this:

1. **Turn off your PC, unplug it, and remove its cover.**

   If you've never gone spelunking inside your computer before, check the cheat sheet at the front of this book. It offers complete cover-removal tips.

2. **Unscrew one of the cards and remove any cables from it.**

   You'll find complete instructions in Chapter 14. Basically, you need to remove that little screw along the top that holds the card in place. Then unscrew or pull out any cables connected to the card.

3. **Pull the card from its slot and clean the card's contacts.**

   Pull the card straight up out of its slot, being careful not to damage any of the electronic gizmos hanging on to it. It's best to handle the card by its edges with clean hands.

   Now, see the little copper-colored connectors on the card "tab" that plugs into the slot? Take a pencil eraser and carefully rub it against the tab until the copper-colored connectors look shiny.

   Be careful not to bend the card while cleaning the contacts; doing so can damage the card.

**4. Replace the card and cables. Then repeat the process with the next card.**

By removing any corrosion from the cards, you let your computer talk to them more efficiently.

Be sure to screw the cards back in. That single screw provides an electrical connection between the card and the computer.

# Install a New Power Supply

When older computers simply refuse to turn on and do anything fun, it's probably because the power supply died.

Power supplies have gotten increasingly reliable over the past few years. Still, be sure to replace the power supply, which costs less than $100, before replacing the entire motherboard, which always costs *more* then $100.

Chapter 13 provides complete power-supply replacement instructions.

# Run the Weird-Sounding CHKDSK Program

Here's a quick fix that's free! If your computer's sending weird error messages or you're running out of hard disk space, give this trick a try. It doesn't hurt anything, and it can often help.

Type the following command at the C:\> prompt:

```
C:\> CHKDSK /F
```

That is, type **CHKDSK,** a space, a forward slash, and **F.** Your computer responds with some computer jargon. But if the program asks you whether you want to Convert lost chains to files (Y/N)?, press Y.

Your computer then gathers any file scraps and stores them in files with names like FILE000.CHK, FILE001.CHK, FILE002.CHK — you get the picture. Feel free to delete those files. They don't contain anything worthwhile, as you'll soon discover if you try to open them with your word processor.

If your computer doesn't ask you for permission to convert lost chains to files, CHKDSK won't fix anything for you — it didn't find anything wrong.

Still, feel free to run CHKDSK /F every couple of weeks, especially if your computer was turned off while a program was still running.

# Chapter 19
# The Ten Hardest Upgrades

*In This Chapter*

▶ Upgrading older computers like the PC, XT, or PCjr

▶ Adding internal modems

▶ Putting in a motherboard

▶ Adding a second hard drive

▶ Adding more memory

*E*verybody wants to save money by avoiding the computer repair shop. But how can you tell which fix-it jobs you can do on your dining room table and which ones require experienced technicians who work in sterile rooms, drinking out of Batman coffee cups while holding expensive probe things with curly wires?

Turn to this chapter when trying to decide whether *you* should hold the screwdriver or pass the job on to somebody else.

## Upgrading Ancient Computers Like the Original IBM PC, XT, or PCjr

Unfortunately, the computers most in need of upgrading are the hardest machines to upgrade. These oldsters set the stage for everything to come.

But just as the Wright brothers would have trouble finding parts for their old Kitty Hawk cruiser, you'll have increasing trouble finding parts for your old IBM PC, XT, or PCjr. These computers won't accept most of the latest cards. They're too old to run most of the latest software, too. You can forget about Windows and OS/2.

Sure, you can scrap together a few parts here and there from garage sales and mail-order outfits. After all, the Wright brothers built their airplane from scratch in their bike shop. But if you decide to keep your oldster going, you're tossing your money down a hole. Consider saving your money and buying a new computer. That's usually cheaper than keeping the old one running.

So what do you do with your old computer when you get the new one? Hang onto it. It's destined to be a collectible.

- ✔ A German calculator from the 1820s fetched $11.8 million at Christie's in London, a record auction price for a scientific instrument. How many calculators have you thrown away in the past ten years? (Including the free ones that come with magazine subscriptions?)

- ✔ The Altair, the first personal computer, is now selling for thousands of dollars as a collector's item.

- ✔ Your old computer may have to be passed down for several generations before it can be cashed in as a collectible. And your great-grandchildren will always remember you as a technoweenie. But at least they'll be able to live comfortably.

# Installing Those Confounded Internal Modems

Ask any grizzled, back-room repair shop technician about the computer upgrade that causes the most problems. The words *internal modems* will be mumbled with the fullest force.

Modems toss out obstacle after obstacle. You need to plug them into the right place on your computer and make sure that the modem's software is working. Then you need to make sure that the software's working on the other side — on the computer you're trying to call. And all the while, the phone line itself can toss in some glitches, with occasional crackling sounds or background voices.

With an internal modem, the problems loom larger. Is the modem card pushed far enough into its slot? Is it assigned the right COM port, one that no other parts have already staked out? Many internal modems don't even label their telephone jacks, so you can't tell whether or not you plugged the phone cord into the right jack.

Yes, internal modems cause the most headaches of any upgrade by far. (However, you can cut through most of the fat by checking out Chapter 14 and then flipping to Chapter 17 if the thing doesn't work.)

# *Replacing the Motherboard*

Conceptually, replacing a motherboard isn't too difficult. You merely unscrew one part and screw a new part in its place. The problem comes with all the stuff that's *attached* to the motherboard.

It's like replacing the shelves in a bedroom closet. The project sounds simple at first: just pull out the long board that's sagging over all the shirts and bolt some newer, fancier shelves in its place. Unfortunately, you have to remove *everything* from the closet — all those shirts, hangers, and boxes of old checkbooks must come down from the top shelf.

Then after the new shelves are up, all that stuff has to go back on. And if you upgraded the shelves, everything's going to be put back in a different location.

When you replace your computer's motherboard, you can simply screw it in using the same screws that held down the old motherboard. But all the little wires will plug onto slightly different connectors. You'll have to move little DIP switches and jumpers around, too. And where does the speaker wire connect? The reset button wire?

Then you have to put all the cards back in their slots, with all the right cables plugged into the back of them. Finally, you have to fill out a new CMOS — your computer's master inventory list. Chances are, it'll be filled with new, upgraded words like `Fast Gate A20 Option`.

No, replacing the motherboard is not for the squeamish. Unless you have a lot of patience, leave it for the folks at the shop. Besides, you can't even add a new motherboard to most XTs; the latest motherboards won't fit inside an XT case.

The Fast Gate A20 Option makes IBM's OS/2 operating system run better, by the way.

# Adding a Second Hard Drive to an Older First Hard Drive

Hard drives have made some great advances in the past few years. Unfortunately, they've also left their predecessors in the dust. Most new hard drives don't get along with the older-style hard drives. To install one of the newer IDE hard drives, you'll probably have to yank out your old drive. The two kinds of drives just don't like to work together.

Adding a second IDE drive to your first IDE drive can sometimes be a problem, too. In fact, your best bet is to buy your second IDE drive from the same manufacturer as the first. That usually guarantees that the two drives will be happy roommates.

When buying a second hard drive, make sure that the salesperson lets you bring it back for a refund if it doesn't get along with your first hard drive.

# Adding Memory to an Old Motherboard

Sometimes a stroke of good fortune greets you when you lift off your computer's case and peer at its motherboard: you find some empty sockets that are ready to accept new memory chips. Other times, you're in for a disappointment. All your computer's memory sockets are already stuffed full of chips.

However, you can *still* add more memory to your computer; that's not the disappointing part. The disappointing part is that you have to *remove* your old chips and replace them with memory chips that have a higher capacity. For example, you have to yank out all eight rows of 256K memory chips — your existing 2MB of memory — and replace them with eight rows of 1MB chips in order to upgrade your computer to 8MB of memory.

Sure, this upgrades your computer to 8MB, and Windows runs much faster. But you're stuck with a handful of 256K chips and no place to put them. If you're lucky, your local chip merchant will let you trade in your older chips, giving you a discount on the new ones. Otherwise, you'll do what everybody else does: stick them in a Ziploc baggie and keep 'em in a drawer somewhere.

Another alternative is to buy a memory card to add more memory to your computer. The card will work more slowly, however, and probably cost just as much as adding memory chips. If you have a tired old XT, however, it's pretty much your only alternative; those old XTs don't have room for any more memory chips on the motherboard.

# Chapter 20
# The Ten Easiest Things to Upgrade

*In This Chapter*

▶ Keyboards

▶ Mice

▶ Cards

▶ Monitors

▶ Floppy drives

▶ Power supplies

▶ MS-DOS

**S**ome of the most effective automobile upgrades are the easiest. You can simply hang some dice from the rearview mirror, for example. It looks cool, it's cheap, and you don't have to read any complicated manual to figure out which direction the dice should hang.

A few computer upgrades are almost as easy. They're collected and listed here for your upgrading pleasure.

## Adding a Keyboard

By far, the easiest computer part to upgrade is the keyboard. Just turn off your computer, pull the keyboard's plug out of your computer, and take your old, coffee-soaked keyboard to the computer store. Buy another one just like it, plug it back into your computer, turn the computer on, and keep typing, being careful to keep the coffee cup a little farther away this time.

You do need to make sure that the little plugs on the end of the cables match and that the number of keys match. If your old keyboard had 101 keys, the new one should have 101 keys as well. The salesperson will be able to tell at a glance what type of replacement you need, so don't bother counting the keys.

Unlike other upgrades, adding a keyboard doesn't involve fiddling with any software, tools, or files. Just plug and play. Yay! Oh, and see Chapter 5 for some more keyboard information — you may be able to fix the keyboard instead of replacing it.

# Adding a Mouse

Adding a mouse can get a little tricky, but usually it's a pretty easy upgrade.

Chances are, you have a COM port on the back of your computer. (Look in Chapter 3 for a picture of a COM port.) If nothing's plugged into the port, just plug in your new mouse and run the little creature's installation program. You don't have to take off your computer's case and run the risk of letting the snakes out. Quick and easy.

You'll find more mice stuff dissected in Chapter 6.

# Adding Cards

Cards often get a bum rap. Adding cards sounds scary because you have to take off your computer's case. Then you have to decipher that inside-the-case vocabulary, which includes words like *slots* and *8-bit* and *16-bit*.

But for the most part, installing a card is pretty simple. Physically, it's kind of like pushing a credit card into an ATM machine. That, and tightening a single screw, is the whole procedure.

Most cards are designed to work with a wide variety of computers. So unless your computer's set up a little differently than most, the card probably will work right off the bat. If it doesn't, head for Chapter 17. You'll find information to help you figure out what the card's manual means when it says to *set DIP switches 2, 4, and 5 to On,* and *set jumpers J2 and J4.*

It's a *lot* easier than it sounds. Promise.

# *Replacing a Monitor*

Adding a new monitor is another easy upgrade, as long as you understand one key point: Monitors work in pairs with *video cards*. Video cards are the things that live inside your computer and give the monitor a place to plug into.

Your video card is responsible for creating an image and spitting it out. Your monitor merely grabs that image and puts it on the screen for you to show your friends. If you're looking to upgrade your monitor, you'll probably want to upgrade your video card as well. Otherwise, your new monitor probably will display the same image that your old monitor displayed.

✔ Even if you buy a huge monitor to go with your VGA video card, for example, you won't be able to see any more information on your screen. The Windows Program Manager will still fill the entire screen, and your windows will still overlap, just as they did on your other monitor.

✔ The solution? Buy your video card at the same time you buy your monitor. Then you can be sure that your monitor can display the highest quality image that the card can spit out.

✔ You'll probably have to buy a new card with that new monitor anyway because some of the newer monitors won't even plug into older video cards.

✔ You'll find more of this video card/monitor stuff in Chapters 7 and 14.

# *Installing a Floppy Drive*

Floppy drives are a snap to install — *unless* you're trying to install a newer, high-capacity floppy drive into an old IBM PC or XT. Those old guys just can't stand the pressure, and you'll have to add a whole bunch of reinforcement parts before they can handle it.

In other computers, new floppy drives simply slide on in. In fact, one of the most popular upgrades these days is installing those new *combo drives*. (You can see a picture of a combo drive in Chapter 11.) These drives squeeze a large, 5¼-inch floppy drive and a 3½-inch floppy drive into a single floppy drive.

By combining the two floppy drives into one little unit, you free up enough room to stick in a new hard drive, a tape backup unit, a compact disc player, or a pencil holder. And best of all, the double-decker drives are easy to install. Details abound in Chapter 11.

# Adding a Power Supply

Power supplies come in zillions of sizes, but even so, adding a power supply is an easy upgrade. How come? Because you install all power supplies in pretty much the same way.

Just unscrew the old one, making sure to save the screws. Then disconnect all the power supply's wires (write down where the different wires connect before you remove them).

Next, drag the old power supply into the store and get another one that's the exact same size. Screw the new power supply in and reconnect the wires. You're done! (You'll find *complete* instructions in Chapter 13.)

While you're shopping, consider buying a power supply with a higher wattage, as discussed in Chapter 13.

Don't ever try to repair or take apart power supplies. They soak up electricity like a sponge and can give you a serious zap if you poke around inside them.

# Upgrading to the Latest Version of DOS

These days, it's easy to upgrade to the latest version of DOS. MS-DOS 6 comes with a built-in installation program that handles all the dirty work.

If you're serious about upgrading your computer, make sure you're running the most recent version of DOS as well. Most of the newest parts are designed around the latest version of DOS. In fact, some of them won't even work unless you're running the latest version.

So minimize your installation problems by running the newest version of DOS. The only difficulty you'll have will be getting the impetus to head to the store and finally buy it.

# Chapter 21
# Ten Ways to Make Your PC Run Better

## In This Chapter

▶ Buying utility programs

▶ Keeping track of your computer's CMOS information

▶ Adding more memory

▶ Buying a graphics accelerator card

▶ Not smoking around your PC

▶ Keeping the Turbo switch on

▶ Avoiding the cheapest parts

▶ Avoiding turning your PC on and off quickly

▶ Keeping your old parts

*I*f you're in an office somewhere and some tired-looking person is responsible for looking after your computer, don't bother browsing through this chapter. That person is paid to keep your PC running smoothly and probably already knows the tricks in this chapter.

But if *you're* the one who has to handle the screwdriver, this chapter's designed to keep it locked up in the toolbox for as long as possible. It shows you some simple ways to keep your computer healthy and happy.

## Buy Some Utility Programs

The words *utility program* reek with a nerdish aroma. Utility programs aren't designed to let people do things; they're designed to let the *computer* do things. What a bore!

That's why the nerds are snapping them up. Norton Utilities, for example, comes with a hard disk defragmentation program. Described more fully in Chapter 12, the defragmentation program organizes your hard drive more logically so the computer doesn't have to work as hard to grab stuff off the drive. Because the computer isn't working as hard, it's less likely to break down.

Bundles of utilities also contain diagnostic programs to help you figure out why your computer's suddenly gone on strike. Still others can examine the way your computer's memory was set up and offer suggestions to make it run faster or smoother.

## Write Down Your CMOS Information

This tip's described in Chapter 17, but it's important enough to emphasize here. Your computer's CMOS works like its secretary. It keeps track of all the parts currently installed inside your computer. Should something happen to your CMOS information, your computer will be as lost as a blue-suited executive whose secretary leaves for three weeks.

Call up your computer's CMOS and copy it into the chart in Chapter 17 while the information's safe. If something dreadful happens, you'll be glad you did.

## Buy More RAM

The advertising on the Windows box says that Windows needs 2MB of RAM. But if you listen to the Windows box, you'll also be listening to your hard drives whir and grind. With only 2MB of RAM, Windows constantly shuffles information back and forth from your hard drive.

If you're using Windows, upgrade to at least 4MB of RAM; better still, upgrade to 8MB. Windows will run faster and smoother. You'll also be able to run more programs at the same time, all the while shifting information between them. And that's the whole point of Windows.

# Buy a Graphics Accelerator Card

Another quick way to add some spunk to Windows is to buy a graphics *accel-erator card.* These small, quick video cards shoulder the burden of updating the screen when you move little windows around on the screen.

That doesn't sound like much to get excited about. But when you see the difference it makes on your screen, you'll be surprised at all the extra zip you get from an accelerator card.

# Don't Smoke around Your PC

You can tell a lot about a PC's owner by looking inside its case. Computer repair folks can quickly tell when someone's been smoking around a PC.

The PC's fan constantly sucks air into the case and blows it out the back to keep the machine cool. If the air's filled with smoke, the PC's internal organs soon are covered with smoke, too.

So smoke outdoors. Ride a horse like the Marlboro man or toss a hat in the air like the Virginia Slims woman. If you can't smoke outdoors, clean the inside of your PC's case regularly. Remove the case and use a can of compressed air to blow away all the gunk, as described in Chapter 2.

# Keep the Turbo Switch On

This one's simple, yet it makes a big difference. Most newer PCs have a *turbo switch* along the front of the case. Don't think that pushing the button puts your PC into high-speed turbo mode. The switch turns *off* the turbo mode.

Look for the little turbo light along the front of the case. When the turbo light's on, the turbo mode is on, too; your computer's already running as fast as its legs will carry it.

# Avoid Really Cheap Parts

When buying computer parts, you'll inevitably come across three brands of parts that look the same and claim to do the same thing. One will be priced sky-high, the other will cost less than dry cat food, and the other will be priced somewhere in the middle.

Don't buy the *cheapest* parts. They're made with the cheapest ingredients tossed together in the cheapest way. They may save you money in the short run, but they cost you in the long run.

For example, the cheapest floppy disks can coat your floppy drives with gunk after a few years of use. The cheapest hard drives won't last as long as the slightly more expensive ones. And the cheapest cables (usually found on the cheapest mice) fall apart more quickly than others costing just a few dollars more.

In addition, some of the cheapest parts aren't as compatible with your other computer parts as the more expensive brands. Finally, if something goes wrong with a cheap part, you'll usually find that its manufacturer has either gone out of business or doesn't have a technical support staff who'll listen to you.

# Don't Flip the Computer On and Off a Lot

Computers tend to go bad when stressed. Because computers don't worry about credit card interest rates, car stereo thieves, or public restrooms, their most stressful experience comes when they're first powered up and a jolt of electricity flashes through them.

To ease the strain, don't turn a computer on and off repeatedly like you did to make "livingroom lightning" as a kid. After you turn your computer off, wait 30 seconds before turning it back on again.

Computers also get stressed when the temperature changes. They heat up when they're running, and they cool down when they're turned off. This makes them expand and contract, no matter how slightly. The expansion and contraction can lead to subtle cracks in the motherboard as well as to "chip creep" — parts slowly lifting themselves from their sockets.

If you live in an area where the temperature varies widely, keep your computer turned on all the time. That keeps it running at a constant temperature.

# Hang on to Your Old Parts for Emergencies

When you upgrade to a newer or fancier computer part, keep your old one in a closet somewhere. Then you'll have something to help test your computer when things go wrong.

For example, I put a new motherboard in my wife's computer, but it wouldn't boot up. Each time I rebooted, the screen came up blank. So I pulled out the video card and stuck in an older video card from yesteryear. The computer worked!

Of course, I spent two hours trying dozens of other tricks before stumbling onto the fact that her new motherboard simply didn't get along with the newer video card. But because I still had my three-year-old video card in the closet, I could fix her computer myself; I didn't need to take it into the shop.

✔ Duplicate parts always come in handy when you're trying to figure out what's wrong with a computer. By swapping different parts one by one, you can eventually isolate the part that's stirring up trouble.

✔ Store your old cards in a Ziploc bag; if they're too big, store them in Saran Wrap or its generic equivalent. Storing cards in this way helps prevent any damage from static electricity.

✔ Got an old monitor in the closet? You may be able to plug it into a laptop to provide a better screen when you're working at your desk.

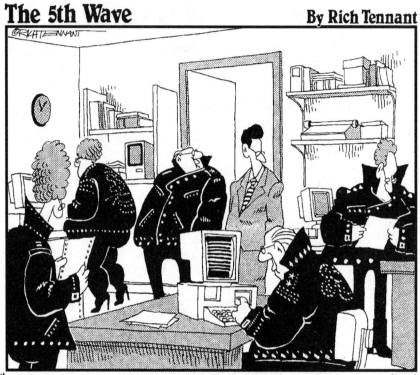

The 5th Wave                                    By Rich Tennant

"A CONSULTANT TOLD US THAT POLYESTER CAN CAUSE SHORTS IN THE SYSTEM, SO WE'RE TRYING AN ALL LEATHER AND LATEX DATA ENTRY DEPARTMENT."

# Chapter 22

## Ten Confusing Things Your Computer May Say When You Turn It On

●●●●●●●●●●●●●●●●●●●●●●●●●●●●●●●●●●●●●●●●●●●●●●●●●●●●●

### In This Chapter

▶ Bunches of confusing little messages

▶ that pop up on your screen

▶ when you first turn on your computer,

▶ as well as tips

▶ on what you're supposed to do to fix them.

●●●●●●●●●●●●●●●●●●●●●●●●●●●●●●●●●●●●●●●●●●●●●●●●●●●●●

*W*hen you first turn on your computer and it wakes up, it scurries around looking at all its parts. If it finds something wrong, it tells you. Unfortunately, it doesn't tell you in English. It sends you some complicated observation about its internal mechanics and then stops working.

This chapter offers some translations for the most common boot-up messages you may see frozen on your screen.

## What Do Those Little Numbers Mean?

Some of the genuine IBM computers and a few older clones just flash some code numbers on the screen if they're having problems getting on their feet. They don't bother listing any more helpful details about what's bothering them and what they'd like you to do about it. Table 22-1 explains what some of those cryptic numbers mean and also tells you which chapters offer more information about fixing the problem.

One note about the table: See how the codes have the letter *X* in them, as in *1XX*? The X stands for *any* number. The code 1XX can mean any three-digit number starting with the number 1, such as 122, 189, or something similar.

Also, some computers flash words on-screen along with the numbers. These words are deciphered in the next section.

### Table 22-1    Numeric Codes and What They Mean

| This Code | Usually Means This Is Acting Up | Comments |
|---|---|---|
| 02X | Power supply | You may need to replace your power supply, described in Chapter 13. |
| 1XX | Motherboard | These numbers often translate to expensive problems. Look up any of your computer's other symptoms in Chapters 23 and 24; Chapter 4 may help as well. |
| 2XX | Memory | Try pushing your memory chips more firmly into their sockets (Chapter 10). If that doesn't work, you probably need to have your memory chips tested by a professional. |
| 3XX | Keyboard | Is a book lying across the keyboard, pressing some of the keys as your computer boots up? Another possible solution is to turn off your computer, unplug the keyboard, shake out any dust, and try rebooting the computer. See Chapter 5. |
| 4XX | Monochrome video or adapter | Only XTs complain about this one. Your monochrome video card is acting up. See Chapter 7 and Chapter 14. |
| 5XX | Color video or adapter | Only XTs complain about this problem. Your CGA video card is acting up. See Chapter 7 and Chapter 14. |
| 6XX | Floppy drive or adapter | Could there be a bad floppy disk in the drive? Is your CMOS set up for the right type of disk? Better start with Chapters 11 and 17. |

*(continued)*

| This Code | Usually Means This Is Acting Up | Comments |
|---|---|---|
| 7XX | Math coprocessor | Is your math coprocessor seated firmly in its socket? Does your computer's CMOS know that the chip's there? Chapters 9 and 17 should help you fix this one. |
| 9XX | Printer port | Your I/O card may be at fault. See Chapters 3 and 14. |
| 10XX | Second printer port | Your I/O card may be at fault. See Chapters 3 and 14. |
| 11XX | Serial port | Your I/O card may be at fault. See Chapters 3 and 14. |
| 12XX | Second serial port | Your I/O card may be at fault. See Chapters 3 and 14. |
| 13XX | Game card | Your I/O card may be at fault. See Chapters 3 and 14. |
| 17XX | Hard drive or controller | Better give Chapter 12 the once-over: make sure that your hard drive's cables are securely fastened and that its jumpers are set correctly (Chapter 17). Also make sure that the controller card is set firmly in its slot (Chapters 14 and 18). |

# When My Computer Boots Up, It Spits Out Weird Words

We're talking gut-level error messages here, the kind your computer spits out before it even has a chance to load DOS. (DOS error messages — the ones that turn up after the computer's been turned on for a while — are deciphered in Chapter 24.)

The error messages described in this section are stored in your computer's *BIOS,* the base-level chip that serves as your PC's nervous system. (Your computer's BIOS is covered in Chapter 9.)

Different brands of BIOS chips spit out subtly different error messages. However, Table 22-2 shows some of the key words and phrases all BIOS chips use when they find something wrong with your PC.

### Table 22-2  Common Boot-Up Messages and How to Get Rid of Them

| *These Key Words* | *Usually Mean This* |
| --- | --- |
| 64K | Some of your memory's probably gone bad. Your best bet is to pull all your memory chips (Chapter 10) and have a professional test them. |
| Bad DMA | Your motherboard may need replacing. Turn to Chapter 9. |
| Bad or missing command interpreter | Your computer's looking for a file called COMMAND.COM, which is supposed to be it its root directory. Copy that file back to your root directory from your System disk, described in Chapter 2. |
| CMOS, Configuration | When your computer mentions CMOS, you need to change some of its settings. Head to Chapter 17 to read about CMOS settings. |
| Drive Failure | Head for Chapter 12 and make sure that your hard drive's cables are plugged in snugly. Is the drive getting power from the power supply? Also check out Chapter 17 to make sure that the drive is listed correctly in your computer's CMOS. |
| Memory and Failure | When combined in the same message, these two words usually mean something's wrong with one or more of your memory chips. Your best bet is to have your memory chips professionally tested (Chapter 10). You may need to replace the motherboard (Chapter 9). |
| Non-system disk or disk error | Take out the disk that's in drive A and press the spacebar for a quick fix. If your computer sends this message about your hard drive, you need to copy COMMAND.COM over to the hard drive from your System disk, described in Chapter 2. |
| Parity | Your memory's acting up. Head for Chapter 10 and try pushing the chips more firmly into their sockets. |
| Partition table | Your hard drive's acting up. Your best bet is to buy a hard drive installation utility, described in Chapters 12 and 17, and let the utility try to fix the problem. |
| Sector not found or Unrecoverable error | This means a disk is starting to go bad. Programs such as Norton Utilities or PC Tools can help recover any information before it's too far gone to retrieve. |
| Timer | Problems with timers usually mean that your computer's motherboard is defective. |

# Chapter 23
# Ten Common Warning Beeps and What They Mean

● ● ● ● ● ● ● ● ● ● ● ● ● ● ● ● ● ● ● ● ● ● ● ● ● ● ● ● ● ● ● ● ● ● ● ● ● ● ● ● ● ● ● ● ● ● ● ● ●

*In This Chapter*

▶ Lists of little beeps

▶ that fill the air

▶ when you first turn on your computer

▶ and what, for goodness sake,

▶ you're supposed to do about it.

● ● ● ● ● ● ● ● ● ● ● ● ● ● ● ● ● ● ● ● ● ● ● ● ● ● ● ● ● ● ● ● ● ● ● ● ● ● ● ● ● ● ● ● ● ● ● ● ●

Anybody who's watched television in the last decade has seen computers that can talk to their owners. Your little desktop computer can talk, too. But instead of using the more common vowels and consonants, your computer does the best it can: it strings together some beeps.

By carefully counting all the beeps, you can figure out what your computer's trying to say. It's no opera singer, but your computer will give you a clue as to what's wrong even if you can't see any error messages on your monitor.

## What's This BIOS Beep Business?

Sometimes your computer freaks out while it's booting up or being turned on. But if it finds something wrong before it gets around to testing the video card, it can't flash an error message on the screen. So the computer beeps to say what's wrong.

Unfortunately, no clearly defined "beep standard" exists. All PC manufacturers know their computers should beep when something's wrong, but because there aren't any hard and fast rules to follow, they all assign different "beep codes" to different problems.

The secret beep codes are stored in your computer's BIOS chip (described in Chapter 9). By figuring out what BIOS your computer uses, you can tell which beep codes your computer uses.

Watch the screen carefully when your computer first boots up or is turned on. Look for some words about BIOS copyright — that legalese stuff you usually ignore.

Do you see a company name? It's probably AMI — short for American Megatrends — or Phoenix. These two companies are the biggest BIOS makers. Don't be confused by the *video card* BIOS copyright stuff that may pop up on the first line; you're looking for the computer's *real* BIOS information. Can't figure out what BIOS you're using? Chapter 9 has more tips.

When your computer makes some beeps and stops working, count the number of beeps you hear. Feel free to turn the computer off, wait 30 seconds, and turn it back on again. When you're sure that you counted the right number of beeps, look in the table in this chapter that corresponds to your brand of BIOS. The table translates different beep codes for you.

- ✔ If your computer's down to the beep stage and you've tried all the "cheap fixes" listed in Chapter 18, something's usually seriously wrong.

- ✔ Many of the errors mean that a chip is bad on your computer's motherboard. Unfortunately, it's usually easier to replace the entire motherboard than to isolate the problem chip, remove it, and solder another one in its place.

- ✔ Still, if you have computer hacker friends, see if you can cajole them into giving you a hand. If you explain the specific problem — a bad timer chip, for example — they may know whether it's something they can fix or whether the whole motherboard's a goner.

# *AMI BIOS Beeps*

Normally, computers using the AMI BIOS don't bother with beeps. When they can't muster the energy to boot up, they flash an error message on the screen. To figure out what the computer's trying to tell you, look up the message in Chapter 22.

But if there's something wrong with the video card or the computer's so confused it can't even put any words on the screen, it falls back on the ol' beep trick. Table 23-1 explains what your AMI BIOS beeps are trying desperately to tell you.

Don't take these beep codes as the absolute truth. They provide a clue as to why your computer's acting up, but they don't always finger the exact culprit.

| Table 23-1 | AMI BIOS Beeps and What They Mean |
|---|---|
| *Number of Beeps* | *What It Means* |
| No beep | You're *supposed* to hear one beep. If you don't hear anything, your computer's suffering from a bad power supply, a bad motherboard, or a speaker that doesn't work. |
| 1 beep | Normally, computers issue one self-assured beep when everything's working fine. But when nothing appears on the screen, you'd better check your monitor (Chapter 7) and your video card (Chapter 14). If those two parts seem to be working well, the single beep can mean that your motherboard's struggling with some bad chips. This is a job for the men in the white lab coats. You probably can't fix it yourself. |
| 2 beeps | Your computer's complaining about its memory. Make sure that the chips are seated firmly in their sockets (Chapter 10). If that doesn't fix the problem, you probably need to pull out the chips and have them tested at the chip store. If the chips are good, you may need a new motherboard. Again, this problem may be beyond your help. |
| 3 beeps | Same as the 2 beeps message. |
| 4 beeps | Almost always the same as the 2 beeps message. |
| 5 beeps | Your motherboard's acting up. Try reseating all the chips, especially your CPU. If that doesn't work, you may have to spring for a new motherboard. |
| 6 beeps | The chip on your motherboard that controls your keyboard is acting up. Try reseating it (if you can find it) or try a different keyboard. You may want to take this one to the shop. |
| 7 beeps | Your motherboard's acting up. Try reseating all the chips, especially your CPU. If that doesn't work, you better spring for a new motherboard. |
| 8 beeps | Is your video card installed correctly? Better hit Chapter 14; you may need to replace your old video card. |

*(continued)*

| Table 23-1 | AMI BIOS Beeps and What They Mean *(continued)* |
|---|---|
| *Number of Beeps* | *What It Means* |
| 9 beeps | Your BIOS (Chapter 9) is acting up; you'll probably have to replace it. |
| 10 beeps | Your motherboard (Chapter 9) is acting up; if this problem persists, you'll have to replace the motherboard. |
| 11 beeps | Your motherboard's cache memory has problems. You'd best take this one to the shop. |

# Genuine IBM BIOS Beeps

If you have a "True Blue" IBM computer, the kind that says *IBM* on its case, Table 23-2 lists some of the beep codes you may hear.

Don't take these beep codes as the absolute truth. They provide a clue as to why your computer's acting up, but they don't always finger the right culprit.

| Table 23-2 | Beep Codes for *Real* IBM Computers |
|---|---|
| *These Beeps* | *Mean This* |
| No beep | You're supposed to hear one beep. If you don't, your computer either has a bad power supply, a bad motherboard, or a speaker that's broken or not connected. |
| Constant beep | Your power supply (Chapter 13) isn't working right. |
| Short, repetitive beeps | Your power supply (Chapter 13) isn't working right. |
| One long beep, short beep | Your motherboard (Chapter 9) isn't working right. |
| One long beep, two short beeps | Your video card (Chapters 7 and 14) or its cables are messing up. |
| Long beep, three short beeps | Your EGA card (Chapters 7 and 14) or its cables are messing up. |

# *Phoenix BIOS Beeps*

If you see the word *Phoenix* on the screen when you reboot or turn on your computer, your system uses the Phoenix BIOS.

So? Well, Phoenix honed the beep code concept to a fine art. Listen to the beeps carefully: the computer's giving you *three* sets of beeps, with a pause between each set.

For example, if you hear BEEP BEEP, a pause, BEEP BEEP BEEP, another pause, and BEEP BEEP BEEP BEEP, that translates to two beeps, three beeps, and four beeps. That all boils down to this code: 2-3-4. You need to look up 2-3-4 in Table 23-3 to find out what your Phoenix BIOS is complaining about this time.

Don't take these beep codes as the absolute truth. They provide a clue as to why your computer's acting up, but they don't always finger the right culprit.

| Table 23-3 | Phoenix Beep Codes |
| --- | --- |
| *These Beeps* | *Usually Mean This* |
| 1 - 1 - 3 | Your computer can't read its CMOS (Chapter 17), so your motherboard's complaining (Chapter 9). |
| 1 - 1 - 4 | Your BIOS probably needs to be replaced (Chapter 9). |
| 1 - 2 - 1 | A timer chip on your motherboard is acting up; you'll probably have to replace the motherboard (Chapter 9). |
| 1 - 2 - 2 | The motherboard is bad (Chapter 9). |
| 1 - 2 - 3 | You have a bad motherboard (Chapter 9) or memory (Chapter 10). |
| 1 - 3 - 1 | The motherboard (Chapter 9) or memory (Chapter 10) is bad. |
| 1 - 3 - 3 | The motherboard (Chapter 9) or memory (Chapter 10) is bad. |
| 1 - 3 - 4 | You probably have a bad motherboard (Chapter 9). |
| 1 - 4 - 1 | You probably have a bad motherboard (Chapter 9). |
| 1 - 4 - 2 | Some of the memory is bad (Chapter 10). |
| 2 - ? - ? | Any beep series starting with two beeps means some of your memory is bad (Chapter 10). Better get the chips tested professionally. |
| 3 - 1 - 1 | One of the chips on your motherboard is acting up; you'll probably have to replace the whole thing. |

*(continued)*

| Table 23-3 | Phoenix Beep Codes *(continued)* |
| --- | --- |
| *These Beeps* | *Usually Mean This* |
| 3 - 1 - 2 | One of the chips on your motherboard is acting up; you'll probably have to replace the whole thing. |
| 3 - 1 - 3 | One of the chips on your motherboard is acting up; you'll probably have to replace the whole thing. |
| 3 - 1 - 4 | One of the chips on your motherboard is acting up; you'll probably have to replace the whole thing. |
| 3 - 2 - 4 | Your keyboard (or the chip on the motherboard that controls it) is acting up. Visit Chapter 5. |
| 3 - 3 - 4 | Your computer can't find its video card. Is there one in there? (See Chapter 14.) |
| 3 - 4 - 1 | Your video card is acting up (Chapter 14). |
| 3 - 4 - 2 | Your video card is acting up (Chapter 14). |
| 3 - 4 - 3 | Your video card is acting up (Chapter 14). |
| 4 - 2 - 1 | Your motherboard has a bad chip; you'll probably have to replace the whole thing (Chapter 9). |
| 4 - 2 - 2 | First, check your keyboard (Chapter 5) for problems; if that doesn't fix the problem, your motherboard's probably bad. |
| 4 - 2 - 3 | Just as with the beeps above, first, check your keyboard (Chapter 5) for problems; if that doesn't fix the problem, your motherboard's probably bad. |
| 4 - 2 - 4 | One of your cards (Chapter 14) is confusing your computer. Try pulling your cards out one by one to isolate the culprit. |
| 4 - 3 - 1 | Your motherboard's probably gone bad. |
| 4 - 3 - 2 | Again, your motherboard's probably gone bad. |
| 4 - 3 - 3 | One of the timer chips died. You'll probably have to replace the motherboard. |
| 4 - 3 - 4 | Try calling up your CMOS (Chapter 17) and checking the date and time. If that doesn't fix the problem, try changing your computer's battery (Chapter 9). Still acting up? Try a new power supply before breaking down and buying a new motherboard. |
| 4 - 4 - 1 | Your serial port's acting up; try reseating (or replacing) your I/O card (Chapter 14). |
| 4 - 4 - 2 | Your parallel port's acting up; try reseating (or replacing) your I/O card (Chapter 14). |
| 4 - 4 - 3 | Your math coprocessor's acting up. Run the program that came with it to see if it's *really* fried or just pretending. |

# Chapter 24
# Ten Common Error Messages (and How to Avoid Them)

## In This Chapter

▶ Oodles of error messages

▶ that seem to pop up

▶ when you're trying to finish

▶ up some work

▶ and turn off the darn computer.

**D**OS has more than 100 error messages. You'll find the ten most popular — actually, the most *un*popular — error messages in this chapter. You'll also find some tips on how to shut 'em up.

## Insert disk with COMMAND.COM in drive A Press any key to continue

This message means your computer can't find DOS. Stick a system floppy in drive A and press Enter. Or, if you want to boot off your hard drive, remove the disk from drive A and press Enter. Dunno how to make a system floppy? Troop back to Chapter 2.

# Invalid media or Track 0 bad disk unusable Format terminated

When your computer hides its most important files on a system floppy, it sticks them in some front-row seats called *Track 0*. If those seats are damaged — they're full of gum or something even worse — the computer can't stick its important stuff on them.

That's what happens when this message appears. Throw the disk away and try another. If you get this message when you're trying to format your hard drive, you're in *deep* trouble. Head for Chapter 12 for some possible fixes.

# Access denied

You're probably trying to write (or delete) something on a write-protected floppy disk. If you're *sure* that you want to change the disk, disable its write-protection. On a 5¼-inch floppy, remove the little piece of tape from the edge of the disk. If you're working with a 3½-inch disk, slide the little tab away from the hole in the disk's top corner.

You may also receive this message if you try to delete a protected file on the hard disk. Or perhaps you're trying to read or write to a file that is used or manipulated by another program in Windows.

# Divide Overflow

This one leaves you no choice but to reboot the computer. Your computer's fine, but the software did something that's confused everybody since their first math course: it tried to divide by zero.

Try reinstalling the software onto your hard disk from the original disks. If that doesn't work, try cajoling the folks on the software's tech support line to send you a new, working copy of the program. Also, make sure that you have the most current drivers, as discussed in Chapter 15.

# Drive not ready
# Abort, Retry, Ignore, Fail?

The computer's probably startled because it didn't find a floppy disk in one of the drives. If you put a floppy in there, is the drive's latch closed? Is the floppy right-side up? Make sure that the floppy's in the right drive and press R for Retry.

# Insufficient memory

Your computer doesn't have enough memory to run this particular program. Or perhaps the memory you do have isn't set up right.

Your best bet is to put your System disk (described in Chapter 2) in drive A and reboot your computer. When your computer reboots from the boot disk, it'll come up "clean" of anything that's sucking memory from the available pool.

Don't try to run Windows after this trick, though.

# Track 0 Bad — Disk Unusable

You're probably trying to format one of those high-density, 1.2MB floppies in a 360K floppy drive. It just can't be done.

If you're *not* using a 360K drive, the floppy disk itself is probably bad. If the message refers to your hard drive, however, it's particularly bad news. Head to Chapter 18 for a cheap fix and then see Chapter 12 for some more detailed tips.

# Bad command or file name

You probably typed something at the C:\> prompt, and DOS couldn't figure out what you were trying to do. You may have spelled something wrong or typed in the name of a program DOS couldn't find.

If you see these words when your computer's first booting up, one of the lines in your AUTOEXEC.BAT file is confusing your computer. (That weird-sounding file's described in Chapter 15.)

# Bad or missing filename

If you see this message when you boot up your computer, it probably means that the computer couldn't find a driver listed in your CONFIG.SYS file. Check Chapter 15 and then check your CONFIG.SYS file to see what's amiss. Otherwise, your computer's telling you it couldn't find a file. Check out the information on *paths* in Chapter 15.

# General failure

When DOS has trouble trying to read information from a hard drive or floppy disk, it offers a specific error message. But when it's *really* confused, it slings out this one. Check to make sure that your hard drive is configured correctly (Chapters 12 and 17). On a floppy drive, check to make sure that your disk's formatted properly, that it's inserted right-side up, and, if you're using a low-density drive, that the floppy isn't a high-density disk.

# Incorrect DOS version

This message usually pops up when the commands and programs in the computer's DOS directory come from a version of DOS that's different from the version that boots up from its hard drive.

Suppose that your hard drive is formatted to boot up and start running under DOS 3.3. Then you take a friend's backup disk of DOS 6 and copy all those DOS 6 commands to your DOS directory.

The computer still thinks that it's running in DOS 3.3. When you type one of the DOS 6 commands, the computer gets confused: the two versions of DOS don't match each other. The solution? Buy DOS 6 (or the latest version of DOS) and run the installation program that comes with it.

# Insufficient disk space

When you see this message, your disk — hard drive or floppy disk — doesn't have enough room on it to store the incoming files. You have to delete some files from it to make room. Of course, you could just put in a clean floppy disk or buy another hard disk, described in Chapter 12.

# Internal stack failure, system halted

Reboot your computer. You may need to use a System disk, described in Chapter 2, before the computer will stop flinging out this message and come back to life.

Next, add the following line to your hard disk's CONFIG.SYS file, a process described in Chapter 15:

```
STACKS 9,256
```

When you reboot your computer, it should be back to normal. If not, try changing the 9 in the STACKS line to 12. Still getting the message? Then increase the number to 15. Don't change the 256 number, though. That won't help.

# Sector not found

DOS is having trouble finding information on a disk. Try running CHKDSK, described in Chapter 18. If you haven't backed up your disk — whether it's a hard disk or a floppy — do it as quickly as possible. Your hard drive (Chapter 12) may be on its last legs or in need of reformatting.

# Index

## • Symbols •

1.2MB disk, 177
1.44MB disk, 177
101-key enhanced keyboard, 43, 86
1200 baud modems, 97
14,400 baud modems, 97
16-bit card, 51, 216, 222
   Video Graphics Array (VGA) monitor, 47
16-bit slot and Video Graphics Array
   (VGA) monitor, 47
2.88MB disks, 177
2400 baud modems, 97
300 baud modems, 97
32-bit slots, 52
360K disk, 177
386 class computers, 31–32
   32-bit slots, 52
   CMOS, 265
   CPU, 32
   hard drives, 32
   memory, 32
   upgrading, 32
   video cards, 32
386DX chips, 139
486 class computers, 31–32
   CMOS, 265
486 chip, 139
   in 386 computer, 142–143
486DX chip, 139
486SX chip, 139

487 chips, 139
586 class computers, 31–32
   CMOS, 265
64K error message, 296
720K disk, 177
8-bit cards, 51, 215, 222
84-key keyboard, 86
8514/A monitors, 47
9600 baud modems, 97

## • A •

A/B serial port switch, 255
A/B switch box, 126
AC adapter, 100
accelerator cards, 47, 107, 289
   built-in graphics chips, 47
   video, 219
   wisdom in buying, 110–111
Access denied error message, 304
access time, 191
addresses and hardware, 259
AMI BIOS beeps, 298–300
analog, 106
arrow keys unable to move cursor, 83
ASCII text file, 233
AT-style (standard) keyboard, 42
AUTOEXEC.BAT file, 76, 91, 227,
   229–230, 238
   backups, 230, 232
   card drivers, 218

editing, 232–236

mouse driver, 91

path, 231

PATH statement, 231

REM statement, 235

root directory, 230, 232

SETCLOCK program, 134

starting Windows automatically, 236

unable to locate, 138

backups

  CONFIG.SYS and AUTOEXEC.BAT files, 230, 232

  power supply, 208

Bad command or file name error message, 230, 305

Bad DMA error message, 296

Bad or missing command error message, 296

Bad or missing file name message, 235, 306

Ballpoint trackball, 92

bandwidth, 106

batteries, 54, 134–138, 207–208

  CMOS, 264, 266

  Dallas Real Time chip, 135

  dead, 72

  IBM XT, 135

  installing, 136–138

  location, 135–136

  Old IBM PC, 135

  soldered, 136

bay, 179

beeps, 72–73, 297–302

  AMI BIOS, 298–300

  counting, 73

  genuine IBM BIOS, 300

  Phoenix BIOS beeps, 301–302

  when pressing keys, 85

bidirectional parallel port, 41

BIOS (Basic Input/Output System), 50–51, 150–151

  AMI BIOS beeps, 298–300

  beeping while booting up, 297–298

  begins, 236

  genuine IBM BIOS beeps, 300

  notched end of chip, 153

  Phoenix BIOS beeps, 301–302

  replacing, 151–154

  types of chips, 150

boards. *See* cards

Boot disk. *See* System disk

boot sector, 237

boot-up messages, 293–296

  color video or adapter, 294

  floppy drive or adapter, 294

  game card, 295

  hard drive or controller, 295

  keyboard, 294

  math coprocessor, 295

  memory, 294

  monochrome video or adapter, 294

  motherboard, 294

  numeric codes, 293–295

  power supply, 294

  printer port, 295

  serial port, 295

bus, 217
  EISA, 217
  ISA, 217
  MCA (Micro Channel Architecture), 217
bus mouse, 44, 93
  mouse port, 93
buttons on computer case, 35–37

cables, 37–42
  fastened securely, 68
  keyboard cord, 39
  power cord, 37–38
cache, 164
  settings, 144
call waiting, 98
capacity, 191
cards, 53, 72
  16-bit, 51, 216, 222
  8-bit, 51, 215, 222
  adding, 284
  bus mouse, 44
  cleaning connectors with eraser, 276–277
  controller, 53, 219
  DIP switch, 218
  doesn't fit, 215–217
  doesn't work, 218
  driver program, 218
  full-length, 217
  hard cards, 62
  I/O, 53, 219

IBM XT, 31
installation program, 218
installing, 220–223
interface, 220
internal modems, 46, 219
ISA (Industry Standard Architecture), 53
jumper, 218
memory, 219
miscellaneous, 53
motherboard, 51–52
not bending stuff on it, 26
original IBM PC, 30
PCMCIA, 33
PS/2, 33
reseating, 276
scanners, 45
sound, 219
static electricity, 220
types, 218–220
video, 53, 218
vs. memory slots, 221
case, 34
  big, 34
  digital readout, 37
  floppy drive lights, 36
  hard drive light, 36
  key and lock, 37
  power light, 35
  power switch, 35
  reset button, 36
  small footprint, 34
  tower, 34

CD command, 232
CD-ROM drive
    device driver, 201
    external, 200–201
    installing, 200–202
    internal, 200–202
    SCSI ports and cards, 202
central processing unit (CPU), 47, 49–50
    386 class computers, 32
    chip megahertz, 49
    design number, 49
    IBM AT, 31
    IBM XT, 31
    matching math coprocessor, 139
    upgradable, 143
cheap fixes, 273–277
    booting from System disk, 275
    checking for overheating, 275
    cleaning card connectors with eraser, 276–277
    installing new power supply, 277
    plugging it in, 273
    removing floppy then turning on computer, 274
    reseating cards, chips, and connectors, 276
    running CHKDSK program, 277
cheap parts and your computer, 290
chips
    memory, 54
    reseating, 276
CHKDSK command, 179, 187–188, 277
CMOS, 144, 263–265
    386, 265

486, 265
586, 265
assignments, 264–265
battery, 264, 266
Configuration error message, 296
configuring for new drive, 197
date, 267
floppy drives, 267
hard drives, 267
IBM AT, 265
IBM XT, 265
keeping settings in place, 207
math coprocessor, 269
memory, 268
monitors, 269
motherboard, 268, 281
Old IBM PC, 265
Pentium, 265
setting, 198
time, 267
updating, 265–269
user-defined area, 198
viewing, 265
writing down information, 146, 288
color, 105
    looks awful in programs, 109
Color Graphics Adapter (CGA) monitor, 46
Color video or adapter boot-up messages, 294
COM ports, 40, 91, 94. *See also* serial port
    A/B serial port switch, 255
    assigning, 254, 256
    don't get along, 253–256
    needing more, 255

COM1 port, 95, 99

COM2 port, 95, 99

Combo Drive, 59, 179, 201, 285

COMMAND.COM program, 238

commands
    automatically executing, 229
    CD, 232
    CHKDSK, 179, 187–188, 277
    FDISK, 198
    FORMAT, 23, 176, 199
    Print, 76

communications port. *See* COM port

compact disc (CD) drives, 61
    access time, 61
    CD-I (Compact Disc-Interactive), 62
    Kodak Photo CD, 62
    MPC, 62
    ports, 42
    sound cards, 61
    WORM (write-once read-many), 62

compact discs (CDs), ISO-9660/High Sierra standard, 62

compressed air canister, 22–24

computer
    386 class, 31–32
    486 class, 31–32
    586 class, 31–32
    accidently destroying, 9–10
    batteries, 134–138, 207–208
    beeps, 72–73
    BIOS begins, 236
    cables fastened securely, 68
    can't find memory, 159–160
    card doesn't fit, 215–217
    case, 34
    changing location on desk, 70–71
    cheap parts, 290
    constant whining noise, 205–206
    doesn't work anymore, 67–69
    DOS boot sector, 237
    EISA (Enhanced Industry-Standard Architecture) slot, 53
    fishing out dropped screws, 27
    forgets date, 207–208
    frozen, 85
    garage, 20
    hanging on to old parts, 291
    hard drive type number, 137
    how much memory it has, 158–159, 188
    IBM AT, 31
    IBM XT, 31
    IBM-compatible and Macintosh, 176
    information about it, 75
    lack of mystery, 12–13
    laptops, 33
    local bus video, 110
    lost hard drive and doesn't know date, 134–138
    making it run better, 287–291
    math coprocessor for older, 140
    MCA (Micro Channel Architecture) slots, 53
    messages when you turn it on, 293–296
    modular, 10
    narrowing down the problem, 69–71
    no video card, 110
    nothing happens when turned on, 206–207

original IBM PC, 30
overheating, 275
PCjr, 33
Pentium, 31–32
plugged in, 68, 273
potential problems, 1
Power On Self Test (POST), 236
proprietary memory slot, 219
PS/2, 32–33
RAM (random access memory), 158, 288
removing cover, 19
removing floppy disk before
   turning on, 274
removing old and inserting new item, 19
replacing motherboard, 281
reset button, 274
restarting with Windows, 248
retesting, 20
road map, 230–231
sharing printers, 126
slot types, 53-54
smoking around, 289
temperature changes, 290
time and date queries, 138
"to-do" list, 229
tower props, 34
turbo buttons, 36, 289
turning off and unplugging, 19
turning off then back on, 68–69, 274, 290
types, 29–33
unable to locate mouse, 90–91
upgrading, 11, 17–20, 143, 279–280
vents, 22

VL-bus, 54
watching screen while turning on, 71–72
what happens when you turn it
   on, 236–238
which parts do I have, 64–65
writing down CMOS information, 288
computer chips and static electricity, 10
CONFIG.SYS file, 76, 91, 227–229, 238
   backups, 230, 232
   card drivers, 218
   device driver names, 228
   editing, 232–236
   mouse driver, 91
   path, 231
   REM statement, 235
   root directory, 229, 232
connectors, reseating, 276
controller card, 53, 177, 189–190, 219
   floppy and hard drives, 53
conventional memory, 158-159, 162
cordless mouse, 92
CPU. *See* central processing unit (CPU)
cursor
   disappears, 111–112
   jerky mouse cursor, 89–90
cylinders, 198

● *D* ●

daisywheel printers, 47
Dallas Real Time chip, 135
data transfer rate, 191

date
  CMOS, 267
  computer forgets, 134–138, 207–208
  queries, 138
daughterboards. *See* cards
DEFRAG program, 189
detachable hard drives, 61
device driver, 150, 201
  names, 228
diagnostic programs, 73–74
digital readout, 37
DIP (dual in-line package) switches, 21, 55, 173, 260–263
  flipping, 262–263
  rocker controls, 262
  sliding controls, 262
DIP chip, 161, 165
  installing, 172
directories
  moving around, 70
  renaming, 70
  viewing files on floppy disk, 6
disk drives, 57–62
  burning out frequently, 208
  combo drives, 59
  device drivers, 150
  floppy drives, 57–58
  forgetting what it has, 177
  hard drives, 59–60
  light flashing, 72
  low-density, 176
  old and Windows, 249–250
  out of alignment, 175
disk rescue program, 178

disks
  formatting, 23
  volume label, 24
Divide Overflow error message, 304
DMA (Direct Memory Address channel), 259
DOS
  memory manager program, 160
  Setup program, 243-245
  upgrading to latest version, 286
DOS 6, built-in defragmentation program, 189
DOS boot sector, 237
DOS text file, 233
dot pitch, 106
dot-matrix printers, 47
dots per inch (dpi), 122
double-density disks, 177
DRAM (dynamic random-access memory), 57
Drive Failure error message, 296
Drive not ready Abort, Retry, Ignore, Fail? error message, 305
drivers, 91-92, 107
  printer, 122
  Windows, 239
Dvorak keyboard, 84

# ● *E* ●

Edit program, 233
EISA (Enhanced Industry-Standard Architecture) slot, 53, 217
empty egg carton, 22–24

emulation, 121

Enhanced Graphics Adapter (EGA) monitor, 46

enhanced keyboards, 240

Epson, 121

ERROR Code 161, 72

Error in CONFIG.SYS line 13 message, 235

error messages

64K, 296

Access denied, 304

Bad command or file name, 230, 305

Bad DMA, 296

Bad or missing command, 296

Bad or missing filename, 235, 306

boot-up, 293–296

CMOS, Configuration, 296

Divide Overflow, 304

Drive Failure, 296

Drive not ready Abort, Retry, Ignore, Fail?, 305

during boot-up, 295–296

Error in CONFIG.SYS line 13, 235

FAT Is Bad, 178–179

General failure, 306

Hard Disk Failure, 134

Incorrect DOS version, 306

Insert disk with COMMAND.COM in drive A, 303

Insufficient disk space, 306

Insufficient memory, 305

Internal stack failure, system halted, 307

Invalid, 176

Invalid Configuration Information, 134

Invalid media or Track 0 bad disk unusable, 304

Keyboard Not Found, Press <F1> to Continue, 81

Memory and Failure, 296

memory mismatch, 173

Non-system disk or disk error, 68, 237, 274, 296

Parity, 156, 296

Partition table, 296

Sector not found, 178-179, 307

Sector not found or Unrecoverable error, 296

Timer, 296

Track 0 Bad — Disk Unusable, 305

Unrecognized command in CONFIG.SYS, 235

ESDI hard drive, 190–192

expanded memory, 157, 162-163

expansion bus, 52

expansion cards. *See also* cards

memory, 56

expansion slots, 51–52, 217

retaining brackets, 152

extended capacity disks, 177

Extended Graphics Adapter (XGA) monitor, 47

extended memory, 158, 163

extended-capacity disk, 178

external hard drive, 194

external modems, installing or replacing, 98–101

EZ-Drive, 197

# • F •

F11 key not on keyboard, 84

F12 key not on keyboard, 84

Fahrenheit video card, 53

fans, 62

Fast Gate A20 Option, 281

FAT Is Bad message, 178–179

FDISK command, 198

file allocation table (FAT), 179

files

  AUTOEXEC.BAT, 91, 227, 229–230

  CONFIG.SYS, 91, 227–229

  IBMBIO.COM, 237

  IBMDOS.COM, 237

  IO.SYS, 237

  moving around, 70

  MSDOS.SYS, 237

  README.COM, 18

  README.TXT, 18

  removing unusual, 70

  renaming, 70

  road map to location, 230–231

flash BIOS, 151

floppy disks, 175

  1.2MB, 177

  1.44MB, 177

  2.88MB, 177

  360K, 177

  720K, 177

  bad, 177

  file allocation table bad, 178

  different formats, 176

  double-density, 177

  extended capacity, 177-178

  formatting, 176–177

  high-density, 176-177

  low-density, 177

  removing before turning on computer, 36, 274

  sector not found, 178

  unable to read new, 176–177

  unformatted, 176

  viewing files in directory, 6

  volume label, 176

  won't work in my PC but will in friend's, 175–176

floppy drive or adapter boot-up messages, 294

floppy drives, 36, 57–58

  CMOS, 267

  Combo drive, 179

  controller card, 53

  DS switches, 186

  full-height, 57

  half-height, 57

  high-density, 58, 179

  installing, 179–185, 285

  lights, 36

  mounting brackets, 180

  Original IBM PC, 30

  removing disk, 36

  power cable, 180, 183

  ribbon cable, 180, 183, 186

  Terminating Resistor jumper, 180

  turning lights on/off, 192

fonts, 122, 125

form feed, 122

FORMAT command, 23, 176, 199

forms, filling out, 85

fragmentation, 189

full-height drives, 57

full-length cards, 217

## • *G* •

game card boot-up messages, 295

game port, 41, 53

   doubling as MIDI port, 41

   sound cards, 41

garage, 20

General failure error message, 306

genuine IBM BIOS beeps, 300

graphics accelerator card, 289

graphics accelerator chip, 111

## • *H* •

half-height drive, 57

handheld scanners, 45

hard cards, 62, 194

Hard Disk Failure error message, 134

hard drive or controller boot-up messages, 295

hard drives, 59–60, 187

   386 class computers, 32

   access time, 191

   adding second with old first drive, 282

   backing up before upgrading, 17

   breaking in new, 198–199

   cache programs, 189

   capacity, 191

   CMOS, 198, 267

   controller card, 53, 60, 189–190, 195

   cylinders, 198

   data transfer rate, 191

   detachable, 61

   ESDI, 190, 190–192

   external, 194

   file allocation table bad, 178

   forgetting where files are, 187–188

   formatting, 199

   fragmentation, 189

   has slowed down, 188–189

   heads, 198

   IDE (Integrated Drive Electronics), 60, 190–197

   Invalid message, 177

   jumper, 192

   laptops, 33

   light, 36, 192

   Logical DOS Partition, 198

   lost, 134–138

   master, 193

   MFM (Modified Frequency Modulation), 60, 190

   MTBF (Mean Time Between Failures), 192

   optimized, 189

   partitioning, 198

   Primary DOS Partition, 198

   RLL (Run-Length Limited), 60, 190

   SCSI (Small Computer System Interface), 60, 190–192

sectors, 178, 198

size and storage space left, 188

slave, 193

ST506, 190–192

System disk during replacement, 23

tape backup unit, 18

turning computer on its side, 34

type number, 137, 268

unable to find, 72

vs. power supply fan problems, 206

hardest upgrades, 279–282

    adding memory to old motherboard, 282

    adding second hard drive to older drive, 282

    ancient computers, 279–280

    installing internal modems, 280

    replacing motherboard, 281

hardware

    addresses, 259

    buying replacement parts, 74–75

    DMA (Direct Memory Address channel), 259

    I/O addresses, 259

    incompatibility chain reaction, 15

    serial number, 75

head-cleaning disks, 26

heads, 198

Hercules monitors, 46

high memory, 158

high-density disks, 176-177

high-density drives, 58, 179

HIMEM.SYS program, 160

## ● I ●

I/O addresses, memory and hardware, 259

I/O cards, 53, 95, 99, 219

IBM AT, 31

    286 CPU, 31

    CMOS, 265

    motherboard, 31

    power supply, 31

    upgrading, 31

IBM Graphics, 121

IBM XT, 31

    486 motherboard installation, 143

    battery, 134-135

    CMOS, 265

    CPU, slots, and cards, 31

    memory card, 157

    upgrading, 31, 279–280

IBMBIO.COM file, 237

IBMDOS.COM file, 237

icons, 5

IDE (Integrated Drive Electronics) hard drives, 60, 190–192

    adding, 197, 282

    CMOS, 197-198

    controller card, 193, 195

    formatting, 199

    installing, 192–197

    master/slave jumper, 197

    partitioning, 198

    power cable, 194, 196

    ribbon cable, 194, 196

Incorrect DOS version error message, 306

infrared cordless mouse, 92

inkjet printers, 48

input devices, 44–46

    modems, 46

    mouse, 44

    scanners, 45

Insert disk with COMMAND.COM in drive
    A error message, 303

Insufficient disk space error message, 306

Insufficient memory error message, 305

interface cards, 220

interlaced, 107

internal modems, 46

    installing, 280–281

Internal stack failure, system halted error
    message, 307

interrupt (IRQ)

    address, 219

    assignments, 256-257

    hardware arguing over rights, 256–258

Invalid Configuration Information error
    message, 134

Invalid media or Track 0 bad disk unus-
    able error message, 304

Invalid message, 176

IO.SYS file, 237

ISA (Industry Standard Architecture)
    cards, 53, 217

itty-bitty flathead screwdriver, 21

## • J •

jacks. *See* ports

jumpers, 260–263

    moving around, 260–261

    open and closed circuits, 261

    removing, 261

## • K •

key and lock, 37

keyboard, 42–44, 81

    101-key enhanced, 43, 86, 240

    84-key, 86

    adding, 283–284

    AT-style (standard), 42

    boot-up messages, 294

    buffer, 85

    checking plugs, 81

    cord, 39

    Dvorak, 84

    introducing to Windows, 240–243

    keys sticking after spill, 82–83

    letters and numbers wore off, 83

    lights flashing, 72

    no F11 and F12 keys, 84

    trackball, 43

    unable to find, 81–82

    XT-style, 42

Keyboard Not Found, Press <F1> to
    Continue message, 81

keys
  beep when pressed, 85
  Ctrl, Alt, and Delete (Reboot), 85, 274
  letters and numbers wore off, 83
  Num Lock, 83
  sticking after spill, 82–83
kilobytes (K), 177


• *L* •

labels and laser printer, 124
laptops, 33
  screen looks weird, 113
laser printer, 48
  cartridge, 120, 125
  labels, 124
  memory, 125
  paper jams, 124
  smelling funny, 126
  upgrading, 125
LaserJet adding PostScript, 125–128
lights on computer case, 35–37
line feed, 122
local bus video, 110
Logical DOS Partition, 198
low-density disks, 177
low-density drives, 176


• *M* •

magnetized screwdriver, 22–24
math coprocessor, 50, 139
  adding speed, 138–142
  boot-up messages, 295
  CMOS, 269
  CPU matches, 139
  for older computer, 140
  installing, 140–142
  marked corner, 140-141
  speed, 141
MCA (Micro Channel Architecture) bus,
    53, 217
medium Phillips screwdriver, 21
megabytes (MB)., 177
memory, 107, 162
  386 class computers, 32
  banks, 170
  boot-up messages, 294
  cache, 164
  CMOS, 268
  computer can't find, 159–160
  conventional, 158-159, 162
  DIP (dual in-line package), 55, 161, 165,
    172
  DRAM (dynamic random-access
    memory), 57
  expanded, 157, 162-163
  expansion boards, 56
  extended, 158, 163
  high, 158
  how much computer has, 158–159, 188
  I/O addresses, 259

installing more, 168–173

laptops, 33

laser printer, 125

monitor, 107

motherboard capacity, 167–169

moving old to new motherboard, 161–164

nanoseconds, 166

needing more, 275

not enough for Windows, 156–157, 160

parity error, 156

RAM (random-access memory), 54–57, 162, 288

RAM disks, 164

ROM (read-only memory), 57, 163-164

SIMMs, 55–56, 161, 165, 171

SIPPs, 56, 161, 166, 172

speed, 166–169

SRAM (static random-access memory), 57

telling programs about, 160

terms, 162–164

types, 165–166, 169

upper, 162

virtual, 163

what should I buy, 164–168

Memory and Failure error message, 296

memory cards, 219, 282

proprietary, 157

memory check, 72

memory chips, 54

memory manager programs, 160

memory mismatch message, 173

memory modules, 156

memory slots vs. cards, 221

messages. *See* error messages

MFM (Modified Frequency Modulation) hard drives, 60, 190

Micro Channel Architecture (MCA), 32

Microsoft mode, 240

Microsoft Windows. *See* Windows

MIDI (Musical Instrument Digital Interface), 41

miscellaneous

cards, 53

ports, 42

MNP4 modems, 97

MNP5 modems, 97

mode, 105-106

modems, 46, 89, 219

1200 baud, 97

14,400 baud, 97

2400 baud, 97

300 baud, 97

9600 baud, 97

AC adapter, 100

cable, 100

call waiting and, 98

external, 98–101

hanging up on calls, 98

I/O card, 99

installation software, 101

installing, 280–281

internal, 46

laptops, 33

MNP4, 97

MNP5, 97

mouse cursor goes crazy, 91–92

phone line, 100

PS/2, 33

SatisFAXtion 400 internal, 53

serial port, 40, 46, 99

terms, 96–97

V.42, 97

V.42bis, 97

modularity, 10

money, saving, 11–12

monitors, 46–47, 103

8514/A, 47

accelerator, 47, 107, 110–111

analog, 106

bandwidth, 106

brightness and contrast knobs, 108–109

CMOS, 269

color, 105, 240

Color Graphics Adapter (CGA), 46

don't open up, 27

dot pitch, 106

driver, 107

dust all over screen, 103–104

Enhanced Graphics Adapter (EGA), 46

Extended Graphics Adapter (XGA), 47

Hercules, 46

installing, 113–115

interlaced, 107

introducing to Windows, 240–243

makes weird noises, 112

memory, 107

mode, 105–106

multifrequency, 106

multiscan, 106

multisync, 106

new but programs look the same, 111

noninterlaced, 107

pixel, 105

plugs, 104

refresh rate, 107, 110

replacing, 285

resolution, 105, 110, 240

screen, 108–109

screen burn-in, 112–113

swivel-mounted, 71

terms, 105–107, 106–107

video card, 47, 108, 110–112, 285

video port, 42

Video Graphics Array (VGA), 47

monochrome video or adapter boot-up messages, 294

motherboard, 48–57, 133–154

486 chip in 386 computer, 142–143

486 slower than 386, 144

adding memory to old, 282

adding speed with math coprocessor, 138–142

banks, 170

battery, 54

BIOS (Basic Input/Output System), 50–51, 150–151

boot-up messages, 294

cache settings, 144

cards, 51–53

central processing unit (CPU), 49–50

CMOS, 144, 268, 281

DIP switches, 159, 173

expansion bus, 52

expansion slots, 51–52

Fast Gate A20 Option, 281

IBM AT, 31

installing, 145–149

math coprocessor, 50

memory capacity, 167–168

miscellaneous parts, 56–57

moving old memory to new, 161–164

Overdrive chips, 145

removing everything attached, 146

removing memory chips, 147

replacing, 281

ROM chips, 51

should I install it, 144

spacers, 148

standard sizes, 143

mouse, 44, 89

adding, 284

another won't work on my computer, 92

bus, 44

bus versus serial, 93

cleaning, 89–90

cordless, 92

cursor goes crazy after modem installation, 91–92

drivers, 91, 92

exotic species, 44

I/O card, 95

installation program, 96

introducing to Windows, 240

jerky cursor, 89–90

Macintosh, 45

Microsoft mode, 94, 240

number of buttons, 45

optical, 92

PC unable to locate, 90–91

PS/2 style, 44

serial, 40, 44, 95

small, round PS/2-style port, 95

mouse port

bus mouse, 93

PS/2, 33

MSD (Microsoft Diagnostics) program, 64, 74

how much memory you have, 159

MSDOS.SYS file, 237

MTBF (Mean Time Between Failures), 192

multifrequency, 106

multiscan, 106

multisync, 106

## • *N* •

nanoseconds, 166

Non-System disk or disk error message, 68, 237, 274, 296

noninterlaced, 107

Norton Utilities, 74, 178, 288

Num Lock keys, 83

numeric boot-up messages, 293–295

## • *O* •

online services and Windows forums, 249

operating system version, 75

Optical Character Recognition (OCR), 45

optical mouse, 92

original IBM PC, 30

    486 motherboard installation, 143

    battery, 134-135

    cards, 30

    CMOS, 265

    floppy disk drives, 30

    upgrading, 30, 279–280

OS/2

    memory manager program, 160

    mouse buttons, 45

Overdrive chips, 145

page description language (pdl), 121

pages per minute (ppm), 121

parallel ports, 40, 53

    bidirectional, 41

    detachable hard drives, 61

    printer, 40–41

Parity error message, 156, 296

Partition table error message, 296

parts

    hanging on to old, 291

    serial number, 75

path, 230–231

PC. *See* computer

PC Tools, 178

PCjr, 33

    upgrading, 279–280

PCMCIA cards, 33

pencil and paper, 22

Pentium, 31–32

    CMOS, 265

Phoenix BIOS beeps, 301–302

pitch, 122

pixel, 105

Plain Text file, 233

plugs. *See* ports

point size, 122

ports, 37–42, 53

    compact disc drives, 42

    game, 41

    keyboard cord, 39

    miscellaneous, 42

    parallel, 40

    power cord, 37–38

    RS-232, 40

    RS-232c, 40

    serial, 39–40

    sound cards, 42

    video, 42

PostScript, 121

    adding to LaserJet, 125–128

power cord, 37–38

power light, 35

power supplies, 62–64, 205

    adding, 286

    as line conditioner, 208

    backup, 208

    boot-up messages, 294

    burning out disk drives frequently, 208

    constant whining noise, 205–206

    don't open up, 27

    fan, 62, 205

IBM AT, 31
installing, 209–213, 277
reconnecting cables, 212
undependable, 207–208
uninterrupted power supply (UPS), 208
unplugging cables, 210
voltage, 10, 212
wattage, 63
what kind to buy, 209
power supply fan vs. hard drive
    problems, 206
power switch, 35
power-on self test (POST), 72, 236
Primary DOS Partition, 198
Print command, 76
printer mode, 121
printer port boot-up messages, 295
printers, 47–48, 117
    adding new, 250–251
    air ventilation, 118
    black streaks, 118
    built-in fonts, 124–125
    cable, 118, 126
    creased paper, 119
    daisywheel, 47
    DIP switch, 119
    dot-matrix, 47
    dots per inch (dpi), 122
    double-spaced or everything prints on
        same line, 119
    driver, 122
    emulation, 121
    Epson, 121
    faded print, 118

    fonts, 122, 125
    form feed, 122
    IBM Graphics, 121
    inkjet, 48
    installing, 127–128
    laser, 48
    line feed, 119, 122
    page description language (pdl), 121
    page looks blotchy, 118–119
    pages per minute (ppm), 121
    paper jam, 118
    parallel port, 40–41
    pitch, 122
    point size, 122
    PostScript, 121
    power light, 118
    printer mode, 121
    printing greek, 123–124
    refilling cartridges and ribbons, 127
    self-test program, 128
    shared by computers, 126
    skip perforation, 122
    switch box, 118
    terms, 121–122
    toner cartridge, 120, 122
    typeface, 122, 124
    won't print anything, 117–118
problems
    narrowing down, 69–71
    trying different parts, 71
programs. *See also* software
    adding new, 69–70
    color looks awful, 109

COMMAND.COM, 238

DEFRAG, 189

diagnostic, 73–74

disk rescue, 178

Dvorak keyboard layout, 84

Edit, 233

exiting, 19

EZ-Drive, 197

forcing monitor display mode, 112

hard drive cache, 189

HIMEM.SYS, 160

memory manager, 160

MSD (Microsoft Diagnostics), 64, 74, 159

Norton Utilities, 74, 178, 288

PC Tools, 178

printing from, 118

screen blanker, 112

SETCLOCK, 134

SmartDrive, 189

telling them about more memory, 160

utility, 287–288

wrong printer driver, 124

proprietary memory slot, 219

PS/2, 32–33

PS/2-style mouse, 44

**• R •**

RAM (random-access memory), 54–57, 162

   computer doesn't count it call, 158

   the more the merrier, 288

RAM disks, 164

README.COM file, 18

README.TXT file, 18

Reboot (Ctrl, Alt, and Delete) keys, 274

refresh rate, 107, 110

replacement parts, buying, 74–75

reset button, 36, 274

resolution, 105, 110

RLL (Run-Length Limited) hard drives, 60, 190

ROM (read-only memory), 51, 57, 163, 164

ROM shadows, 269

root directory

   AUTOEXEC.BAT file, 230, 232

   CONFIG.SYS file, 229, 232

RS-232 ports, 40

RS-232c ports, 40

**• S •**

SA bus, 217

SatisFAXtion 400 internal modem, 53

scanners

   cards, 45

   handheld, 45

   Optical Character Recognition (OCR), 45

   serial port, 40

screen

   burn-in, 112–113

   looks ugly, 108–109

   washed out, 108–109

   watching while turning on computer, 71–72

screen blanker, 112

screws, fishing out dropped from PC, 27

SCSI (Small Computer System Interface) hard drives, 60, 190–192

Sector not found error message, 178–179, 307

Sector not found or Unrecoverable error message, 296

sectors, 179, 198

serial mouse, 44, 93

   installing or replacing, 94–96

serial port, 39–40, 44, 53, 91, 94

   big, 95

   boot-up messages, 295

   fighting over, 254–256

   modems, 40, 46, 99

   no extra available, 93

   scanners, and mice, 40

   small, 95

SETCLOCK program, 134

SIMMs (single in-line memory modules), 55–56, 161, 165

   installing, 171

   mixing varieties, 55.

SIPPs, 56, 161, 166

   installing, 172

slots and IBM XT, 31

small flashlight, 22

small Phillips screwdriver, 20

SmartDrive, 189

smoking around PC, 289

software. *See also* programs

   adding new, 69–70

   diagnostic, 73–74

sound cards, 219

compact disk (CD) drives, 61

   game ports, 41

   IRQ address, 219

   ports, 42

spare computer parts, 22–23

SRAM (static random-access memory), 57

ST506 hard drive, 190–192

static electricity, 10, 25, 146

surge suppressor, 64

switch box, 118

swivel-mounted monitor, 71

system board. *See* motherboard

System disk, 159, 199

   booting from, 275

   creation, 23–24

## • T •

tape backup unit, 18, 202–203

technical support, calling, 75–76

temperature changes, 290

time

   CMOS, 267

   queries, 138

Timer error message, 296

toner cartridge, 122

tools, 20–23

   compressed air canister, 22–24

   empty egg carton, 22–24

   itty-bitty flathead screwdriver, 21

   magnetized screwdriver, 22–24

   medium Phillips screwdriver, 21

pencil and paper, 22

small flashlight, 22

small Phillips screwdriver, 20

spare computer parts, 22–23

tower case, 34

Track 0 Bad — Disk Unusable error
  message, 305

trackball, 43-44, 86, 92

turbo buttons, 36

turbo switch, 289

typeface, 122, 124

# • *U* •

unformatted disk, 176

uninterrupted power supply (UPS), 208

Unrecognized command in CONFIG.SYS
  message, 235

unusual files, removing, 70

upgradable computers, 143

upgrading

  386 class computers, 32

  backing up hard disk, 17

  cards, 284

  chain reaction, 15

  doing one thing at a time, 25

  don't bend stuff that comes on cards, 26

  don't force parts together, 25–26

  don't open up monitors or power
    supplies, 27

  don't use head-cleaning disks, 26

  ease, 11

  easiest things to add, 283–286

  exiting programs, 19

  hang on to your old boxes and
    manuals, 25

  having tools ready, 19

  IBM AT, 31

  IBM XT, 31, 279–280

  keyboard, 283–284

  laser printer, 125

  monitor, 285

  mouse, 284

  original IBM PC, 30, 279–280

  PCjr, 279–280

  power supply, 286

  PS/2, 33

  putting PC back together, 20

  reading part instructions, 18

  removing old and inserting new item, 19

  removing PC cover, 19

  retesting PC, 20

  room to work, 19

  saving money, 11–12

  static electricity, 25

  steps, 17–20

  taking your time, 26

  testing new item, 19

  to latest version of DOS, 286

  tools necessary, 20–23

  turning off and unplugging PC, 19

  when you should or shouldn't, 13–15

upper memory, 162

UPS (Uninterrupted Power Supply), 64

utility programs, 287–288

## • V •

V.42 modems, 97

V.42bis modems, 97

vents, 22

VGA video port, 42

video cards, 53, 103, 108, 218

   386 class computers, 32

   accelerated, 219

   changing video modes, 244

   drivers, 240

   Fahrenheit, 53

   introducing to Windows, 240–243

   monitors, 47, 110–111, 285

   more colors and higher resolution, 244

   none in computer, 110

Video Graphics Array (VGA) monitor, 47

   16-bit card, 47

video modes, Windows won't work, 245–246

video ports, 42

virtual memory, 163

VL-bus, 54

volume label, 24, 176

## • W •

warning beeps, 297–302

Windows

   adding printer, 250–251

   Change System Settings command, 241

   changing video modes, 244

   Control Panel, 246, 250–251

   directory, 245

   Display options, 240

   DOS version of Setup program, 245

   drivers, 239, 249

   Drivers icon, 247

   introducing mouse, keyboard, video card, or monitor, 240–243

   introducing to hardware, 246–249

   mouse buttons, 45

   not enough memory, 156–157, 160

   old drivers, 249–250

   online service forums, 249

   Options menu, 241

   parts in a different mode, 240–243

   Printers icon, 250

   Restart Windows command, 242

   restarting computer, 248

   screen blanker, 113

   Setup icon, 241, 243-244

   Setup window menu bar, 241

   starting automatically, 236

   telling about new parts, 239–251

   won't work in new video mode, 245–246

Windows 3.1, Dvorak keyboard layout program, 84

Windows' Notepad editing CONFIG.SYS or AUTOEXEC.BAT file, 233

WordPerfect, starting, 303

## • X •

XT-style keyboard, 42

# Order Form

**Order Center: (800) 762-2974** (8 a.m.-5 p.m., PST, weekdays)  or (415) 312-0650

**For Fastest Service:** Photocopy This Order Form and FAX it to :  (415) 358-1260

| Quantity | ISBN | Title | Price | Total |
|----------|------|-------|-------|-------|
|          |      |       |       |       |
|          |      |       |       |       |
|          |      |       |       |       |
|          |      |       |       |       |
|          |      |       |       |       |
|          |      |       |       |       |
|          |      |       |       |       |
|          |      |       |       |       |
|          |      |       |       |       |
|          |      |       |       |       |
|          |      |       |       |       |
|          |      |       |       |       |
|          |      |       |       |       |

## Shipping & Handling Charges

| Subtotal | U.S. | Canada & International | International Air Mail |
|----------|------|------------------------|------------------------|
| Up to $20.00 | Add $3.00 | Add $4.00 | Add $10.00 |
| $20.01-40.00 | $4.00 | $5.00 | $20.00 |
| $40.01-60.00 | $5.00 | $6.00 | $25.00 |
| $60.01-80.00 | $6.00 | $8.00 | $35.00 |
| Over $80.00 | $7.00 | $10.00 | $50.00 |

In U.S. and Canada, shipping is UPS ground or equivalent.
For Rush shipping call (800) 762-2974.

Subtotal _____

CA residents add applicable sales tax _____

IN residents add 5% sales tax _____

Canadian residents add 7% GST tax _____

Shipping _____

TOTAL _____

## Ship to:

Name _____

Company _____

Address _____

City/State/Zip _____

Daytime Phone _____

Payment:  ❑ Check to IDG Books (US Funds Only)    ❑ Visa    ❑ MasterCard    ❑ American Express

Card # _____    Exp. _____    Signature _____

Please send this order form to: IDG Books, 155 Bovet Road, Suite 310, San Mateo, CA 94402.
Allow up to 3 weeks for delivery. Thank you!

**BOBFD**